IT'S ONLY A GAME

JASON MARRINER

IT'S ONLY A GAME

"When we're good they never remember.
When we're bad they never forget."

MAINLAND GB PUBLISHING

© Jason Marriner 2006

Published by
Mainland GB Publishing
P.O. Box 21
Dulverton
TA22 9YN
www.jasonmarriner.com

ISBN 0-9552682-0-6   978-0-9552682-0-5

Printed and bound in Great Britain

To my beautiful Julie and our sons,
Connor, Mason and Billy-boy –
I love you all.
To Mum, Dad, Father-in-law Stan, Mother-in law Silvia,
brothers Mark and Paul and sister Nikki,
who also stood by me throughout.

In Loving Memory:
My lovely Nan, I miss you every day.

CONTENTS

INTRODUCTION   1

1 A STRAIGHT RED   5
2 GREAT SKILLS (by the camera)   12
3 OFFSIDE   19
4 ROUTE ONE   25
5 TWO DIFFERENT KITS   35
6 THE SLY FOXES   40
7 PLAYING A RINGER   52
8 "WHO'S THAT TEAM THEY CALL THE CHELSEA?"   61
9 THE MEET   69
10 LOCAL DERBY   78
11 HOME OR AWAY   87
12 WANDSWORTH AWAY   95
13 IN THE AWAY END   103
14 USING YOUR FULL SQUAD   108
15 MOVING TO A BETTER CLUB   114
16 MOVING THE GOALPOSTS   120
17 INJURY TIME   127
18 HOME WIN   139
19 PREMIERSHIP *V.* MACINTYRE   143
20 WHAT'S THE SCORE?   212

ACKNOWLEDGMENTS   271

IT'S ONLY A GAME

INTRODUCTION

"My name is Donal MacIntyre and I'm a BBC reporter. I work undercover . . . to expose worlds that ordinary journalism couldn't reveal. My only protection has been my cover story and my secret camera. And my most dangerous assignment was to uncover the world of organised football violence.

"The only way to get to the ringleaders who orchestrate the violence is to use exceptional methods and I spent over a year of my life infiltrating one of the country's most notorious gangs."

Well my name is Jason Marriner and I'd guess you're one of the 7.4 million viewers who saw me on the 'MacIntyre Undercover' programme in November, 1999. You might still remember the speech above as part of the commentary for the opening scenes and for the next hour or so you saw some 'sexy' television, didn't you? It was exciting, all-action stuff (I might've enjoyed it myself if I hadn't been in it!) but so it should have been as it cost the BBC £300,000, about three times more than a typical episode of Panorama and the most they'd ever spent on a single documentary.

I don't know about you but I'm not in to all that 'fame and celebrity' bit, I find it embarrassing. I mean, who am I? I'm just a kid who ran a tyre and vehicle recovery business and when I wasn't working I lived for football, either playing the game at least three times a week or following Chelsea, which is something I've done since I was five years old. Was I really important enough in life to make a documentary about? They seemed to think so, as the impression they wanted to give you was that they were lifting the lid off the 'ugly face of football violence.'

But listen, don't kid yourself any of the programmes in the "MacIntyre Undercover" series were made from some 'moral high-ground.' They weren't made to expose 'wrong-doing' in the world, for fuck's sake, they were simply made for commercial reasons, to attract as many viewers as possible and that's the bottom line.

For decades the BBC had been trading off the reputation it built up in its heyday as the pride of journalism and to far too many, the BBC is still a by-word for integrity and honesty as far as its reporting goes. Good old 'Auntie Beeb' doesn't get up to any dodgy tricks when it broadcasts its news and documentaries, it tells us the truth, right? Wrong! You must be living in the Dark Ages if you still believe that.

Back in the 90s we all started fixing satellite dishes on our walls or plugging in to cable and now there are so many different TV channels out there you'd go boss-eyed just flicking through them all. So the BBC's been facing a shrinking audience for years, but it's still got to justify its licence fee and the only way to do that is give the public what they want: 'sexy TV.' Forget the truth as far as documentaries and the news are concerned, just keep it exciting, keep the viewers' entertained and make sure they don't change channels.

This kind of thinking soon seeped through to the corporation's news coverage. I'll give you an example of how the BBC now presents its news: a kid I know went on holiday with his missus to Sicily in 2001 just weeks before Mount Etna erupted. They did the whole tourist bit, taking a trip to the top of the volcano and on the way up the tourist guide's pointed out the devastation caused by the last big eruption back in 1991. The blast that year had sent molten rock all the way down to a village below making a right mess of the houses and the guide this geezer's with has pointed out one of them because it's become a bit of a tourist spot, being covered in volcanic rock right up to the roof.

But the eruption in 2001 was much smaller, not as eye-catching – it just wasn't sexy enough – so the BBC film crew sent out there to cover it filmed a few dramatic shots of Mount Etna throwing out the lava, then cut to the houses ruined 10 years before as if they were now a part of what was going on and the people there were fleeing for their lives while their homes burned to the ground. This kid's seen the news report back in England and laughed. He knows it's made up because he's just come back from the area and he's even recognised the house with volcanic rock up to the rafters that the BBC crew has filmed. It's like he said to me, "The house they showed on the news was covered in cold rock from a decade ago, not molten lava, did no-one else spot that?"

I won't lie to you, if I'd heard that story a few years back I'd have probably just laughed. So the BBC have been a bit cheeky with their footage, they've cut and edited it to make it a bit more exciting for the tele. Well, who'd have thought it? But now I do think about it and I know they were prepared to do all that just to fill a 20-second slot on the evening news. It doesn't even scratch the surface of what you're about to read because what do you think they'd be prepared to do, what corners would they cut – and what lies would they tell – to make a series of 'ground-breaking,' hour-long, undercover documentaries?

It's no secret the BBC regarded 'MacIntyre Undercover' as it's flag-ship series for 1999, it was the 'big one' that was going to get everyone talking and win back all those lost viewers. It worked, you all tuned in in your millions, didn't you – and the BBC conned you all.

Because what you probably don't know is Donal MacIntyre, along with the documentary's co-producer Paul Atkinson and their undercover crew, secretly shot 344 hours of tape to make the programme on football violence and every single second of film shot was all in an attempt to get anything on me – anything at all.

You only saw 60 minutes' worth and yet at NO time did you once see me or Andy Frain, a good mate of mine who I've been going to Chelsea with for years, commit a single crime – you still wouldn't have even if you sat through the other 340-odd hours – but if you weren't paying attention it didn't seem that way, did it?

Because there was only one approach left for MacIntyre, Atkinson and Philip Clothier, the programme's producer and editor, to get a ratings-winning documentary out of their dressed-up, sexed-up flop: cut, edit, alter and distort whatever scraps of film they'd secretly got over 18 months until they finally had the programme they wanted – one that would sell. So that's 344 hours of tape, £300,000 of licence payers' money and it was all total bollocks from start to finish. Conning a viewing public of millions and charging them through their licence fees for the privilege is bad enough as it is, but there was so much more to it than that.

As the misreporting in the MacIntyre Undercover programme would ultimately put me in prison for six years and Andy, my co-de, away for seven.

The night that programme came out I decided right there and then I'd have my say – listen, if I have an argument I've always got to have the last word but there was no point in me screaming and shouting at the tele, was there! – they've started an argument and now it's my turn to finish it. Because what MacIntyre and Atkinson have done isn't just about football, it could have been about anything as the rest of their heavily criticised series showed. It seems these days that if programme makers decide to target someone, for whatever reason, they'll put that much effort into trying to find material against the person that when they finally find they've got nothing they're still prepared to distort it all, rather than cut their losses and admit they've got nowhere. And what's more, it seems there's nothing or no-one out there who's prepared to stop them from doing this.

I've been bang to rights before but this was the first time I'd been set up, so what was it all about? It was all about realising that light-weight reporters like MacIntyre and Atkinson will go to any lengths once they've put their minds to it and while I'm quite a strong kid a weaker man might have buckled going through what I've had to, knowing all the while they were innocent.

You're now holding in your hands the truth behind "MacInlies" and what his under-cover reporting did to me. I haven't written this to earn a pound I've done it as a warning for everyone, for the nation needs to know they should be very, very careful about taking at face value what they see, hear or read in the news, or in some 'investigative' documentary.

So while you're reading this book just remember one thing, what happened to me could have happened to anyone. Don't kid yourself it was a one-off or that all the 'fly-on-the-wall' documentaries you've seen since weren't made in exactly the same way because believe me, there will be someone else maybe five years, 10 years down the line, who goes through exactly the same as I did – and it could even happen to you.

1

A STRAIGHT RED

The night 'MacIntyre Undercover' came out on television I watched it with my local solicitor – I'd had a tip-off it was going to be shown, but more of that later – and my phone did not stop ringing. It's like everyone said to me at the time, "you've got nothing to worry about, have you," but for me it was always going to be very uncomfortable viewing.

So I went away for a couple of weeks after that, just to let the dust settle a bit and then after I'd got back and a couple of months or so had passed, I started to think I was home and dry. Well you would, wouldn't you as it was like everyone had said at the time, I hadn't actually done anything wrong at all, however bad the programme makers had tried to make me look. Surely even a blind man could see that much. Yet during that time, oh let me tell you, I'd got sick to fucking death of hearing MacIntyre's name. To me he'll always be a prick and a proper mongrel, sneaking around and screwing up people's lives then passing it off as undercover journalism to an unsuspecting public. He must have had his dinner money taken off of him at school to make him the way he is now – nothing more than some bitter and twisted 'wannabe cozzer,' still waiting to arrest his tormentors from nursery.

Talking of cozzers in March, 2000, four months after the programme was aired, I went to Twickenham police station and requested information on Donal MacIntyre. The reason I gave them was that I believed he was involved in terrorism – well why not? He'd done the same sort of thing to me as how else do you think he got the information he needed? Do you remember at the start of the programme when they showed all those pictures from police files of the suspected football hooligans? Exactly!

I'd sort of guessed the Old Bill weren't going to plonk a big fat file on MacIntrye in my hands and say 'help yourself,' but listen, they only had the front to tell me they didn't give out information on other people. I said to them, "How can you stand there and tell me that when this film crew's come in here and got all the information under the sun on me, handed to them on a plate by you lot? You bent over backwards to help MacIntyre and his pals make their programme and yet I'm not a terrorist, I'm just an alleged football hooligan.

"What is it? One rule for one and one for another?" I told them as I was leaving the station and just to let them know I added, "Well, I've made my point and I'll see you later" – I couldn't have guessed at the time I'd see them all again the next morning.

Wednesday 22nd March, 2000, not a day I'll forget. Well, for starters Chelsea were playing Lazio in the Champions League that evening and I was really looking forward to it, but first I had a business to run.

A kid called Aaron works for me and I went 'round his house at about 8 o'clock just to make sure he was ready for work, as he's a typical young man, he didn't need a reason to have a 'light ale' but he sort of looked up to me as a father-figure. It just so happened Aaron was ready and he was all set to drive off from his house when his mum came out and said Porky's on the phone.

Porky's an Indian fella who has an M.O.T. station next to my tyre business so I couldn't work out at first why he would call me when he knew me and Aaron would be at work any minute. Well, these things get your nut working don't they and it soon dawned on me – I knew the 'other' people were there.

I was keeping a serious eye out as I drove up to the main gates and just as Aaron drove on into the yard I noticed a typical Old Bill car opposite. So it was unmarked but c'mon, it still stood out like a pork pie at a Jewish wedding. Porky's made his way over to my car window and said "Fucking hell mate, what have you done, they're everywhere!" and then for a minute it's all gone absolutely fucking mental.

I looked in my wing mirror again and I could now see two of the ugliest men I've ever seen in my life, because before they'd been out of sight lying down in their 'haddock.' So straight away I've rammed my motor into reverse, swung out on to the main road and don't ask me why because I couldn't tell you – maybe it was just a rush of blood to the head – but I started laughing like mad as I was overtaking all the other cars.

When I finally pulled over well, talk about something 'on top,' it was like something out of 'The Sweeney.' I'd been chased by the Tactical Support Group, the Football Intelligence Unit and the two 'unnoticeable' cozzers in their Vauxhall. Altogether there must have been 25 Old Bill all for one person which was ridiculously over the top. I'd sort of guessed by now it was more than my tax disc they wanted a word about and don't forget Andy was getting the same treatment at exactly the same time in Reading, so that's 50 Old Bill all told between the two of us – PATHETIC!

I had a quick look across the road where there were a few shops including my mate Mark's caff – which I must say don't go to if you're expecting any bills in that month as it's probably cheaper to pay off your mortgage – and there were photographers and TV crews everywhere. I didn't really have time to count them all so I don't know how many there were, but I think I made my feelings towards them all clear enough before one of the cozzers came up to me and said, "Jason Marriner, I'm arresting you on conspiracy to cause violent disorder and affray." I just laughed at the Old Bill first of all and when he tried to explain what it was all about I was laughing even harder: "Conspiracy my bollocks, what are you talking about?"

However, another one of the cozzers started to get a bit fresh as he must have spotted the cameras as well and wanted to make a big show for them by forcing my arm up my back – it seems everyone needs their '15 minutes of fame' except me, doesn't it – so I just shouted, "What are you doing, you fucking prick."

I'm not a fool, the Old Bill must have leaked my arrest to the press for there to have been all those newspaper reporters and film crews just waiting across the street to capture it all as it happened. You'd have thought I must be a mass-murderer or something, to get that kind of media attention. I couldn't do anything about that and, as for the Old Bill, well apart from the one trying to take my arm off they were only doing their job (although it's not a job I'd choose myself, though, would you?)

Yet there was still to be no getting away from the cameras even when I was inside the police van, as when I turned around there's this great big zoom lens being stuck right in my face. He was that close filming me I felt like I was the best man at a wedding.

Now, if he was a police cameraman there wasn't much I could complain about but if he wasn't police then he was trespassing, he shouldn't have been allowed inside the police van – and more than that, he was really giving me the zig – yet if he's not one of MacIntyre's film crew and he really is a police cameraman, who was it who later gave this footage to MacIntyre to use in his follow up programme? Yeah, tricky one that.

You have to ask yourself just how close was the link between the police and the programme makers. Well, I'd already worked that bit out so if you saw the results in the MacIntyre update you'll know by this time I was really spitting mad. Well, sometimes it just makes you feel better to get it off your chest, doesn't it?

Yet because they've made their arrest the police now had an excuse to spin my yard and we all went back there in one big show convoy. They went through my tyre shop searching for anything and do you know what they found? Yeah, tyres, unbelievable isn't it, I couldn't have worked that one out. The only thing they 'found' was my book of phone numbers, you know, work contacts and friends, that sort of thing. So to everyone reading this book be very careful about keeping people's numbers as it can lead you into a lot of trouble – no, I'm not joking and I'll explain what I mean a bit later – I might add that a lot of the numbers were connected to football but hey, I have got a life outside of work.

I've also got close links with Travellers, a lot of Travellers are good friends of mine and I've lived on Travellers' sites on and off over the years. So having just seen the cozzers spin my yard I didn't want them spinning my mate Cliff's trailer just because I'd been staying there. Not that they'd have found anything if they had, but you know what they're like.

I shouted out to the lads in Romany to warn him and they were staunch, I also told one of the kids to let Andy Frain know what had happened but although I didn't know it then, he'd been nicked at the same time as me. I was finally taken to Staines police station and during the journey the cozzers made a few comments and asked a few questions, but I wasn't interested, I didn't respond at all.

Well, not quite, for as anyone who knows me will tell you I'm a piss-taker, I can't help myself, whatever's going on around me and I started making a few sarcastic comments such as, "I haven't been to Staines for a while but no doubt I'll make up for it with my length of stay today." One copper replied, "No, you'll be bailed in a few hours." I just laughed (there's something about cozzers, they're always funny went they aren't trying to be) and told him straight, "I've got as much chance of that as your old woman not letting the milkman in to tuck under her belt."

The cocky desk sergeant at Staines said, "So here he is then, the famous Jason Marriner," as I was led through (they just aren't funny, are they) and he followed it up by saying "I bet you've got a police record." So I said "Yeah, I've got a few as it happens and my favourite is 'Walking On The Moon,' but I always preferred The Jam, myself!" By the look on his face I don't think he was up on his music and his sense of humour was obviously different to mine so I made some remark like, "Fuck me, this gaff's changed, it's massive," to which the desk sergeant replied, "Yes, it's been done from top to bottom, they spent £18 million on it." Was I supposed to be impressed? So I just said, "Well, it's nice to know I'm staying in a new hotel as I'd have been very disappointed if I'd not been given a top of the range suite."

After I'd been searched I had to sit on a bench with two ugly plain-clothes gavvers when in comes this other geezer wearing a right dodgy Mr ByRite suit. His first words to me were, "Do you know a Gregory?" If some stranger came straight up to you on the Tube and said that, you'd think 'nutter' wouldn't you, so because I'd never even seen this geezer or spoken to him before in my entire 'straight and natural,' I just thought "who the fuck is he and what the fuck is he talking about?"

I turned to the cozzer sitting beside me and asked him, "Who's that geezer in the dodgy whistle?" He started laughing and replied "so you don't like his suit, then?" Well, I had to be honest so I said, "No, not much and not only that he wants to put some jam on his shoes and invite his trousers down for tea." That really sets this cozzer off, he's pissing himself laughing but he still just about manages to blurt out, "I can't wait to tell him that, because he's our boss and he's the one leading the case," so I told him, "Oh well that explains it, what chance has he got in life." Probably more than the desk sergeant. I couldn't believe it when he called me up for my details and asked me if I wanted a solicitor. What kind of a stupid question is that? My brief was just waiting to hear what station I'd been taken to.

So while I waited for him I thought I'd go off to my 'peter' for a lie down (for those of you who don't know already, a peter's what we call a cell because years ago there used to be a safe called a Peter and you couldn't crack the thing no matter how hard you tried).

"Chicken Neck" told me I'd get bail so I just laughed and said "'Course, I will. Give us a blanket and pillow and don't be late for court in the morning." My brief arrived a few hours later, so now it's interview time.

"Chicken Neck," as me and my co-de Andy Frain later nicknamed the officer in charge of the case, came out with all his reasons why I was there, how he was going to play a video and then ask me some questions. I read out a short statement put together by me and my solicitor denying any conspiracy to commit violent disorder and stating my rights not to answer any questions.

So, is that it, can I go home now? Can I fuck, because while I had the right to remain silent that didn't stop Chicken Neck from carrying on with his endless questions, did it. On and on he went trying to get a reaction, but I just sat there staring at him, smiling every now and again. Well, I wasn't going to make his job easy for him was I, because if you answer just one question they'll twist it, they'll say why didn't you answer any of the previous questions as if you have something to hide.

I had a DNA sample taken along with my photograph, while my brief said he was going to try and get me bail. And he did try, but after Chicken Neck had had his tuppence-worth what chance was I ever going to have?

Later on that night a gavver and two other people came to my cell. They turned out to be the Friends of Prisoners volunteers and they'd come 'round to make sure I was being treated fair and square. "Well I'm not getting treated at all," I told them, "because I ain't seen no cunt for hours!" All I really wanted to know was the Chelsea-Lazio result and I told them I'd really appreciate it if they could find out. They just laughed as if to say 'is that all you're worried about?' but they did come back with score 10 minutes later – it was 1 – 1.

The next morning I was off to West London Magistrates Court in the sweat-box, with Andy Frain. Now, for those of you who don't know what a sweat-box is, it's a segregated box within the bus and in the summer it gets so hot in there you'd sweat your grandmother off ,so that's why it's called a sweat-box, of course!

So the next time you spot one of these vehicles in the street heading to or from a court, each window you can see from the outside is a separate sweat-box and your 'vulnerable prisoners,' or 'bacons' as they're known to us normal people – as in 'bacon bonce': nonce – are always at the back of the bus.

I shook hands with Andy when we got to the court just before we were banged up in single cells. My solicitor Huw Jones came to my cell and we laughed over lots of little things, but especially the charges that had warranted myself and Andy getting arrested. Even at this early stage Huw said MacIntyre's documentary had already caught his eye, as he'd seen nothing illegal in it, nothing at all. I remember to this day him saying that was the most over-hyped documentary he'd ever heard of with no substance to it.

He also said, "Jason, when I first saw the programme I was going to write to the BBC because I had never seen so much shit in all my life and why you got arrested is beyond me, we'll try and get you bail." Like I'd told the cozzer earlier I said, "come on son, there'll be no 'six inch nail' for me today" and I'd be right about that, as I knew I would be. Sometimes you just know they've got '12 men on the pitch,' don't you.

Listen, a Magistrates Court is nothing more than a kangaroo court. Did you know the percentage of those getting a not guilty in there is just 0.1%, so what chance has me, you or anyone else got against three beaks, one of whom is a church goer, one owns a corner shop down the road and the other one does Neighbourhood Watch. Because don't forget they're doing this as a hobby and what kind of people do you think do this for fun?

Oh yeah, you can tell your side of the story but it's only ever a short adjournment before they come back and say you're guilty. They don't believe a single word you say yet they're happy to believe every word the copper says. And why's that? Simple, it's because he's got a uniform on so he must be telling the truth. It's just one reason why so many people have lost all confidence in the legal system and because of the current state it's in more and more people are thinking of leaving this country, if they haven't done so already, because they're sick and they're scared of the stitch ups which happen here. Whether it's the police, the prosecution lawyers, whoever, they want you so much that they'll do anything to get a conviction. And justice? No, it doesn't even come into it. I mean listen, the Crown Prosecution Service must have realised there was absolutely no evidence in this case so why did they even progress with it this far? That's easy, because this was a high profile case and they know juries are not sympathetic towards those facing charges like football violence or terrorism. They know the defence faces an uphill battle from the start, so the police had it easy convincing the CPS they can win at trial, because once you get someone into court the prosecution can lie through their teeth. Like I say, forget 'innocent until proven guilty,' you're guilty in their eyes and somehow you've got to prove your innocence.

In the courtroom Andy stood beside me (which I can assure you wasn't the first time!) and there's the prosecution telling the bench what the case is all about, that me and Andy had featured in the 'MacIntyre Undercover' documentary. My brief did make an application for bail but what chance have you got with Miss Piggy, Kermit and Fuzzy Bear on the bench?

I'll give you an example of how desperate the prosecution were: they said I'd given MacIntyre death threats. Now, when I first found out what he'd done I did phone him up and said "I know about the programme you dog, are you happy with what you've done" and put the phone down. I've had no contact with him since, why should I have, I don't want anything to do with him so if he really has received death threats it's got fuck all to do with me.

But do you remember what I said about keeping people's names and addresses? Well here's why because the funniest thing ever, which I had to laugh out loud at even in the courtroom, was when the prosecution told the three muppets I had MacIntyre's name and address on a bit of paper in my pocket . What the fuck do I want his name and address in my pocket for when he's been living in the same block of flats as me as a neighbour for the past 18 months! And what a coincidence that the police even lost the piece of paper. Great police work, I only got nicked the day before.

Yet just having his phone number was still enough to get me and Andy remanded for a week so no surprise there then, it was going to be 'plenty of jail and no bail' as I arrived at 'sunny Wanno.' But listen. I didn't tell you , as we left for Wandsworth in the sweat-box I had to laugh – and I swear this is the truth – I could hear Billy Joel's 'I'm An Innocent Man' playing on the radio.

After I was let out of the sweat-box I had to go through the strip search and past the box which had V.P.U. (vulnerable prisoners unit) marked up in chalk. I just glared at them and thought 'fucking nonces, I hope they get all they deserve.' And while most nonces go into their secure unit there are still some who get put on the normal wings because they haven't put themselves on the 'cucumbers,' the numbers, Rule 43.

But they'd normally get sniffed out sooner or later, or you might get the nod from a 'kanga' ('kangaroo': a screw) due to them always screaming to their solicitors about how they're treated. It's why they now get wrapped up in cotton wool whereas I would like to see them get wrapped up in a body bag.

Yeah, I'd arrived at Wanno and I'd be there for the best part of 10 months before my trial started. It turns out the prosecution would still be trying to get their evidence together three weeks before the start. So answer me this, if the prosecution didn't have a case all that time later how did the police feel they had enough evidence to nick me in the first place?

Yet for now I was 'Marriner FR 4629.'

2

GREAT SKILLS
(by the camera)

Like I said, the 'MacIntyre Undercover' programme on me and Andy was nothing more than an hour's worth of sweet F.A., just piles of distorted footage resulting in character assassination and one long clever lie to entertain you, the watching millions . But then I would say that, wouldn't I and if there's one thing all of this has taught me it's not to trust anyone so why should I expect you to believe me?

Well, I'll go through the programme and explain what they did and then you can make your own mind up, can't you. Just don't forget, what you read next became the sole basis of mine and Andy Frain's arrest and it would later be used as evidence in our trial:

So, do you remember the 'rogues gallery' from the opening shots? This is what MacIntyre said in his voice-over about it:

MacIntyre's voice-over: "This is a sheet from police files. It's a rogues gallery of some of the most dangerous hooligans in the country and what is more remarkable, they all follow one team. Collectively they are known as the 'Chelsea Headhunters.' The files reveal an intimidating record of violence."

And the Old Bill don't give out information on people, do they. Wake up at the back, of course they do. How else do you think the programme makers got access to these police files, they must have liaised with them at some point. I mean, they also included filmed interviews with Chief Supt. Bryan Drew of the Police Football Intelligence Unit so isn't it obvious?

But more importantly MacIntyre's already 'sewn the seed' and any casual viewer eating his dinner and not paying full attention has been taken in right from the very start. MacIntyre now only has to say the words 'Chelsea,' 'hooligan' or 'Headhunters' at any point in the programme from then on and whoever he's referring to will be seen as guilty in the viewers' eyes. Now listen, this is supposed to be an all-action documentary isn't it, so he needs something to grab the viewers' attention – what better than footage of fighting in the street during the France '98 World Cup?:

MacIntyre's voice-over: "Ok, Ok, there are bottles flying and it's kicked off again, the fighting started on Friday night, Saturday night and has continued on to Match Day. The violence has taken over the city with English hooligans and is now a full riot with bottles and flares being thrown."

They way he describes it you'd think he was Kate Adie reporting from a war zone. Brave, isn't he and I had to laugh about the next bit where he says feels like a real novice and he tries to fit in by pretending to smoke. Fuck knows why he did that if it was to later try and impress me because I don't smoke. My missus does and I can't stand it. But listen to what he says after all the 'action':

MacIntyre's voice-over: "My journey begins, I need to get a taste of how hooligans look and behave close up and the only place to be in the summer of '98 is France and the World Cup....Even before England's first match the country's reputation is tarnished. But who's behind the violence and are there any Chelsea hooligans here?"

Ok, but what has any of that fighting being shown got to do with Jason Marriner? I couldn't tell you for the simple reason they were showing scenes shot in Marseilles and I never even went there. Funny how that didn't stop these scenes later being used against me in court. 'MacInlies' then goes on to say how he's got his covert camera on and he enters a bar to find a group of Chelsea fans there:

MacIntyre's voice-over: "....in the middle of them holding court in a bright yellow jacket, I spot a Headhunter. I instantly recognise him from police files. He and his friends are casually snorting cocaine off the tables. It is clear his violence isn't being fuelled by alcohol alone. His name is Stuart Glass, leading Headhunter and a friend of Jason Marriner."

With this shot they show one person, not the whole group, taking cocaine and claim the violence is not just fuelled by alcohol. They also throw my name in as well and not only am I not even there but everyone who knows me knows I don't touch cocaine. So once again, what has any of this got to do with me? Absolutely nothing that's what and being fair to the bloke filmed taking the stuff he's then not shown taking part in any violence – you can't miss him, he's got a bright yellow jacket on! – Don't you think if they'd spotted him fighting they would have filmed him? Because to get the brief shot they used in the programme of Stuart they secretly filmed him in that bar for the best part of an hour. According to MacIntyre, Stuart was supposed to have been 'holding court,' as if he's plotting some sort of trouble but if you see the rest of the tape it's clear him and his pals were just sitting there having a chat and a laugh. There's a young couple sat just a few seats away from them and they aren't bothered by Stuart and his mates, they hardly pay them any attention at all because they're just not doing anything.

And as for 'MacIntyre Undercover' and drugs that's a story in itself. Don't worry, I'm going to tell you all about it later.

So far all they've shown is trouble in Marseilles that I wasn't even at and then go on to show MacIntyre in a bar with a bunch of blokes watching the England v. Argentina game. And I'll tell you why I wasn't in the bar with them, I was actually in the ground watching the match. Yeah, paying £300 off a tout's a sure sign I'm a hooligan who's only there for the trouble, isn't it, so don't ever let them tell you those who may have been involved in trouble don't care about the game itself, because that's more bollocks than a David Batty penalty.

MacIntyre then claims England's exit from the World Cup after losing to Argentina gives the hooligans one last chance for some violence. Now, as he says this he shows a group of English supporters coming around the corner not causing any trouble and then – blink and you'll have missed it – he cuts to a bunch of Moroccans and Turks fighting in Marseilles. So tell me, what's that got to do with Jason Marriner or even English 'football thugs' for that matter.

This is all still early on in the programme but already MacIntyre introduces the idea of conspiracy to cause affray when he says, "a world dominated by a small group of hard core thugs who organise violence through a sophisticated network....and who are always one step ahead of the police."

What's he talking about there? I mean, apart from some firms occasionally contacting each other on mobile phones, something the police are more than well aware of and know how to deal with it, it's all pot luck. It's just a bunch of geezers who are up for it if anything happens, there's no planning behind it. MacIntyre's just trying to fill gaps in his programme and because he's not actually interviewing anyone he's just making his own comments to camera, he can lie through his teeth without anyone there to contradict him. So that's exactly what he does, time and time again, like when he next claims these 'hard core thugs are one step ahead of the police.'

Maybe you don't know about these things so let me tell you how it really works. The police have got their spotters at every game, we know them and they know us and they're watching us all the time, they know exactly what we're doing every step of the way. At the end of the day, I was a season ticket holder at Chelsea which means, as anyone who goes to games these days knows, I'm only allowed to sit in the one seat in the ground and that's the same seat for every game. For argument's sake, the Old Bill could put a camera on me for the whole 90 minutes if they wanted to – and we've all been to games where the crowd's more interesting so maybe that's not such a bad idea after all – but tell me, how I'm supposed to stay 'one step ahead' while I'm in the ground? Yeah, exactly.

Does he mean outside the ground? Maybe he does but come on, let's have it right, Stamford Bridge on a match day isn't exactly Hackney Marshes, is it? (even if some jokers reckon the playing surface is better over there – cheeky bastards!). Chelsea's in the West End and it's hard to get a parking space so if you're lucky enough to find a little spot where you know you can get a regular space…well, it ain't rocket science, you aren't going to go and look for somewhere else to park are you. So I'm parking my car in the same place and walking down the same way to the ground for every game.

Listen, all football fans have their routines before a match, football is a routine the whole day home or away, we are creatures of habit. You'd have to be a really shit policeman not to pick up on this if you wanted to trail someone. Even a Keystone Cop could've picked up that clue so, 'one step ahead? highly organised gang of dangerous people'? Those of you who go to football regularly already know the answer to this but to those of you who don't and lapped up every word of MacIntyre's lies along with your egg and chips sat in front of the tele, are you now starting to see what's going on here?

Because what he's doing in this part of the programme is building up a false picture and when he says, "There's a hard core few who spoil it for the majority of decent fans," he gives his little speech over footage of young fans in club shirts making their way to the ground with their mums and dads. It's as if hooligans are putting them all in some danger – and he's already claimed I'm one – but it's just not the case, absolutely far from it.

Those who've ever been involved in trouble have a name for the average supporter, it's a 'barmy.' The barmys wear all the shirts, bobble hats, scarves etc. and let me tell you if anyone out of a firm ever gave a barmy a clump the others would go mad about it. We only fight our own kind otherwise we'd give ourselves a bad name. Listen, If I was respected at football and the pal I'm with is respected, we're 30 – 40 handed or whatever and then all of a sudden one of you hits a barmy you'd be called a cunt by the rest of the firm and that's the truth, it's an unwritten rule. Believe me, no dad just taking his kid to watch the game has ever been in any danger because those who know about this know one thing: you don't get caught up in the trouble, you have to go looking for it.

Now, after the stuff filmed in France MacIntyre really starts in with his acting, it's like he's trying to build himself up as some big investigative journalist or some James Bond-type figure, just trying to find out where I live. And to make it all sound even more exciting he makes me out to be some kind of sinister villain:

MacIntyre's voice-over: "I face the task of befriending Headhunters, can I really convince them I'm one of their own? Hampton Hill, a pleasant suburb of

West London. An unlikely place to go looking for a hardened thug, but this is where Jason Marriner lives. He is a well-known figure in the pubs and bars.

"The locals think he's a regular guy but I still don't know exactly where he lives. While I try to find out all I can do is hang around the streets in the hope of bumping in to him. I hear he keeps strange hours and I keep my watch around the clock."

What is this about? Let me tell you mate, if he couldn't have found out my address from the police files that they'd been only too happy to hand over it wouldn't take a lot of work to find out where I lived. There aren't many people around my area who don't know me, so he's not much of a detective is he. Sherlock Homes? More like Eammon Holmes, let's have it right. Maybe he should have looked elsewhere, other than just in the pubs and bars because I never drink during the week nor the night before I play football, which is most Saturdays and Sundays.

Out of season? Yeah ok, so I'll drink more and I do drink on Sundays after playing but that's about it – I don't want to shout it out too loud, but I reckon I could be within the government's guidelines on safe units of alcohol a week. Anyway, as for working 'strange hours,' I'm a businessman for fuck's sake and there's 24 hours in the day. I work when I can and when I have to, there aren't any strange hours for me.

Now this is where the sequence of the programme really starts to get cut and mucked about with to suit the makers' purpose of blackening mine and Andy's names and it carries on like that right to the very end. So pay attention.

Let me give you an example: the first bit of trouble they show from this country is inside the ground at a Man City – Millwall game. Yeah, I know, what's that's got to do with me, I'm a Chelsea supporter remember, I must have been at home washing my hair while that game was on! But I'll bet some of you thought that must have been a Chelsea match and it was Headhunters involved in the fighting because when they cut to show trouble outside that same game the voice over used on the programme comes from a Radio 5 Live phone in about the Leicester–Chelsea game, the game which would later be used as evidence against me an Andy to put us away.

MacIntyre then switches to Andy Frain saying 'this man's name keeps cropping up in police files, they've been after him for years, his nickname is 'Nightmare' and he's linked to another hooligan, Jason Marriner.'

MacIntyre's voice-over: "Over the next year I was to get to know Andy Frain and he was to tell me how he once tried to kill a policeman by slashing his throat."

The film then cuts to a small part of the car journey up to Leicester which is repeated later, it's just a brief shot of when Andy's in the back of the car and he jokes about slashing that copper's throat, you know that bit:

Andy Frain: "we was laughing at him, he said 'you can't do that I'm an off-duty policeman.' I said shut up, it's one o'clock in the morning, nobody can see us, and his bird's run off hysterical."

Now let's get a couple of things straight here, Andy only met MacIntrye and Atkinson twice – once in the back of the car to Leicester and once on the anti-Bloody Sunday demonstration – they never got to know either of us and he has now served a seven-year sentence just for having met them. But Andy doesn't hold it against me at all, he knows we've been very unlucky and he's been good as gold, sweet as a nut.

The incident MacIntyre's brought up is something which happened before a friendly between Chelsea and Hibs at least 14 years ago and someone did stand trial for it, but they were acquitted because the policeman was so pissed at the time of the attack he couldn't remember who'd slashed his throat. It wasn't Andy who was acquitted, Andy didn't even stand trial for it because Andy never had anything to do with it.

So why was he sat in the back of a car boasting about slashing someone's throat if he didn't do it? Well, for those of us who know Andy the answer's simple, it's written all over his face: it's one of his wind-ups, he's just having a laugh. As for the other seven million people who saw it on the tele, they don't know Andy so they might just have missed that.

And the real reason Andy was happy to play up to them was because I'd asked him to, I'd told him MacIntyre and Atkinson were a free meal ticket as I knew those two wanted to hear a lot of stuff about the 'good old times' because they were always asking about it all. They loved it and in return they kept offering us all their free stuff, lifts, match tickets or whatever. In the same circumstances anyone would have done exactly the same as us.

Little did I know then, however, just how much they wanted to hear these stories or why. Little did I know either that these two strangers were secretly filming us mucking about – well, it's not the kind of thing that usually crosses your mind when you accept a lift to an away game by a neighbour – but hindsight's a lovely thing, isn't it? And don't tell me the camera never lies because in the hands of people like that it doesn't even begin to tell half the story.

Listen, like I said with all that stuff filmed in France, 'what has it got to do with me?' well when the programme cuts to Gerry Gable, a journalist who writes for the Left Wing 'Searchlight' magazine I had to ask myself, 'what has it got to do with him?' yet here he is giving his opinions on Andy:

Gerry Gable: "He's the kind of guy that will lead a mob on the rampage and people, especially young kids, are prepared to follow him because of his reputation. That reputation and the nickname Nightmare is very well deserved."

But Gable's not qualified to make the accusations he does, he's no-one and he doesn't know the first thing about Andy. He's just some second-rate journalist they've included in the programme to try and get some sort of Left Wing sympathy vote with all the champagne socialist middle-class viewers. And there would have been a lot of those because they get as much of a buzz out of 'football violence' stories as MacIntyre and Atkinson did.

It was next said that if this 'tight, close knit group of thugs' found out someone had infiltrated their number, someone like a journalist, they would get done. Oh MacIntyre and Atkinson would have got done, fuck me, I'm not going to deny that, they'd have been ironed out good and proper. But let me tell you now, I know a million and one people who hate the sight and sound of MacIntyre I don't need to do anything and I really don't care that much about him to do anything. I laugh at him these days and I'm not letting him live in my head rent-free because all the time he's doing that I'm not getting a pound note and he's cost me enough already. No, fuck 'im, he's a mongrel.

I've had the cards dealt to me and I've done my bit of bird. So along with Andy Frain I'm one of the two people who's been hurt by this man's so-called 'work,' but I'm not interested in hurting him. I am not spending my life in prison over pricks like him and Atkinson because I've got bigger and better things to do – exposing the truth is my main priority in life, that's the only revenge I want.

3

OFFSIDE

MacIntyre's voice-over: "Any spare time is spent learning the history of Chelsea Football Club, I need to know my stuff if I'm going to make it as a Headhunter . . . it's time to put my newfound knowledge to the test."

So for the cameras 'MacInlies' pretended to learn about Chelsea and our history. Did he really? I couldn't answer you that one as I very rarely saw him and when I did, he never spoke to me about anything that ever happened on the pitch. Yet the shot they showed in the programme was of him studying a Chelsea v. Arsenal game from the early 70s. I was only three years old when we won the cup in 1970 so I'm not going remember too much about that time in the club's history anyway. I suppose it helped to waste a few more moments in his programme though, by making it seem he'd done some thorough research on the subject. Let's face it, he really was struggling to fill it with anything worth watching, as shown by the next clip:

MacIntyre's voice-over: "August, the first home game of the season for Chelsea....Among the fans I get my first glimpse of Jason Marriner harassing a man in a phone box. He's a committed Chelsea supporter and has a season ticket, but he's also committed to violence, which is just as important."

Once again MacIntyre gives his little speech, another of his lies which goes uncorrected, to further blacken my name. This time I am allegedly harassing a man but that just isn't the case, I was actually having a general conversation with the geezer. I mean, he doesn't look intimidated and nor did he need to be. I can't remember the exact conversation, I think I was having a laugh about the prostitutes' cards but at one point I have my arms outstretched and that's just not an aggressive gesture. So you tell me, where's the violence or even the signs of violence I'm supposed to be committed to? There aren't any, not even in the clip shown in the documentary, but what you wouldn't know is that the whole sequence has been cut from minutes' worth of film down to about just 20 seconds and it's cut before you see me hold the phone box door open for someone else – funny that.

MacIntyre then claims he gets a vital breakthrough from his surveillance of Hampton Hill, as he's now found out where I live. I'll tell you more about his so-called surveillance later:

MacIntyre's voice-over: "He lives in Chelsea Close, I should have guessed – I hire a flash car, hoping that when I run into him he'll be impressed and, like Jason, I wear designer clothes and make sure I'm seen – and his flat has the same number as his favourite position on the football field."

It's true I like my clothes, I spend a few quid on Prada and Armani , so what, don't a lot of people or am I the only one who likes nice clothes? But MacIntyre tries to make out like this is the sign of someone up to something dodgy, it's as if he's trying to portray me as some big underworld figure and he hadn't even met me at this point. As for the F-reg Porsche he reckoned he hired to impress me, well, you couldn't even hire one of those in the first place but I drive a van, for fuck's sake. Do you really think I cared what he or anyone else was driving?

And then having a go about me living at No.7, Chelsea Close was desperate, even by MacIntyre's low standards. So yeah, a lot of my heroes wore the number seven: Kenny Dalgliesh, Tommy Baldwin, Kevin Kegan, Paul Gasgoine, they didn't have to have played for Chelsea as I'm a fan of football first and foremost, an out-and-out football fan. But did I buy a flat because it was in Chelsea Close? No of course I didn't. Oh yeah, I had a million and one of my pals laugh with me about it but come on, don't be silly. It just happened to be on the market in the area I wanted to live in, right place, right price and that was it. If the same 'bowler hat' had been 'No.42, Fulham Close' or what-ever I'd have bought that one instead, but MacIntyre just wanted to make me out to be some kind of unhinged obsessive fool.

It all sounds too stupid to take seriously and I'd be laughing too if it wasn't for the fact that all the while, what he's doing is everything he can to build a distorted view of me as a person, a false impression that would not only drag my name through the mud in front of millions of viewers but would ultimately send me to prison for years. You just think about that for a minute.

Now, talking of obsessive fools, what do you make of this?:

MacIntyre's voice-over: "And then another breakthrough, a flat in Jason's block comes up for rent and I move in.....I've just moved in to Jason's block of flats and he doesn't know it, but I'm about to move into his life."

Ask yourself, how long did they wait to rent a flat in the same block as me because I'll never know. Maybe they put their names down at an agency and said they only wanted a flat in that block, so it wasn't me who wanted a flat in Chelsea Close so much after all was it, it was MacIntyre and Atkinson. But the serious point I'm making is I'm just living my life and these two are doing all they can to worm their way into it and then deliberately try and set me up, it's not normal behaviour it's creepy. And they wonder why no-one in the London area talks to their neighbours anymore. I'll tell you something though, MacIntyre makes out we become good mates after he's moved in and that's absolute bollocks. They never set foot inside my flat at Chelsea Close, I never invited them inside which shows how close we really were as friends. I mean, if you've got a pal living in the same block as you you'd have them in for tea or coffee every now and again, wouldn't you? But no, not once did they ever come in my flat.

And from creepy behaviour, boomf, it's back to time wasting again. Do you remember the farce about him having a Chelsea tattoo done? Well, if not, I'll remind you:

MacIntyre's voice-over: "Now it's time to take the ultimate step, it's drastic but necessary, if Jason's going to take me seriously. There is no way I could be accepted as a hooligan without a tattoo, with one, I'd be 'proper' Chelsea. Much to my embarrassment I pass out on the counter, but the job had to be completed, nothing would give me away faster than a half-finished tattoo."

That was just total acting. And if he did it to impress me, like he did with his smoking, he shouldn't have bothered as you only have to see later on when he tries to show it off to me I take no notice, I'm just not interested. Maybe it's because I'm covered in tattoos, I've got my back done, my shins, my leg, places that hurt. But the first tattoo doesn't hurt as much as the others because you're expecting the unexpected, you don't know how much pain you will go through so you tense up for it. And then afterwards you think 'that wasn't so bad after all.'

Now I know a few tattoo artists and I say please don't be fooled that this man passed out after having his done, because if he really did not only is he the biggest prick I've ever come across, but secondly no tattooist in the country would have carried on after he'd passed out..

It's just another example of his staged footage and this is supposed to be part of the best of 344 hours of filming. Who's this film about, me or him? It looks like he didn't have enough exciting footage on me to fill an hour's worth after all, doesn't it?

Ain't it funny how we don't actually see him pass out, one minute he says he's feeling a bit faint and then 'boomf,' we cut to him flat out – it's all just total bollocks. And to put the icing on the cake a pal of mine from Manchester later went to the same tattooist and asked him if he was the man who'd "famously" tattooed MacInlies when he was supposed to have passed out and the tattooist confirmed that MacIntrye never passed out, it was all an act for the cameras. And from that bit of play-acting he's straight back into his 'serious' stuff reading old newspaper cuttings.

MacIntyre's voice-over: "I've still not tracked down Andy Frain. I learn that he lives in Reading and a trip to the local library reveals more details about him – 'eight in the dock after attack on supporter, seven accused after West Ham fan seriously hurt . . . Among those charged with the alleged offences is Reading man Andrew Frain, . . . other defendants are Vincent Drake, David and Ian Sim, Anthony Covele and Mark Alloway. These are all Headhunters and six of the seven were remanded in custody."

Yeah, that eight in the dock cutting does apply to Andy but he and all of the other seven were acquitted, but MacIntyre forgot to tell you that fact and also, once again, it's got absolutely nothing to do with me.

Yet if you've got a copy of this programme have you noticed that all the while the minutes are clocking away, it's nearly half-way through a 60-minute programme and he hasn't even met us yet? If he had so much stuff on us, real stuff that showed me or Andy actually committing an offence – even just one – wouldn't he have used it by now?

So it's back to Hampton Hill where MacIntyre claims we're now on nodding terms because he's my neighbour. He says he meets me regularly at McDonalds because that's one of my frequent haunts. What's that all about, is he trying to say I have frequent meetings there to 'arrange' things or is he just saying I'm fat!

What the viewer wouldn't know is there was a team from the programme tracking my every move, so when they'd see I was near a McDonalds they'd call MacIntyre who in turn would then call me to see if I wanted a coffee or whatever and more times than not I'd say no. But the implication was that I had some 'HQ' at a fast-food place where I regularly held meetings, plotting conspiracies to commit affray.

The next shots are important as it's the point in his programme where 'MacInlies' really starts to try and link me to football violence. Well, he had to start at some point and it's at the Fulham Dray pub:

MacIntyre's voice-over: "The next step is to meet in one of his favourite pubs near the Chelsea ground. I choose the day of the Chelsea match against Aston Villa, but the pitch is flooded and the game has been called off....the match is off, but Jason is still keen on picking a fight if he can."

Right, now that day in the Fulham Dray I was gutted because you're talking about a Premiership club and the game against Villa's been abandoned because the pitch is water-logged. That's terrible, we were the only game to be called off that day and it was an embarrassment to Chelsea Football Club.

The early days: Milwall in The Shed, 1977

▲ Brighton, first game of the season.

◀ Seats litter the pitch as police appeal for order. 300 broken seats as Derby beat us in the FA Cup.

▼ We're Up! fans celebrate Chelsea's promotion to the First Division by invading the pitch.

▲ Gate 13, Eaststand Lower, guaranteed to have fun in them days. Me in the middle.

▼ Rome was brilliant, I've not seen the game to this day.

▲ Real Zaragoza, we took the gaff over. ▼ The old bill were sweating like Harold Shipman in the dock.

▼ After another altercation.

▲ Lansdowne Road, England v. Rep. of Ireland. The game got abandoned, well, call it an English win ay?

▼ All the right faces in the right places. Spain, Real Zaragoza.

▼ Stuart, Me, Gerti, and Andy Lagging in Saville.

▲ This cozzer didn't find me amusing, but he wasn't drinking Champagne at three quid a bottle.

▼ SuperAli McCoist at parkhead for an Old Firm game.

▲ Poland, it's always eventful.

▼ Austria, thirty of us in Vienna's seats.

▲ Chelsea v. Real Zaragoza 1995. Plenty of fun in the sun.

▼ Against the Argies in St Etienne.

But the comments I made next was just pub talk, you have to remember that all I've had off MacIntyre and Atkinson, when I've seen 'em, is their non-stop talk about the 'good old days,' the fighting and that:

Male Anon: "Are you staying 'round here or what?"

Jason Marriner: "I'm fucking gonna have a walk about see if they're about."

Male Anon: "They'll be up in Victoria, the twins and that."

Jason Marriner: "Yeah, but you know what it is though, he'll go over there, Victoria."

MacIntyre: "I'll bet Villa's scarpered."

Jason Marriner: "No they're about. Fulham Old Bill have already pulled one of our lads."

MacIntyre: "Where are they?"

Jason Marriner: "They'll go over to Victoria, but all my lot are over Victoria....they'll get smashed to pieces, smashed to bits."

I already knew the kind of stuff those two wanted to hear, you know what I mean, pub-talk, a lot of bragging as it's what we do when we're talking in the pub, isn't it? Yet when I was talking about people getting 'smashed' I was actually talking about a boxing do from the night before when there was some trouble, but I wasn't talking about the Villa supporters.

And when I did talk about them I said there were Chelsea at Victoria Station but the Villa weren't going to hang around. An Old Bill had told one of our lot Villa had a little firm down, that's how I knew, but I've been going to football long enough to know they weren't going to hang about so I was actually saying there wasn't going to be any trouble.

I'm like any other man I like a light ale, but on that day I wasn't even drinking alcohol and when I left the Fulham Dray I dropped my mate Girty off at his home because he was going for a meal with his wife and he said as much in court. This is what he said in his witness statement: "He dropped me off at home about 6pm...at no time while Jason was in my company did he go looking for any Aston Villa supporters or have a fight with any Aston Villa supporters. I have been to a lot of football matches with Jason and have never seen him involved in any violence. I have often seen him giving it a large one. He has plenty of spill. I find Jason to be a good bloke who would do anything for anyone."

It's just like Girty said, I never went anywhere near Victoria I never even saw any of Villa's lot, never mind have a fight with 'em, but it didn't seem that way on the programme, did it?

More importantly, did you spot that it was MacIntyre who brought up the subject of any trouble, it was him who says 'I bet Villa scarpered.' Now this is really serious because it's a BBC journalist asking a leading question in order to prompt the false reaction he wants for his programme, not to get at the truth. Asking leading questions is supposed to be against the BBC's guidelines but it didn't stop them from broadcasting it all. So much for the BBC's journalistic integrity then, eh?. All I've done is answer it by saying I think Villa are still about but I never mentioned any trouble, MacIntyre did. Oh, and just one other thing which we later proved in court, there wasn't even any trouble that day – are you listening jurors? It's a bit late now though, isn't it.

All the while the minutes have been clocking up on this documentary to 'expose vicious football hooligans' and what have you seen of me so far? Yeah, that's right, absolutely nothing illegal and even all the 'big' talk I've been giving isn't incriminating.

The trip to Copenhagen's coming next and according to MacIntyre's voice-over:

"This trip to Copenhagen could be crucial, it will be my first real chance to get to know Jason as a hooligan."

So half the way through a programme watched by around seven and a half million people and costing £300,000 to make, these two have done their level best to make me look as bad as they possibly can. Yet not only have they edited the film so it's so far from the truth it's distorted, they haven't actually got any footage of me saying or doing anything wrong. So tell me, was it worth your licence fee?

Yet this stuff would not only later be used in a court of law as the prosecution's main exhibit – this farce was going to send me to prison.

4

ROUTE ONE

I really wanted to go on the trip to Copenhagen but I couldn't tell those two how I was supposed to be getting there for the simple reason I didn't know myself. All I knew was I had to get back at some point on the Friday as I was playing football in a big game on the Saturday. Not only that, I also had to pay the lads' wages, I couldn't just let them fucking roast over the weekend.

So although I wanted to go it was looking impossible, that was until 'MacInlies' and Atkinson turned up at my work and said they'd found a route to Copenhagen via Amsterdam that would get me back in time. Not only that, they even paid for it all as well so who was I to say no.

I went with Atkinson and MacIntyre met us at Copenhagen, although I didn't even know he'd be meeting us there. See if this next extract from their programme shows this:

MacIntyre's voice-over: "Jason runs a tyre business near his West London home and I visit him there to see if I can find out more about his travel plans for the match. The authorities are trying hard to prevent the hooligans from travelling and I want to learn how he avoids being stopped by the police....

"The first thing I discover is that he only uses travel agents based abroad, I also learn he never takes a direct route to a game in an attempt to throw the police off his trail."

MacIntyre's little speech about me never taking a direct route is just a total lie as Miles Saward, another witness, later confirmed in court. And Miles should know as he just happens to be the travel agent who books a lot of my football trips abroad, through a company called Flight Options. During his evidence he stated, "Jason has flown with us to many games on direct routes and he's never been in any trouble." Miles also told the court how he speaks to the Football Intelligence Unit before each trip and has to provide a full list of who's travelling. Miles then told them that not once have the police ever made an inquiry about me, so if the police aren't even interested in my travel arrangements what does that tell you?

But that's not what MacIntyre and Atkinson want you to hear so instead you get their edited version from my yard, done to try and make me look like I'm guilty of something:

Jason Marriner: "Then on the Friday it was 'come home at twelve fifteen, Brussels at ten to two, Heathrow at twenty to three, so obviously you get your hour back – happy days!'"

MacIntyre's voice-over : "By the end of the meeting we persuaded Jason to let my colleague Paul travel with him. Jason usually travels alone to avoid attracting the attention of the authorities."

Never mind that I didn't even know McIntyre was going to have anything to do with the trip to Copenhagen, so I didn't need persuading to let 'Paul travel with me,' but on the programme when I say 'happy days,' the way it's shown you'd think I'd just thought up some way clever way to dodge the police. Yet all the while it's just me being happy because I'm going to the game, those two have booked the flight, they've paid for it and made sure I'd get back on the Friday, they'd sorted it all out so of course I was happy about that at the time. But like I said, hindsight's a lovely thing.

MacIntyre is obviously struggling to get anything on me at all so what can he do to fill in the gaps in his patchy programme? He has to switch the focus to some kid called Danny Walford And I don't know him, so whatever Danny Walford talks about has got absolutely nothing to do with me:

MacIntyre's voice-over: "Weeks spent hanging around the pubs in Reading finally pay off when I meet someone who knows Andrew Frain. His name is Danny Walford, he's only 21, but he's already a hardened hooligan.

"I become Danny's drinking partner, Danny and his friends look up to the older hooligans like Frain and Marriner and Danny seeks them out, just as I've sought him out. He sees the respect and fear they command and he wants a piece of the action, he's one of a new generation of hooligans."

According to MacIntyre Danny Walford looks up to people like me and I've never met the geezer in my life, but every bit of footage of him from now on gets linked to me and Andy Frain, we're being lumped in with the whole package to make us look as bad as possible, it's a straightforward example of 'guilt by association.' And not only that, the implication is that I've somehow got a hand in creating the next wave of football hooligans. I ask you, what else is he going to accuse me of without any proof? But the idea of 'there's no smoke without fire' is what he's based his whole documentary on because if you spread enough lies about someone without giving them a chance to answer back, they can be as innocent as a lamb and they're still going to end up looking as guilty as sin.

Next the programme switches back to Copenhagen and MacIntyre claims again that I'm going to be his guide to 'English Hooligans' abroad, he makes out like I've got the whole trip planned. It's like when I said, 'what we want to do is look for a pub with a few English in it and see what the ticket situation is," and MacIntyre's voice over to the camera is "And Jason knows exactly just the place," like I'm up to something.

What's that about? I mean, this ain't rocket science, where do you think I'm going to go when I'm meeting someone who's supposed to have tickets for the game? If you're English following an English team abroad you go to an English pub, don't you, and what was the name of the one we ended up in? Yeah, that's right, it was called "The Old English Pub," so if this is supposed to be 'highly organised football violence' I bet that had the police fooled.

Now, we'd been in the pub for a while when MacIntyre says, "We're surrounded by Chelsea supporters and Jason is in his element." Once again, he implies I'm up to something sinister but hang on, I'm a Chelsea supporter aren't I, and I'm in a pub singing with other Chelsea supporters, of course I'm in my fucking element. I've had a few 'light ales,' I've taken my jacket off and I'm getting into the swing of things, but do you see any violence at all? Of course you don't, it's just a bunch of blokes in a pub singing a bit loud, that's all. I've got a good singing voice though, haven't I.

And I'll tell you something else, something you didn't see on the television, MacIntyre had a few drinks too many and I remember at one point he went behind the bar where he started getting a bit boisterous, so I ended up having to calm him down. They're an embarrassment these undercover BBC reporters, you just can't take 'em anywhere.

Something else men do when they're in the pub with their mates is have a chat and a laugh, maybe brag about this and that. You go to any pub in any county all over the country and you'll hear the same kind of conversations, time and time again, like "Fuck me, do you remember the time we did this and we did that?" That's just what I was doing that night in Copenhagen only I was being filmed with a hidden camera, the film gets edited, MacIntyre gives his little secret speeches and all my pub talk ended up on national television – before I ended up in court:

MacIntyre's voice-over: "Jason knows it's my first time abroad with Chelsea and he wants to tell me all about the history of the Headhunters."

Jason Marriner: ". . . his brother when they done the first football raid, 10 years ago man, his brother got done for football violence, he got £100,000 compensation from 'em for fabricated evidence. He done four years, his brother was a well, well known head man, his brother got killed not long ago with a hammer, big row, big row, yeah."

MacIntyre's voice-over: "Jason was talking about the so-called Own Goal trials, the result of the last big attempt by the police to target hooligans with an undercover operation back in the 1980s. Some Chelsea fans were jailed, but then set free with substantial compensation payments after the police evidence was questioned.

"The cost was enormous and put an end to large scale police undercover operations of that kind."

First off, I didn't have a clue if it was MacIntyre's first time abroad or not as we never spoke about it, but more importantly, have a think about that last line of his when he says about the end of undercover police operations of this kind because of the enormous costs involved. Well, do you now reckon the police might have been involved in MacIntyre's programme? Think about it, they get someone else to do their undercover job for them for just £300,000 – a fraction of what it would have cost the police themselves – so it sort of makes sense to have someone else do the legwork for peanuts, doesn't it?

But the reason I'd been telling him 'the history of the Headhunters' as he called it, was because Steven 'Hickey' Hickmott's brother Sam was in the pub. I was only talking to MacIntyre at all because I was letting him think he was getting closer to me. I'd already had months of him and Atkinson acting like 'Joe The Champs' and by the time we were in Copenhagen I'd thought of a way to show them what I really thought of them. And I'll explain all that a bit later.

But the chat about Hickey, isn't me revealing anything new to MacIntyre, everybody knows about what happened to Hickey and I was just explaining how he'd been targeted in the first football raids during Operation Own Goal. Hickey's even written a good book – 'Armed For The Match' – about how he got sentenced to four years before finally being released and receiving compensation. Hickey won his appeal because of the all fabricated evidence against him. Little did I know then that history was about to repeat itself.

And talking of fabricated evidence the next bit of editing is just a fucking liberty:

MacIntyre's voice-over: "Jason is now in full flow and tells me other stories:"

Jason Marriner: ". . . his brother, you read any football violence book, anything like that, he is one of the most well known football thugs you'll ever come across."

MacIntyre's voice-over: "His stories are cut short only by his enthusiasm for the task at hand."

Jason Marriner: ". . . here we go, we've come to have a war."

MacIntyre's voice-over: "I don't want a war but I can't say goodbye to Jason as we have tickets together for the game."

You can clearly see the tape's been cut here as the 'brother' I'm talking about is still Hickey, Sam's brother, and me saying 'here we go, we've come to have a war' is all part of the story I was telling. Hickey's a really funny geezer and he has this way of talking, it's like no-one else I know. I wasn't taking about what was going to happen in Copenhagen that night I was telling a story and quoting Hickey from years ago, the Milk Cup semi-final against Sunderland in 1984.Anyone who knows me knows that's not how I speak it's how Hickey does, but then how many of the 7.4 million viewers know me personally?

There's not any violence being shown on the screen whatsoever because there was none happening, but then straight after I've quoted Hickey and they've made it seem as though I've come to start a 'war,' the sound of sirens are dubbed onto the soundtrack as if some trouble's just broken out.

Yet one thing you couldn't have known unless you were there is that those sirens weren't even Old Bill, it was the sound of a fire engine going past the pub. They're clever these film makers aren't they, and it doesn't stop there as you'll now see when we finally enter the ground:

MacIntyre's voice-over: "Inside the ground I stick as close as possible to Jason so that all the other Chelsea assume that I'm his friend. There's plenty for Jason to be pleased about as his team scored the winner. But even now I'm not sure I'm cheering convincingly.

"Half way through the match Jason and his friends produce an offensive banner, their aim is to cause trouble and they succeed. But in true Marriner style it's the man standing next to Jason who gets arrested while Jason stays to wallow in the glory. I'm beginning to understand what hooliganism is all about. For a few brief moments Jason is the king of the terraces.

"The Danish police sense that arresting Jason would only cause more trouble. The next day the headlines said it all. Jason starts making Nazi salutes in an attempt to wind up the stewards. But Jason's fascist salute is more than just show; I've learnt that he's close links with the Far Right group, Combat 18, links he shares with a small group of other Headhunters."

Right, so I'm in the ground and I'm singing. The stand given to the Chelsea supporters had four tiers and the top and bottom ones were empty. The third tier was full but the second tier, the one I was in, wasn't even half full yet we've still made more noise than the Copenhagen lot. And let's face it, unless you're

one of those in the executive boxes with your fat face stuffed full of prawn
sandwiches isn't singing what we all do when we're supporting our teams, it's
not a crime to belt out "Can you hear the Danish sing" is it? MacIntyre claims
he sticks close to me so the people around us will assume I'm his friend but I
don't even know the other people around me and let me tell you, no-one in the
entire ground is paying him any attention when Chelsea score, so when he says
he doesn't know if he's cheering properly what's that all about? It's just more
wasted seconds of film because he's got nothing to say about me, it's got no
other purpose than to talk about MacIntyre again as the big undercover journalist. It's all a bit sad, really.

Now, the so-called offensive banner he refers to wasn't even mine and there's
no way you could describe it as offensive, not in a way which was likely to incite
any trouble. It read "Laudrup fuck off home you cunt" and it's about passionate supporters being pissed off with a player sitting on the bench for ridiculous
amounts of money, yet still having the front to say he was homesick. I've got
strong links with Glasgow Rangers but no disrespect, how can Laudrup talk
about being fucking homesick when he's just left Glasgow to live in London's
West End – you tell me where you'd rather live, Bridgeton or the King's Road?

People definitely had the hump about it as most supporters don't earn those
kind of wages let alone get the chance to play for the team they love. A steward's
come over, made himself busy and tried to take the flag so I've had a few words
with him, because let's have it right, this prick's on three euros an hour,
however many hamburgers he can eat and a programme for the day, he doesn't
know what being passionate's all about. Yet MacIntyre then has some dig at me
saying it's typical the bloke next to me gets arrested but the bloke wasn't being
arrested at all, he was being led away by a steward. Now the smoke bombs have
gone off but they weren't mine – I've already told you I don't like smoking – and
I didn't light them either, I can't help it if there's smoke around me. So the
reason I've got my jacket up over my face is because of all the smoke. I'm not
trying to hide my face because I'm doing something illegal, I'm just trying to
fucking breathe.

Anyway, there's a line of Old Bill and stewards within arm's length of me and
if I had been doing anything wrong there's no way I wouldn't have been
arrested for fear of it causing further trouble, as 'MacInlies' claimed. Instead
the Old Bill all turn their backs on us and start watching the game because
they're all happy nothing's going on and nor is it about to. It was just MacIntyre
twisting everything again to try and make me look bad.

Which he carried on with when he claims I'm making a fascist salute associated with Combat 18. Let's make one thing clear, I've got absolutely nothing to
do with Combat 18 and as for the 'fascist salute' well, I could have been hailing
a cab, waving to my mum or drying my armpits – them Stone Island coats are
warm, let me tell you – as far as MacIntyre could tell. But you've read this far so
I'm not going to lie to you. Unlike the programme makers I'm going tell you the
truth instead whether you like it or not – because I was making a salute.

What I was actually doing there was making an Ulster salute, showing the Red Hand of Ulster. I'm a staunch Loyalist and I'll make no apologies for that, they're my beliefs and I'm entitled to them. Yet every time politics is mentioned we have to hear the view from Searchlight's Gerry Gable, don't we? Though why was he picked in the first place I don't know, what's he got to do with anything? They might as well have picked my mum or your mum for their political views. So, c'mon Gerry, tell us what you think:

Gerry Gable: "One of the first things the police found when C 18 came into existence, around '92, was visiting cards from 'Chelsea Headhunters C18,' where people were assaulted, very seriously assaulted, pubs were attacked and smashed up with the occupants.

"Men, women and children were attacked by these gangs and they'd leave behind a calling card that would say 'you've been visited by Chelsea Headhunters – Combat 18.' So from the very early days of Combat 18, Chelsea Head Hunters like Frain and his crew were in there operating with them."

Did you notice even Gable wouldn't mention me by name – and believe me activists like him drop more names than Seaman did crosses – but it's because he knows I've got absolutely no Right Wing connections. As the editor of Searchlight Gerry Gable would definitely have mentioned my name if he'd have had even the slightest suspicion of me being involved in Far Right violence, yet even he knows the be-all-and-end-all for me is that I support Chelsea.

Back to the Copenhagen trip and once again 'MacIntyre Undercover' resorts to dodgy editing, when its 'star' claims the next shots came from after the game:

MacIntyre's voice-over: "In a bar after the game he describes a visit he and Andy Frain made to the Nazi concentration camp at Auschwitz."

Not only does this footage come from before the game, it was filmed in a pub we went to before we even got to the Old English Pub, before the game. Now, in the Old English Pub I can clearly be seen wearing a St. George's Cross jumper, but in this one I've still got my jacket on as it's earlier in the evening and we went to a couple of pubs before the Old English, because there was no 'organised' meet and we were looking for tickets.

Also in this first pub, you can see it's nearly empty but if you go to a pub after a game you can't move because they're packed. Yet I'm being portrayed as if my behaviour might incite a riot after the game and it's totally out of context. What really happened is that I'd seen a couple of kids I know in there and we're having a few cheeky beers before the match, we're talking about old times which we do, week in week out. It's something I still do, I will tomorrow, next week and forever. What I talk about here is when me and Andy went to Auschwitz, which we did do:

Jason Marriner: "They have a tour thing, right, and they're talking to all these Jerries about what happened, blah, blah. Frainey says 'take a photograph, Jase,' there he is and the Jerries start going divvy."

Male Anon: "So you had a good week then?"

Jason Marriner: "Absolutely superb. I think I put the final nail in the coffin when I tried to get in the oven."

Right, I went to Auschwitz because I was interested in seeing it. I've been to Paris and seen the Eiffel Tower, I've been to Rome and seen the Cathedral, I've been all over the place and this is all with football, following Chelsea and England. I'd been to Poland before and I went to Poznan, so this time I went to Katawice and Auschwitz is just 45 minutes away in a taxi. It's a major part of history and who's to say I'm ever going to go to Poland again so I had to go and have a look at it.

But when I'm telling the tale in that pub I'm not giving a history lesson I'm having a laugh, it's just pub chat. Yeah, I did take a picture of Andy but when I then said I'd tried to get in an oven do you reckon I might have been joking? If anyone thinks I really tried to get in an oven they can't have seen them, because the ovens are so small it's unbelievable, I couldn't have got in one if I'd wanted to. Like I said I'm a piss-taker, whether anyone thinks what I said was funny or not is irrelevant. Having a laugh isn't a crime, is it?

But it gave the programme makers an excuse to trot Gable out once more:

Gerry Gable: "The group for the Chelsea Headhunters led by Frain paid a visit to Auschwitz concentration camp. I got a postcard from them, picture of the camp and on the back it said 'Combat 18 Headhunter division, wish you were here. We've just dug up the bones of your grandmother and pissed all over them'."

So Gable reckons he got offensive postcards from Auschwitz? It's shocking he could make a claim like that without any proof because if he'd really been sent offensive postcards why didn't he show them? If he couldn't do that he should have kept his mouth shut and not only that, he's talking about cards which were supposed to have been sent to him in 1991, but what's that got to do with the game in the documentary which was from 1998? Yet Gable can say what he wants to can't he, and there's no-one else in the programme there to contradict him.

But while Gable's good for keeping the Left Wing viewers on their side MacIntyre and Atkinson know they need more than just some chat, so it's time for more action and this time at least it really is from after the game:

MacIntyre's voice-over: "Outside tension is mounting, as Danish start targeting Chelsea. I don't make it, I'm attacked by a Copenhagen fan.....One of the unfortunate consequences of pretending to be a football hooligan is becoming a target for violence off other football hooligans.

"I've just been beaten up, kicked, punched and thrown on the street by a bunch of football supporters from FC Copenhagen, so have some of my travel companions. I'll be leaving Copenhagen with just a few bruises, but apart from that I'm alright."

So even MacIntyre points out that Danish fans were targeting Chelsea yet if I'd had anything to do with organising trouble in Copenhagen, as MacIntyre has implied throughout, surely I'd have got my 'firm' together, I'd have been prepared for it and I'd have started it?

Now, MacIntrye claims he was beaten up after the game and I don't believe that he was, it looks like more 'sexy TV' to me. Yeah, you see a bit of a scuffle and he falls to the ground and then he gets up all breathless, but it's all over in seconds. As far as I'm concerned he got one of his mongrels to act for the camera because if you'd looked carefully in the background you'd have seen people walking past close by as if nothing's happening, it's not like they're concerned that they're so close to a fight taking place. Maybe 'McInlies' staged it, it would be easy enough to do because he's filming it from a camera inside his coat so all he needs to do is get another cameraman to pretend to ruffle him up a bit, just to make it look like he's been in the thick of it. And why would he do that? Well, firstly it makes for good tele and further boosts MacIntyre in the viewers' eyes as a brave undercover journalist and secondly, it serves to blacken my name just that bit more as I'm the first person he refers to afterwards, as if I'm somehow responsible:

MacIntyre's voice-over: "Our trip to Copenhagen has brought me closer to Jason's inner circle and also shown me a more sinister side to his hooliganism, a side I hadn't seen before – his extreme right wing views. For him, politics, patriotism and loyalty to the Headhunters form a dangerous mix. In Jason's hands they add up to violence."

The funny thing is after the game in Copenhagen I was involved in a bit of an altercation. I was on my way to have a booze with my pals and I walked into a few of their firm as I turned the corner. There must have been a good 20 of them, they decided they weren't gonna give me a squeeze and one's thrown a punch. I started having a row with him but I got outnumbered and I'm not too proud to say I got punched and kicked all over the shop and only managed to escape by jumping in a cab. The cab driver spoke good English and he apologised for people acting like that in his country and said not all Danish people were like that. While I didn't want to go the hospital the cab driver wouldn't have it, I think he was worried for me so and drove me straight there. I ended up being treated for my injuries as I was a bit concussed and I had a few cuts and bruises. It almost sounds like one of 'MacInlies' stories, doesn't it, but unlike him I've got proof as translator and witness Heidi Lund's statement and hospital records show:

"I am a Danish national but lived in England for a number of years and speak fluent English.

I have received hospital records from Amager Hospital relating to a man called Jason Marriner and his treatment on 5th – 6th November, 1998. I attach a copy of those records as exhibit HL/1 and a translation of those records as exhibit HL/2" :

Copenhagen 1st Dec 2000
Translation of medical record from Amager Hospital E.R.

Surname: Marriner
First name: Jason

Arrival: 23.51pm
Treatment started at 23.51pm on 5th Nov 1998. Treatment ended at 00.50am on the 6th Nov 1998.
British citizen – been to a football match, where Chelsea won 1 – 0 over FC Copenhagen.
Apparently some of the FC Copenhagen fans got angry and hit the patient in the head and in the face.
He has not been unconscious or sick.

Objective: Blood pressure 115/80 Pulse 104
Awake and clear. Warm and dry
Face: Moderate haematom of the nose, bluish discolouring on the left side.
No immediate signs of fracture. Clear air passage.
Eyes: Pupils round and a natural reaction to light.

Treatment: Observation, to contact ear, nose and throat specialist in own country in 3 – 4 days, to reassess nose.
Leaving for London tomorrow.

But the truth of me being a victim of football violence rather than a highly-organised hooligan who conspires to commit affray didn't really fit in with the picture MacIntyre wanted to paint of me. So you didn't see or hear anything about the attack on me in the programme, did you? Funny, that.

5

TWO DIFFERENT KITS

MacIntyre voice-over: "Jason and I fly back to London. I have been bloodied and Jason is happy to tell me about his past glory."

Jason Marriner: "No-one on their day can take Chelsea. I've been to Millwall, last game of the season we played, we got off at Elephant & Castle and we marched. Our snipers marched, we was 500-handed. One of their top boys, said to him, he phoned me up and said 'what's happening, Jase?'

"He said 'none of our lads are here now.' They are there, I said. We're looking over the bridge. I said they're in there. 'Not ours,' I said they are and you've got a firm in The Lillypot and all, I'm telling you. "It's too early, it's too early, you can't have it now, you can't have it now.'

"What do you mean too early? We're calling the shots now, we're on your manor we're in and we're calling the shots,' so I said it's never to fucking early, it's never too early. It was never too late after a game of football was it. The game finished at quarter to five and we're around until 10 at night, it ain't too late and it ain't too early. I put the phone down, I was fuming."

Now, according to MacIntyre we're supposed to have just got back to the airport in London, but when I was at Copenhagen did you see me with a bag or anything? No, you didn't, because I never took one, I didn't bring a change of clothes. So while I was wearing the St. George's Cross jumper throughout the time in Copenhagen I'm now being shown in a Dolce & Gabbana jumper, totally different clothes and we're not travelling in a Merc like we were leading up to the Denmark trip, we're in a Jeep Discovery with Atkinson driving.

That's because this was filmed on a totally different trip, we were on our way to Manchester. Every now and again the pair of them would come and watch me play football and, because Atkinson's mum came from Manchester, they said they'd give me a lift to the Man. United – Chelsea Cup game.

I was going to meet Trav, Andy Garner, Disco, Andy Turner, 'Kev The Beast' and Swiggy, some pals of mine in Stockport and Manchester, go to the game on the Sunday with them, have a booze after the match and then come home on the Monday. Some time later I found out that Atkinson was a bit nervous about anyone recognising him in Stockport because he's ex-Old Bill. Anyway, on the first night my mate Andy Turner was going to give him his phone number and I warned him not to as I said I just don't fancy either of them. I told him 'I'm just here for the 'Freemans,' which was the name I'd given these two flash strangers who kept cropping up because they were so quick to pay for everything.

Atkinson didn't risk coming back to Stockport and MacIntyre turned up on the Monday alone, making up an excuse for Atkinson saying that his mum's had an accident and MacIntyre will drive me home. He probably thought it would be a chance to get more footage on me but I fell asleep in the car and slept all the way back to London.

Now, the story they did get from me on the way up there is one about the days when I was involved, I'm not going to lie and pretend I never was involved because I was. But this story wasn't from now, it was from 1984 again. It was about us marching down from the Elephant & Castle 500-handed to meet Millwall and no-one's come anywhere near us, so yeah, I was fucking fuming when Lee Parker from Millwall said it's too early. I have some good pals from Millwall and I have respect for them, but for him to say everyone's had a late night on the eve of a massive fixture like Chelsea-Millwall was bollocks as far as I was concerned. And at the end of the day the Old Bill had everything under control within the hour of us being in the pub, so to be honest, unless we were going through the Old Bill it was game over, early doors.

I wasn't telling MacIntyre and Atkinson this because I'd been impressed by MacIntyre in Copenhagen, I wasn't letting him get closer to me. He knows I wasn't impressed by either him or Atkinson at any time and they even admitted this later in court. I was just telling them more of the stories they liked to hear and in all honesty the 80s and early 90s were blinding. But I just wanted the free ride. Let's face it, talk's cheap, money buys houses.

As you've already seen the easiest way for MacIntyre to con most of his audience, to make sure they lose the thread of what's going on in front of them, is to keep switching from one subject to another. So having already implied me and Andy Frain are somehow responsible for the next generation of hooligans it's back to Danny Walford, the geezer from Reading I don't know:

MacIntyre's voice-over: "Jason isn't the only one who's beginning to reveal his world to me....After several months, Reading hooligan and trainee Headhunter Danny Walford takes me into his confidence."

Now, I've nothing against Danny Walford, I don't know the kid and he's got nothing to do with me, he's just another geezer telling stories in the pub, like you do. But what he actually says on camera is more incriminating than anything I'm filmed saying:

Danny Walford: "We call ourselves the Reading Youth Firm. . . . we had Bristol City and they've got a fucking firm and we smashed them at Paddington, eight of us. Their top lad is called Shannon. I smashed him with an iron bar from there to there and he was cut down to there."

Later on in the programme we're shown more of the same from MacIntyre's secret filming of Danny Walford's pub talk. And I'll tell you something, he should count himself lucky he wasn't the one being targeted by the BBC:

Danny Walford: "You know railway tracks, they go like that, don't they, then like that, you know, the coil bits that screw them together?....I threw one of them at a Man U. fan and he fucking, I never heard anyone scream in all my life
". . . he gave as good as he got until I fucking lashed him 'round the head with it. A few times and it snapped, it snapped right, it was about that long and it had a big paddle bit on the end and I fucking hit him about three times and it snapped every time I hit him. I got the paddle bit and I was fucking hitting him with that."

I'm not saying Danny Walford should be prosecuted, of course I'm not, but where's the consistency? They really were targeting me by trying to link Danny Walford to me and Andy and by taping his pub talk for long enough, they finally get Danny Walford to mention Frainey's name. And that lets Gerry Gable from Searchlight back in:

Gerry Gable: "Instead of those kids finding decent role models, the Andy Frains of this world become their role models and that's why it is very important they are removed from society. Because that's a cancer that spreads."

Now it must seem to the viewers that there is some link between Danny Walford, Andy and me and I really don't know the kid at all. But what's the point in being bitter about it they can't have me, I'll take it on the chin and I tell you what, I'll take a lot more on the chin. Fuck 'em.
By the way, I DID set up those three goals from the Sunday game I spoke about, in the car going over to the West Ham game. I had a fucking blinder, if I may say so myself, but to be truthful, when I've had a few light ales I've played even better!
MacIntyre was busy telling you about his rigged-up car as if even the slowest viewer hasn't worked that bit out by now (although I wouldn't have minded

knowing it myself, though, before I stepped inside the thing) and as for me thinking what it cost? No, 'MacInlies,' I never asked you did I, because I just wasn't interested.

MacIntyre's voice-over: "Back at Hampton Hill I drive around in a hired Mercedes trying to look like someone worth knowing well. Jason thinks I've paid £40,000 for it. The reality is, I hire it for £35 on days I know Jason will see it. But the car has another purpose, it's rigged with secret cameras, so I can record my conversations with Jason and his friends.

"I take the car to watch Jason play football. When he was younger Jason had been offered professional trials. He still believes he has some of the old magic left, but sadly, things don't always go according to plan."

It's true I was offered trials at certain clubs but I was too busy watching Chelsea. The only trials I turned up for then was when I was in court!

Jason Marriner: "Actually, I just thought, I set up all three of them goals up, didn't I? I never thought of that!"

So now we're on our way to the West Ham – Chelsea game in their car and just like Copenhagen MacIntyre and Atkinson are paying, they got the tickets otherwise I wouldn't have been going them. I know enough people to get my own tickets, whether it be touts or whoever.

And another thing they forgot to tell all the viewers, the kid who gets in the back of the car is a pal of mine called James Bavin. He's also a West Ham supporter. There wasn't any trouble at the game that day and even if there had have been it wouldn't have been nothing to do with me, would it, as I travelled with and sat next to a West Ham fan. But that car journey, like the rest of the programme, was just another opportunity for them to try and make me out to be something I'm not:

MacIntyre's voice-over: "Jason is excited at the prospect of the game, but he keeps up a flow of racist abuse."

Jason Marriner: "Fuck off you black cunt, I've had enough of you's lot around me today. . . . He's fucking got his eyes shut, that old baboon, he thinks he's in the fucking tree. . . . Why you kick my dog and call it 'Fuck Off '?"

Right, first off, can you honestly say you have never said something and then, 10 minutes down the line, regretted you ever even opened your mouth? Maybe you really are one of them lucky people who's never done this, but me? Well, I'm not, am I. And let's face it even the stuff I said taken at it's worst is just part of life. It's like when I lived on the Travellers' site and the Old Bill would always come over and call us all 'Gypsy cunts,' it's just the way it is. But as with the rest of the programme, there was so much more to that car journey than what was shown to you.

First off, I'd played in Southall that morning and I'd had a row with about three or four black players. It didn't matter to me if they were black, white, pink or fucking blue, but it just so happens they were black. Listen, if I have a row with a fat geezer I'll call him a 'fat cunt,' if he's bald then I'll call him a 'bald cunt' and if he's black, yeah, I'll call him a black cunt. It's the way I describe people and that's it. I'm not saying it's right but it's not a racial thing, it's just the way I speak. Many of my black mates who saw the programme just laughed at it, they took it with a pinch of salt because they know me and they knew straight away what was shown on TV wasn't what I'm about.

Now, those of you who live in the London area already know the drive from Southall in the west to Upton Park in the East End is a good hour-and-a-half drive, even more on a match day. I'm supposed to have kept up a 'flow of racist abuse' and yet 'MacInlies' only shows three examples and each of them aren't real. A flow? It wasn't even a trickle and if he'd have had any more believe me, he'd have shown them.

I mean, the 'Why you kick my dog and call him Fuck Off' line, that's one of the oldest jokes going, it's straight out of Bernard Manning who I just happen to think is the 'bollocks.' It's like he tells his audiences at the start of his shows he doesn't care if they're black, white, fat, skinny, short or tall, if they don't think they'll like his jokes they should clear off now because he's not going to go all 'politically correct' just to keep them happy. Everyone gets slaughtered in his shows and that's my sense of humour as well, I find it funny – and so does an Indian mate of mine, he laughs his bollocks off at that 'Why you kick my dog' joke.

And when a BBC journalist starts trying to make a point about your tattoos when he's supposed to be filming you organising and being involved in football violence, well, you have to laugh at that, too:

MacIntyre's voice-over: "I make a regular appointment to watch Jason play football. On the sidelines Jason reveals an impressive spread of tattoos. I realise now why he is so unimpressed with mine. The one on his leg reads like a motto: – 'when we're good they never remember, when we're bad they never forget'."

MacIntyre's only emphasising the fact I've got a lot of tattoos because all the nice, middle-class white people from the Home Counties have always associated tattoos with criminals. It's just another visual technique he's used in his documentary to make me look like I must be guilty of something. As for 'MacInlies'' own tattoo, no, I wasn't impressed. First off, when you've had a few tattoos done yourself you can always spot a new one on someone else so I knew straight away he was lying when he said he'd had it done years ago.

But I'll tell you what the real giveaway was: for such an old tattoo, how come he had the current Chelsea emblem done on his arm? I'm a life-long Chelsea supporter, did he really not think I'd spot that?

6

THE SLY FOXES

Leicester's the game that gets me and Andy put away, no doubt about it, but conspiracy to cause affray? Violent disorder? For fuck's sake, I've seen my young boys have bigger rows than anything you see in that programme and all you didn't see in the unused tapes. Because there wasn't one fight involving me during MacIntyre and Atkinson's entire operation, I was going to go to prison on the back of a programme which doesn't show any evidence of any crime being committed in any way, shape or form from start to finish. There was just a whole lot of talk:

MacIntyre's voice-over: "A few weeks later and I meet Jason outside MacDonalds again, this time to find his plans for the coming match against Leicester."

Yet when it's MacIntyre speaking he can't even tell the truth about something simple like that. The footage from outside MacDonalds was all shot on the same day, they just used a lot of different camera angles to make it seem like different meets. I doubt very much many viewers would have spotted it but I was wearing the same clothes each time and the sequence was split into two.

Now, there's no denying that there is a bit of history between Chelsea and Leicester, there's always been a hostile atmosphere when the two meet and I don't really know how it started but I think some people think of Leicester fans as having a reputation for trouble. It wouldn't have taken much for MacIntyre and Atkinson to find that out and that's why they were so keen to go with me to that particular game, they were adamant. Yeah, they wanted me badly.

But if you watch the programme closely you can clearly see I really didn't even know if I was going to the game or not and this is the 'big one' at which I'm supposed to be organising all the trouble. I did have tickets but I could have got rid of them 300 times over if I couldn't make it. Atkinson and MacIntyre had spares though and, like I've said, it's funny how they always seemed to have spare tickets for Chelsea games:

Jason Marriner: "I don't know, I'm in so many different fucking minds, eh, I was gonna drive up and go on the Friday, see, now I haven't got a game on the Saturday and Sunday, I might fucking . . . I don't know what to do. You know what I mean, 'cos I might have the 'light ale' now."

MacIntyre: "Yeah, yeah."

Jason Marriner: "I might have a drink."

MacIntyre: "Well, that's the thing, you know."

Jason Marriner: "We're meeting, we're meeting early. We're meeting like Loughborough, probably Loughborough, which is one stop before Leicester, as we've got three coaches and a minibus going, it's naughty, Leicester will be naughty."

MacIntyre: "Yeah."

Jason Marriner: "Leicester will be naughty."

MacIntyre voice-over: "Naughty means Jason is planning trouble."

No it doesn't, it doesn't mean that at all. What is he, a mind reader all of a sudden? He assumes he knows what I'm thinking and what I'm planning, but he's way off. 'Naughty' is a word I use a lot to mean any number of different things with one of them being nothing more than a good day out, a good laugh. On one of the many tapes not shown on the documentary I was filmed saying a Traveller's funeral I'd been to had been 'naughty,' I didn't say it to suggest there had been any violence and guess what, there wasn't any there either. Instead, there were over 300 mourners, there was a lot of drink, people having a laugh, getting drunk and having a hangover the next day, yeah, it was 'naughty,' so when I was referring to the Leicester game as looking like it too would be naughty I meant the same thing, that it looked like being a good day out.

Now, here's a BBC reporter, he's made a distorted film about me being a mindless thug while he comes across as spotless. But when I told him about the Traveller's funeral he said 'everyone knows there's always fights at their funerals.' On another of his secretly recorded trips, this time through Brixton, he turned 'round and said with a right sneer, "God, you look out of the window, it's like a different country out there." Once again he was trying to provoke some sort of response from me but I just ignored him, but who's the bigot now? And you didn't see any of that on the television either, did you.

What you saw next was MacIntyre making a point about how I've planned some big operation to get three coach loads up to Leicester without being spotted:

MacIntyre's voice-over: "In order to see his planning in action I offer him a lift on the car. But when he turns up a few days later, he brings two friends.

....One of them is Andy Frain, the most dangerous of the Headhunters and a man with strong links to both extreme loyalists and the Far Right. I've spent months trying to meet him, suddenly he's in the back of my car and it all feels very different.

Andy and Jason are helping co-ordinate 150 Chelsea hooligans as they travel up the M1 for a showdown with the Leicester fans."

Andy Frain: "Hello Dave, it's Nightmare, alright. Are you on the road yet?"

MacIntyre's voice-over: "The coaches start at different points and take different routes. The drivers don't know it, but this is to avoid the police."

So there's around 150 people on the coaches and they took different routes, but what's that supposed to prove? I didn't know where the coaches were coming from because I didn't book them and I can't help it if I'm going to the football and mates of mine who I want to meet up with for a booze are going up on a coach. That doesn't mean I know all the 150 people on the coaches, does it, and as for the different routes they're on, well, it doesn't take an Einstein to work that one out. They're coming from different places and they're taking the easiest way there.

Yet once again MacIntyre's tried to make it all sound as if it's some sinister ploy to evade the police. It's pathetic and it gets worse. They try to make out we're arranging trouble on the mobile phone but the kid called Dave that Andy phoned is a Chelsea supporter. All he's saying is 'have you left yet?' and if you're supposed to be meeting up with a pal you might just phone them up and ask them if they're on their way, that's all Andy's done. Then there's all that stuff about MacIntyre being nervous because Andy's just got in the back of the car but what did he think Andy was going to do to him? Of course he knew Andy wasn't going to do anything, but it made for some exciting television though, didn't it.

I've met up with Andy at the train station in the morning and I've told him all about these two, MacIntyre and Atkinson.

Andy Frain: "He said they're at Hemel Hempstead causing grief. I don't know what they're doing. There's a coach coming from Cheam, somewhere in Cheam. He said they're going the back door, M1, A6 so and so.

"Yes, he said I'm still sat on the coach, he said they're all outside causing trouble, I said how many have you got, he said we're up to full strength, the beers are flowing he said, swigging beer, snorting Charlie and eating sandwiches."

It's a wind-up. Surely anyone can see we're just having a laugh, Andy's almost pissing himself as he says it all but MacIntyre didn't want to get the joke though, did he?:

MacIntyre's voice-over: "I'm beginning to wonder what I've got myself in to. I chew gum and smile nervously to try and cover up how nervous I feel."

Jason Marriner: "It's John – John, where are ya? What coach you on? It's a what? I fucking just passed ya!"......

Andy Frain: "Ask does it have London Coaches, Kent on the side.....ask is it a white transit?"

Jason Marriner: "John, listen to me, are you in a white London Coach, Kent Coach? I mean, I'm just in front of ya!"

Seeing as we're supposed to be organising all this trouble how come there's a coach coming from Cheam Andy's never even heard of, and we don't know if it's left or not. And when we do pass a coach we're laughing because we've just passed our mate, I'm just breaking up a boring car journey chatting with my friends and because we didn't know one of them was on that coach we're genuinely surprised. Not half as surprised as we would be, when we were later charged with conspiracy to commit affray for what happened next.

MacIntyre's voice-over: "Frain has brought the number of a Leicester contact in order to confirm the details of the fight."

Andy Frain: "Dalby, it's the Nightmare calling. Are your boys ready? We'll have starters before the coach gets there. We'll have a one to one with you, Dalby."

Jason Marriner: "Don't tell him where we are. Tell him we're 30-handed and tell him there's only 30 or 40 of us if they turn up, because they like to out-number us. Phone him now, get him on the phone. Get the man out of bed; start terrorising him before he's even had a cup of tea. He won't be able to eat, he'll be physically sick."

Andy Frain: "We'll go to his house now."

Jason Marriner: "We're outside your front door mate. Open the door."

Andy Frain: "Postman's arrived, special delivery for Mr. Dalby."

Dalby is one of the Leicester people and Andy's got to know him through England games while I met him in Poland in '97. He gets mentioned in the car because he's the only Leicester supporter I used to know, it's as simple as that, but I don't know where he lives and he might not even live in Leicester for all I know.

For those who don't know it's an unwritten rule you never go around someone's house. Football's for football, family's for family. We're not organising anything all that talk about going to his house and terrorising his family is just that, all talk, it was all part of the wind-up for those two mongrels, MacIntyre and Atkinson.

Later on we'd be told 'there's your conspiracy,' meaning the phone conversation with Dalby. But there was no phone call at all, no number was dialled and Andy's pretended to make the call by holding the phone to his ear. It's still all part of the joke, we were pretending to be on the phone to Dalby to talk up in front of those two and that's the worst thing that's happened to us.

Surely to conspire to commit a crime you have to talk with each other but because we never actually spoke to Dalby can you tell me where the conspiracy is? I bet MacIntyre must have been lapping this stuff up, this was just what he needed to keep his programme exciting.

MacIntyre's voice-over: "But the worst is yet to come. Jason reminds Andy of the day he slashed a policeman's neck."

Jason Marriner: "He stabbed the kid, he stabbed the geezer in the face, Andy did and then he said 'I'm a policeman,' so what have some more. He had his throat proper cut."

Andy Frain: "We was laughing, he said 'you can't do that'......"

Andy's really made a big joke of this, he's really playing up to them. You can see he's enjoying himself and it's probably why they used it twice in the film. Like I've already told you, Frainy never did it nor was he one of the ones tried and acquitted of slashing the copper. To the average straight viewer this was probably the most shocking part of the film.

Now, how about this as a plot for some 'highly organised football violence':

Jason Marriner: "Hello mate, alright, listen, you know that boozer, is that, that in Market Harbourough? Oh, Narborough, 'cos we're at the junction now. Narborough, alright then, Ok then."

MacIntyre's voice-over: "Marriner and Frain's co-ordination works and three coach loads of Chelsea meet at a village miles away from the Leicester ground. But the Leicester fans don't show up, instead there's a reception committee from the local police. This outcome is no surprise to Jason."

Now first off, if I'd been organising something wouldn't I have known where the pub was and, when we're filmed meeting up with the coaches outside the place, you can see the police are already there, there's absolutely nothing going on at all. Fuck me, it's just a bunch of blokes meeting up at a pub not some co-ordinated plot that has come together. In fact the only people acting suspiciously were MacIntyre's film crew, hiding in one of the vans parked along the road and what's more, this boozer called The Bell we're meeting at is just down the road from the local police station. I tell you what, for some highly organised war we're supposed to have planned, well, fucking hell, let's have it right – you wouldn't have wanted us leading you into Iraq, would you!

I'll tell you something else, MacIntyre's filming could easily have come to an end when we reached the pub because a pal of mine, Flynnie from Sheffield, was supposed to meet me but couldn't because of work and, if he had turned up that day, those two would have been completely fucked. My pal would have recognised them immediately from another series they did on doormen in Nottingham and those clever undercover journalists would have be exposed in a second. My pal's gutted still to this day that he wasn't there to expose them.

He might not have been there but there were plenty of police inside the pub instead and it's obvious there's a good atmosphere in there, there's no sign of anyone there planning to get involved in any violence. Even so MacIntyre can't stop bringing the subject up, he was like a scratched record. Looks like we were both acting a part, just I didn't know we were being filmed:

MacIntyre: "Are Leicester going to turn up?"

Jason Marriner: "They won't turn up now. Didn't you hear what the Old Bill said, 'haven't you phoned them up yet?' I don't care what they say, some of our phones are tapped, man. They do their fucking homework about ya, they do their homework, man."

MacIntyre and Atkinson secretly shot around an hour's worth of film in The Bell and at one point Atkinson whispers to MacIntyre "They'll bring the bacon home," implying that either me or someone else was bound to mention this big fight that was supposed to have been arranged. They really must have believed their own lies by this point because what's written above is about all I said to them when we were in The Bell. And the simple reason for that is they weren't my pals, I've got my back turned to them as much as possible because I want to chat with my mates, not those two.

Even so, there is one speech caught on that film where I can clearly be heard saying, "If anything had cropped up today I wouldn't have come, it gets harder to get away to games" and I said it after I'd been chatting to my pal Mick, who was 37 with two kids and lived out in the sticks. I was explaining to those two how when you get a bit older things do crop up in life which make it harder to get to all the games you want to. And this is inside the pub on the trip I'm supposed to have organised all this violence. So it's no surprise this clip, showing me to be a regular geezer, ended up on the cutting-room floor.

Instead you, the viewers, got MacIntyre's next comments about me and Andy which were highly inflammatory:

MacIntyre's voice-over: "I say goodbye to Andy Frain, who never had any intention of going to the match. He just came to Leicester for a fight. Jason is travelling the last miles to the ground by coach, his plans for violence temporarily foiled.

I leave him knowing that his pent up violence must find an outlet somewhere and on the way home I listen to the radio with a sinking heart."

Radio Commentators: "A bit of aggravation in the crowd during the game with coins being thrown and I think you're about to see some aggravation afterwards – Absolutely dreadful, David." – "Tell me about it?" – "We were walking up the road and we're charged by a group of absolute thugs." – "How many of them?" – "There was about 20 in the group that I saw in the first sort of wave of shouting and goading, punching and kicking indiscriminately.".....

Radio Commentator: "A chap had a mobile phone and he was in hysterics, laughing away and I think he was possibly giving information to his fellow rabble about the rumble."

Now it's true Andy didn't have much intention of going to the game but he never came up to Leicester for a fight. Andy's the Godparent to one of the children of a pal of ours, Brummy Ian. Birmingham's not that far from Leicester and it was a good excuse for Andy to meet up with him. It's not unusual for people in football circles just to travel to go and have a booze with nice company, I know I love all that 'weekends away' stuff, don't you? But another thing and this is important, Andy did not leave that pub. He hadn't organised any violence and he didn't go off in search of any trouble, he stayed in the pub with our mate who'd come over to Leicester to meet him and was already in the pub when we got there. So what was Andy supposed to have been doing then, what was he guilty of, was he having a fight around the fruit machine or something? Of course he wasn't.

I'd got him a free lift there with those two so now he's only got to get himself a train home, if he goes home that night at all as he might decide to stay at Ian's place in Birmingham. We don't plan these weekends away and that's half the fun, not knowing where you'll end up.

But at no point did Andy say to MacIntyre he was staying for a fight – yet that's what 'MacInlies' tells 7.4 million people.

And as for me and my 'pent up aggression'? Let me tell you what really happened. MacIntyre told me in the pub he'd been drinking and he didn't want to get into his car in front of the police. I didn't want to miss the kick-off so all I've done is get on one of the coaches – which you saw me do all on my own and without any help – I get dropped off outside the ground and I watched the. match. That's it.

MacIntyre's given this big build-up saying there's going to be trouble before the game and there wasn't any, so he's stuck now for something to show. Instead, he goes for chat about trouble from a Radio 5 talk show and dubs it over the top of his footage. It's got absolutely nothing to do with what's being shown on the screen and it's got absolutely nothing to do with me.

But don't just take my word for it this is what Paul Mardle, the landlord of The Bell, said later in his witness statement:

"I am the landlord of The Bell public house and have been so since January 1997. I have been asked about the day Leicester played Chelsea in November, 1998....There were 80-100 Chelsea fans in the pub....There was a fairly heavy police presence outside. The police told me they were present because of their intelligence. (grasses, we call them). They told me that a number of people at the pub were known instigators of violence and were banned from attending games. No-one was pointed out to me.

"None of the fans in the pub caused any trouble. One or two got a bit loud and some of the language was bad, but they seemed to be kept in check by the rest of the group....I think that the fans stayed until about 2.45pm. The majority of them then left. Four or five of them stayed in the pub. I cannot recall how long this group stayed in the pub, maybe an hour or so....

"....my wife Liz rang the secretary of Chelsea supporters club and asked that he passed on a message to the supporters thanking them for their behaviour and custom.

"I do not know and have never had any contact with Jason Marriner....I am of good character. I am willing to attend Court and give evidence if necessary."

So now I'm inside the ground and I'm filmed while there's a fight going on not more than 10ft away from me. There's a bloke next to me who is on a mobile phone – and why shouldn't he be anyway, people do get calls during football matches – but I don't use one, I'm not involved in any of the fighting and yet I'm supposed to have been the one who's organised it all. After the game I went straight to the train station and got the first train home. I've since found out there were at least two BBC reporters there at the station who saw me get on the train and once again, there was no trouble. They failed to mention that in their programme as well, didn't they?

Oh yeah, and one other thing, that Radio 5 caller who spoke of some geezer after the match who looked like he was arranging trouble on a mobile. Well, two months after my arrest I had to take part in an I.D. parade at Brixton police station so this fella can pick out the man he saw on the phone. And do you know what, he never picked me out even though he admitted watching the documentary.

As for Macintyre and Atkinson, well, having made all this effort they needed something for their programme because if they relied on just the truth it was falling apart around them. But never let the truth get in the way of a good story, eh! The next scene is supposed to have been filmed after the trouble at the Leicester game but it wasn't. It was filmed the same day MacIntyre tried to show off his tattoo, it was the same meet and once more they dub some more radio chat over the top.

MacIntyre's voice-over: "Later that week, Jason tells me what happened in Leicester."

Jason Marriner: "Ah, it was fucking left, right and centre, it was just happening, do you know what I mean? Just fucking, eh, in the grounds where it normally happens, in the ground….where they're in the corner bit, like. Where they stand there and we're here."

Radio Commentators: "The child we were with was absolutely terrified, he's come home with his hat and scarf down and told his mum he doesn't want to go to football again." – "That's awful, how old is he? – "He's seven."

Now that whole quote from me shown there had nothing to do with Leicester, I was telling them about what happened when I got sent off playing at Yeading Football Club. You also get a slowed-down shot of me and I seem to be roaring twice, as if I'm some crazy maniac who's been let loose onto the streets.

They've taken what I've said, lifted it, enhanced it and then tried to voice match it into the sequence to give the impression they want. It was a totally false impression and like all their other filming tricks I picked up on it straight away, as soon as I saw it the first time. But no-one else watching could have picked up on that, they'd have had to have had it explained to them and that kind of false film-making is an absolute fucking liberty. Next, 'MacInlies' returns to his old trick of saying something so open-ended it can be taken either way and by now only someone who's really been paying attention is going to give me the benefit of the doubt.

MacIntyre's voice-over: "After the violence Jason didn't go home, instead he went for a drink to mark a special occasion. Five Chelsea had been charged with this attack earlier in the year. Two of them were expecting to be sent to prison, The attack was on some Tottenham Hotspur fans in Central London.

"The Chelsea used iron bars to beat the opposing fans and then smashed up the pub. The people leading the charge are two notorious brothers, the Sims twins, vicious Headhunters and close friends of Jason and Andy. Jason and Andy were there, too, masked by the kiosk.

"Not only do the police fail to arrest Jason, Frain and the others, but the twins who led the attack were only sentenced to two and a half years, with parole, they will only serve 15 months."

So you saw the fighting at the Argyle in the West End and you saw the big white kiosk which hid me and some others. Well, I'll tell you now, I was exactly where they said, blocked from the cameras by the kiosk. But I never got arrested or charged for this and there was never any Queen's evidence against me or I'd have been sent to prison for these offences.

'MacIntyre Undercover' then showed a lot of footage of Danny Walford and Gerry Gable gives us more of his informed comments. You can't shut the man up, can you, some people just love seeing themselves on the television. Then MacIntyre heads towards his documentary's conclusion, the Bloody Sunday march in January, 1999.

There isn't much of the programme left but in keeping with the rest of the bollocks that's gone before it, it's so far from the truth of what actually happened it becomes just another 'MacInlies' lie. What's more, it later gets me an extra two years' consecutive thrown on top. So what, I prefer the number six to four anyway.

MacIntyre's voice-over: "Andy Frain seems to have almost a mythical status amongst hooligans. He's at the centre of the most chilling events of my year as a hooligan.

"This march commemorates 'Bloody Sunday,' the day 27 years ago when 14 Catholics were shot dead in Northern Ireland. But these Far Right supporters will do anything they can to disrupt the march. The police are out in force trying to protect the marchers. They stop and search other Far Right thugs as they arrive, that includes Andy Frain, Jason Marriner and me.

"I've arranged to meet Jason in a pub nearby, where he has already linked up with the leader of the Far Right faction, Combat 18. Jason's been planning to attack this march with them for months. I notice he's drinking mineral water."

With this part of the programme they start by showing a National Front counter demonstration but I'm not a part of that, they were at Downing Street and I was in Trafalgar Square. I don't want to stand with them and I don't want to be penned in with them. I'm not a member of the National Front, Combat 18 or any other Far Right group but of course MacIntyre wants to rope me in with them so he shows their demonstration which has nothing to do with me, I'm not even in the vicinity, just to suggest I'm part of it.

But this was never a march organised solely by the Far Right, it was simply an anti-IRA counter demonstration. What I'm there for is my freedom of speech which, unless I'm mistaken, I'm legally allowed to exercise. IRA sympathisers are marching down my streets and I feel entitled to voice an opinion about that and I was there as a Loyalist objecting to what I saw as an IRA presence. They tried to make out it was all hardened thugs there to cause trouble but I'll tell you who else was there protesting against these marchers and that's members of the armed forces. One of them had had his leg blown off, so don't you think he had the right to protest against terrorist supporters marching down our streets?

MacIntyre also claims he's arranged to meet me and even that's not true. I'd been asked some time before if I was going on the march and to be honest, I hadn't been on one for years, I said I might go but even the day before I wasn't 100% (so much for planning to attack the march for months) all I knew was that if I was going we were to meet at Waterloo. It turns out MacIntyre and Atkinson had an informant keeping them up to date about me – I tell you more about the 'grass' soon – so they were still able to find out my plans even from the day before. And without even trying to, Andy and me made those two's jobs so fucking easy as when I spoke to Andy we arranged to get on the same train together. When we got to Waterloo MacIntyre and Atkinson were already there, all they'd had to do was wait for us to arrive.

Once again, a clever piece of editing from the pub makes it seem I'm about to start some trouble:

MacIntyre: "What's this mineral water?"

Jason Marriner: "I don't give a fuck. That's ammunition mate, a bottle's a bottle to me. I don't give a fuck as long as it hits one of them."

What's been cut from MacIntyre's speech is that after that he also said "It's Ballygowan water, that's Fenian water," before I replied. And once again I'm just boasting, it's just pub talk. But of course MacIntyre uses it to his advantage:

MacIntyre's voice-over: "As the marchers hand in a petition to Downing Street the extremists I'm with are planning to pounce. Leading the attack is Andy Frain, in the front line...is Jason."

To be fair to him he's finally got something right, we were at the front. We later proved in court that no bottle was smashed that day and when I'm next seen running around the corner, it was made to look like we were running to attack the march but really we'd just left the pub too late and there's no bottle in my hand at this point. Now, do you remember when you were at school and there was always some loudmouth teacher shouting, "Don't run – Walk!" at you. If he'd added something like "or you'll end up in prison," I'd have pissed myself laughing at him.

At the end of the day, all you've got on film is the pair of us running 'round a corner. The Old Bill didn't nick anyone that day because nothing happened and there's nothing more to be shown from the march on the programme. So that means I would later get another two years just for running 'round a corner and shouting. A bit harsh that, don't you reckon?

As the programme draws to a close MacIntyre tries to sum up all I'm supposed to have done over the 18 months he's secretly been out to get me:

MacIntyre's voice-over: "There were many more moments that I recorded in my year as a hooligan. I went anywhere where I thought the Headhunters might be.

"To Loyalist marches, to United for a fight that never happened, to Derby in the rain, even to Majorca when Jason failed to turn up . . . Jason continues to evade the police and has renewed his season ticket to Chelsea . . . Jason has taken me to the heart of the Headhunters and, after a year undercover, at last I was able to leave his world behind."

Yeah, I went to the Man.U. game and there wasn't any trouble, Derby I went to but not with MacIntyre and Atkinson while as for Majorca, I never went even though they offered to pay for me for the whole week because they wanted me there so badly. Just think, if you followed the Pope around for a year-and-a-half, secretly filmed him and then edited the film any way you wanted to you could even make him look like a criminal. Man of God? He'd end up looking more like the Godfather.

I'm supposed to have led 'MacInlies' to the very 'heart of the Headhunters' so if that was the case just think how much stuff he should have been able to get on me. And what's he really got? Not much, when you think about it – in fact, he got nothing at all.

So why did he choose me and what set the ball rolling in the first place? It's a story in itself and one which I will now answer, once and for all, how I supposedly let MacIntyre fool me for so long. Believe me when I tell you that's one question I'm sick to fucking death of hearing.

7

PLAYING A RINGER

Do you remember I said I'd had a tip-off that the programme was going to be shown and that I saw it with a local solicitor? Well, the kid who told me the programme was coming out is called Darren Wells. He'd done some work with the BBC before and he had some other mates who still worked there. One of them does the lighting and this geezer has seen a trailer for the MacIntyre programme. He recognised me so he told Wells about it, who then got hold of me.

When Wells said the documentary about me concerned football I just laughed it off, the first thing I said was, "Well what's that going to say, that I support Chelsea? Surely everyone knows that." But then it dawned on me and I asked him, "I don't suppose it's anything to do with those two flash mongrels I've been taking the piss out of, is it?" and when he told me more of what the documentary was about I said, "I think that stinks."

I asked Wells to find out some more details for me – I didn't know he was a 'Bertie' at the time who had grassed me up – and it turned out the programme was due to be broadcast a month later. I went to a local solicitor to get it stopped, or at least to get an advance copy of the programme so I could see for myself what it was all about, but the BBC are very powerful, more than you might realise, so to no avail. I understand that the BBC are powerful but should we really be so scared of them. It really gets my back up because after all, they're funded from money out of yours and my pockets. But all I could do was sit and wait.

With hindsight I'm sure Wells is the one who's set this whole thing up, for me to be 'investigated' by the BBC. I've known this kid for 10, maybe 15 years and I've always had my suspicions about him, he was always up to this, that or the other. He never went to Chelsea that much, he was more involved with a lot of other stuff I'm not in to.

I reckon he must have got himself into some sort of trouble with some of the things he's done and this time he can't get out of it, so he's keen to help the police – which makes him nothing more than a paid informant – and the Old Bill, in turn, have been quite happy to share their information with the programme's makers, just to see where it might lead. MacIntyre and Atkinson start doing their homework after Wells has informed them about me and they find my name keeps coming up. But of course my name keeps coming up, I've been going to football for over 20 years and to be honest, I was a fucking nuisance at football. Those two now know they can use me, they know I can go to Sheffield Wednesday, Man. United, Arsenal, Man. City, Newcastle, wherever, and I know all their boys as they've been pals of mine for years. MacIntyre and Atkinson just thought, 'here's a kid we can make a good story out of,' that's all they were interested in.

Oh yeah, and another thing about Wells, he was the one who kept pressing for me to attend the anti-Bloody Sunday demonstration when I wasn't sure if I was going or not. With Wells as their informant MacIntyre and Atkinson would have found out the day before the march that me and Andy were coming in to Waterloo so all they had to do was wait for us. Wells is in America now and I'm led to believe he got £7,000 for a double-page spread in a national newspaper and I don't know what he got from Searchlight working as an informer for them, but I'm sure he's more than spent it by now.

Once MacIntyre, Atkinson and the BBC had made their decision to target me, from this point on they would not be prepared to admit they'd made a mistake. They were now going to get me for however long and whatever it took – nice to be wanted, isn't it.

But listen, in the programme MacIntyre claims he did all this snooping around just to find me, yet it had nothing to do with that. Like I said, most people know me and where I live, he could have found out easy enough. No, what he wanted was an 'in' and him and Atkinson thought they'd found it through a good friend of mine, Heather Smith. The lengths they went to, to try and find stuff out on me before faking a meet, is laughable but don't take my word for it, here's what Heather later had to say herself, in her court statement:

In the Blackfriars Crown Court:

R – v – Jason Marriner – Statement of Heather Smith

Heather Smith will say as follows:

1 – I am 28 years old and have no criminal convictions.

2 – I met Jason through an ex-boyfriend. This was about six years ago. I

shared a flat with this ex-boyfriend for about two years. Jason lived there at the same time but moved out before I did. Jason has never been my boyfriend.

3 – About two years ago I began working as a barmaid in the Jenny Lind Public house in Hampton Hill.....MacIntyre was the first of them to start coming in the pub. He used to come in on his own. He invariably ordered one bottle of Bud.....for some reason he never finished a bottle and the first conversation I had with him was me asking why he always left most of the bottle. To begin with he used to come into the pub and do this almost every day.

4 – The first time I met Paul Atkinson was one night when he came into the pub with Donal MacIntyre. They sat at a table together. The pattern changed, from MacIntyre being there alone to both of them being there. I got talking to Paul when MacIntyre told me that Paul was not happy as he had split up with his girlfriend....Then Paul started coming in alone...On one of these occasions he asked me if I knew Jason Marriner and I told him that I did.

He asked me for his telephone number but because I did not know him I was not prepared to give him Jason's mobile number, although in fact, I did have it. On that occasion he gave me his pager number and his mobile number, asked me if I would contact Jason and ask Jason to contact him.

I asked him why he wanted me to get Jason to contact him and he told me he was in the process of buying a fleet of vehicles and therefore wanted as reliable supplier of tyres....About a week later Paul came in and told me that he had actually spoken to Jason.

5 – Some days later Paul came in and told me he would like to thank me for putting him in touch with Jason and asked if he could take me out to dinner. I told him that wasn't necessary, as I had only passed on some telephone numbers, but he persisted, he said it was a big favour and that he would really like to take me out for a meal.....It was arranged for the following Saturday night.

6 – ....We went to the Blue Elephant Thai Restaurant in Fulham. We drove there in his Mercedes, but the drive was strange because he kept driving round in circles. I assumed this was simply because he was not familiar with the area, I had noted he had a northern accent and of course, he had already told me he was new to the area.

We got to the restaurant, he behaved flash, we had champagne throughout the meal. We spoke a bit about him and me, but I found it strange and somewhat annoying that he mostly wanted to talk about Jason.....on the way home....his mobile rang and it was MacIntyre.

Paul had a very monosyllabic conversation with MacIntyre and I was very surprised when he then handed the telephone over to me. MacIntyre asked me if I had had a good night, I obviously told him that I had and he told me he would see me soon.

7 – After the meal Paul continued coming into the pub regularly, but my recollection is that I only saw MacIntyre in the pub on one more occasion....Paul came to the pub with another younger man who was from Manchester and introduced me to him. Unfortunately, I cannot now recollect his name, in the rest of this statement I will refer to him as X.

8 – On one of these occasions that Paul was in the pub, he invited me out again.....I told him that on the day in question a friend was having a going away party at the Jenny Lind pub and I suggested we went there first....We were sat with some of my flat mates and X was with Paul. I found it strange that he had brought male company with him.

Paul and I were talking to each other and it was on this occasion that he told me he imported/exported drugs. He told me it was mainly dope, but some cocaine. He had told me when we went out for the meal...that he had a five-year addiction to cocaine, I reacted neutrally to this information.

He also told me he could not read or write and did I think Jason would take him to Copenhagen with him. He gave me the impression that because he could not read or write he could not travel alone. I told him I had no idea, that it would be up to Jason, not me.

Shortly after he told me this four of us left the pub. We were going back to my flat.....We were there for a couple of hours....before Paul and I were alone....We kissed. I actually got his shirt buttons undone. He wanted to take things further but kept saying he could not. He was obviously embarrassed and kept saying he couldn't, he couldn't....it did cross my mind that he might be married.

9 – The next day I had invited X out to meet a friend of mine, my brother and his girlfriend. X had explained to me that he was new in the area and wanted to meet some friends, out of kindness I invited him along....X said Paul would be joining us later. Paul did eventually arrive and we had drinks and food...I now feel very foolish that I read the menu out to Atkinson

.....Before he left he said he would like to go out with me again and asked me to ring him, to tell him when I would be free. I did ring him on a few occasions, but he never responded to his mobile telephone or pager.

10 – After a gap of about one month he telephoned me and we arranged to meet, on a week night at about 7pm. At about 6.30pm, he telephoned me to say he could not make it. I was really quite cross he cancelled this on 30 minutes' notice...I did telephone him on a few more occasions after this, but he never responded and I never heard from him again.

Atkinson was scum doing what he did, the way he grafted my friend Heather, wined and dined her at no expense spared just to get to me – you couldn't make it up, could you – but it gives you a good idea of the extent these two were prepared to use people just to make their documentary. MacIntyre and Atkinson have now done their little bit of homework on me, they now know I run a garage with new and part-worn tyres, that I've got someone working for me with the recovery trucks and someone else as a mechanic. They start asking me about tyres for the courier firm and c'mon, ask yourself, what am I supposed to do to a legitimate business offer? Say 'No, you might be journalists for the BBC who are filming my every move and conversation?'

So to all of you who've since asked me "didn't you ever suspect him?" and "how did you fall for him for so long?" tell me, what did I fall for there? I never did 'fall' for either of them at any time, as you'll soon see.

MacIntyre asked me if I knew anyone who could fit an exhaust on his car and I said "Yeah, my friend Graham can help." Then the next time I saw him MacIntyre offers me this fake Burberry t-shirt to say thanks for my friend helping him out. I said there was no need and I told him straight, "I don't mean to be funny, but I don't wear snide clothes, thanks all the same." MacIntyre told me he's got a mate in the Midlands with a factory churning out this snide gear and that I can have as much as I want of whatever make I liked and again I refused -What is it with him, aren't we speaking the same language? He'd 'bumped' into me just as I was off on holiday, so I went away for a fortnight and never gave it another thought. But this was just the first attempt by the two of them to try and impress me with their dodgy business dealings.

Now, apart from one brief scene in France and MacIntyre trying to make out football violence is now fuelled by drugs as it may be by alcohol, drugs were not mentioned again in the programme. Funny that, because all the while they were secretly filming me those two couldn't stop talking about drugs, that is when they weren't talking about football violence but they didn't show that footage, did they? So why would MacIntyre and Atkinson keep referring to drugs, well, let me tell you.

Those two were never impartially investigating whether or not I was involved in organising football violence. As far as they were concerned I was guilty of this right from the start (sounds like some magistrates, judges and jurors I've met). In their own minds they'd built up a picture of me as some shady under-world figure so they adopted the roles of stereotypical criminals, because they believed it would make it easier for them to be accepted by me. And the act they put on, first hinted at by Atkinson to Heather Smith when he was using her, was of a pair of high level international drug dealers.

They were about six or seven months into their investigation when they first offered me drugs, it happened during the filming they took outside the McDonalds restaurant and Atkinson said he wanted me to shift his cocaine for him. I made it very clear I wasn't interested, you can clearly hear me say on film but they were both very persistent.

They started offering to cut me in to their cannabis business and even then I don't respond positively, despite the fact they're both enthusiastic about it. At one point Atkinson's brought up the subject of drugs yet again and I simply turn away from him without replying. When I do talk, I change the subject to my tyre business. But because they were so sure I was a criminal and bound to be impressed by their easy way to get cash and flash cars, they just couldn't let up. Not only did they offer to set up an off-shore account for me they even offered me a flat in St Johns Wood or Belgravia, if I agreed to get involved in their drug deals. Think about it, those two have offered me everything from snide t-shirts, Class A and Class B drugs to off-shore accounts, all in the hope I'd slip up and show myself to be a criminal and I've constantly said no to everything. Why would I go for it, I had my own business, I wasn't impressed by them at all so ask yourself, were they deliberately trying to ruin my life?

And it wasn't just me they were trying to trap with drugs. I've since heard that when we were in the pub before the Leicester game MacIntyre offered another kid cocaine in the toilets, which he refused. This bloke didn't know who MacIntyre was until the programme was broadcast but as soon as he saw him he recognised him immediately, he was 100% sure it was the same geezer.

Now, you have a think about that. MacIntyre must have had the drugs on him when he offered them because he'd have looked pretty fucking stupid if the bloke had turned 'round and said 'yes' only for MacIntyre to be empty-handed. If this is the case, and from what I know now of MacIntyre's methods I've no reason to I believe it isn't, then does that mean when MacIntyre's conducting his investigative journalism he's above the law?

MacIntyre later claimed in court he is convinced in his own mind that drugs play a major part in the Chelsea Headhunters and whatever other hooligan groups are supposed to be operating nowadays. When he did his programme on doormen he also offered them drugs, the same as when he did the documentary on the fashion industry. But surely, if you keep offering people drugs and they keep refusing when are you going to get the hint? It's just trying to create something which isn't there – just what is it with him and how is he allowed to get away with it?

There are a couple other important points people need to know about MacIntyre and Atkinson's 'drug dealers' act. Later in his prosecution statement MacIntyre claims during his investigation that he did not encourage anyone to do or say anything out of character – hey, hold on, he hasn't done nothing but encourage me to act out of character. The very fact they'd portrayed themselves as major drug dealers meant I felt the need to impress them and exaggerated every story I told them for the maximum impact and I encouraged Andy to do the same before the car journey to Leicester for exactly the same reason, so those two would continue throwing their money about like they had been.

Also, in all the hours of uncut tapes there are so many occasions it's clear to see that MacIntyre and Atkinson repeatedly bring whatever conversation we're having back to football violence, when it's obvious I'd rather talk about something else. A major BBC guideline is that their journalists shouldn't ask leading questions, but leading questions were the only type I was asked for 18 months' solid so don't tell me I wasn't being encouraged to do anything out of character.

But forget about biased reporting and BBC guidelines for a moment, what MacIntyre and Atkinson did was blatant entrapment – ask Sophie Rhys Jones, now the Countess of Wessex, about that when she was set up by tabloid journalists trying to dig some dirt on her. Although all she got was a few days' embarrassing press, she didn't end up doing a six did she? – it still stinks though, doesn't it and how come what happened to her was considered entrapment when my stitch-up wasn't? It looks like another case of 'one rule for one, but not for Joe Public.' Because even if those two had managed to film me committing one single crime during those 18 months (which they didn't), by rights it still shouldn't have been allowed in a proper court of law and wouldn't have been in any other country. But things are different in England where, it seems, entrapment is no defence.

Think about it, someone can worm they way into your life, encourage you to commit a crime you'd never have considered doing without them egging you on and then, boomf, they turn 'round and say they're Old Bill and you're nicked. Whatever evidence they've got against you is then allowed in a court of law if your defence fail to cast any doubt on how the police (or anyone working on their behalf) behaved to get that evidence. And to cap it all, even if the defence do prove the police or their agents have behaved improperly, the evidence can still be used to convict you. All the prosecution have to do is claim that their case will 'resolve any inadequacies' during the course of the trial.

In other words when it comes to entrapment under English law, you, as the defendant, cannot win. I don't believe for a minute my case would have come to court in a country like America, so do you now see why more and more people are getting sick of the legal system in England?

Considering all MacIntyre, Atkinson and their colleagues have done and the way they've gone about it you might not think what I'm about to tell you is that important. But listen, this is the one thing about the programme which I found really fucking insulting: it was the way it was cut to make it seem MacIntyre was my best pal. Because believe me, it was nothing like that at all.

First off, they wanted me to see them moving in to the block of flats at Chelsea Close, they made every effort (including having their own 'spotters' waiting for me and saying 'here he comes! here he comes!') just to bump into me, so they'd have the chance to speak to me. This was a block of only six flats, yet for three months – three fucking months! – I didn't even say as much as 'hello' to either of them. So much for the flash cars they were flaunting to get my attention like the couple of Porsches and Mercedes. And I thought first impressions were supposed to count for something.

Even after we'd first spoken I was very stand-offish with them both for a long time, because I never felt 100% comfortable around them. I just didn't like either of them, it was as simple as that, but they were always willing to spend a few bob whether it was drinks, take-aways, match tickets, plane tickets, or whatever. At the end of the day I didn't have to like them and when you've got a couple of pricks around who want to be flash and spend money like they're Joe The Champs, well, you suffer them. It was as simple as that as far as I was concerned. In fact, they pissed me off so much with their flash routine that by the time we got to Copenhagen I was all set to fuck them and their drug importing – and I mean really fuck 'em.

Listen, let me explain, before we left for Denmark these flash bastards had offered me x-amount of cocaine and I don't want nothing to do with that nor their other cannabis deals, I'm just not interested. But then they've offered me 20 cars at £5,000 a car just to move them from one part of London to another.

According to them, these cars had between 50 and 100 kilos of cannabis stashed inside, which other dealers were then supposed to pick up and serve whoever it is they serve. With my recovery trucks I could have shifted all those cars in a day. So when you see me in the pub in Copenhagen happily talking to them so it seems like we're all becoming good pals, what I'm really doing is playing a little bit of a reverse role. I'm just letting them think they're getting bang in to me because by now I'd already decided 'Right, I'm going to set them up.'

The way I saw it I could move all those cars, take them some place else and then turn 'round and say to those two, 'You're fucked, how about that.' Even if I'd got nicked doing it I could have told the police the truth, that I was moving these cars which had broken down. If it had been cocaine then no, no way, you couldn't give me £10million to get involved in Class A drugs because that could have meant a 25 year sentence, my life gone and you can only spend £15 a week in prison so the money doesn't count. Yet that shows how much they'd annoyed me by this time with their flash, arrogant chat, I'd reached the point I felt it was time to line them up to fuck 'em, they were ready to be rumped. In the end I didn't do it, but it gives you a better idea of what I really thought about them both.

There's still something else you wouldn't know about me and my 'best mate' MacIntyre. I only ever got to know him as 'Macca,' during all the time he was filming me, I never even knew his full name, that's how well I got to know him. And the reason for that? It's simple, I never saw him more than 25 times in the entire18 months, which is only one or two brief meetings a month, because he was off doing more filming for the other programmes in his series at the same time as he was doing mine. Obviously I didn't know that at the time. His excuse for going away, as if I cared, was that he was out of the country sorting out all his big time drug runs, this that and the other. It's why I had no idea he'd turn up at the airport in Copenhagen and when he did, he passed it off as saying he'd just finished doing some drug deal in Amsterdam.

No, it was Paul Atkinson who you don't even see on screen who 'had the talk and had the walk,' it was him I saw the most of even if it was just bumping in to him. When he was Old Bill, Atkinson had worked Moss Side so he'd had to do a few moves in his time and he was definitely better at it than MacIntyre. On a number of their secret tapes, recorded when they were both working together like in Copenhagen, you can clearly hear Atkinson having to keep telling MacIntyre, 'Less is more, less is more,' because MacIntyre kept going way over the top when he was trying to act like he thought a 'hooligan' was supposed to – the prick was an embarrassment to his own colleague.

But most of the time Atkinson was tying up everything this end for MacIntyre while he was out of the country filming more lies for the other documentaries. When they come to show the 'football hooligans' documentary on the tele it's all in MacIntyre's name so he's just taken the cream with his name on the credits while Atkinson's the one who actually did all the legwork. Even so, Atkinson didn't impress me any more than his idiot friend and they both know this because they later admitted as much in court.

Yet what you've got to understand is that even the title of this documentary – shown on the BBC which has always prided itself on its journalistic integrity (their standards must be slipping) – was as misleading as the rest of it.

'MacIntyre Undercover'? No, it should have been called 'Atkinson Undercover.'

8

"WHO'S THAT TEAM THEY CALL
THE CHELSEA?"

I'm not going to pretend to be something I'm not, that's 'MacInlies" game and I think it stinks so I'll tell you now I have been a nuisance and, you know, maybe I was the 'Black Sheep' of the Marriner family. But I was always brought up to have respect for myself and for others at all times, I've never lost my self-respect nor have I ever not shown respect to those who deserve it.

My interest in football's a life-long one thanks to my dad Graham who first took me to Chelsea when I was five years old and Chelsea's been a part of me ever since. But you know how it is, you get a bit older and you want to go with your mates don't you and, let me tell you now, I did become a nuisance at football, I've done more than just serve my apprenticeship at Chelsea, do you know what I mean?

I was about 15 when I first got involved in the violence and went up to an away game at Wolves with about five or six other mates in a motor. On the way up there someone said about me, 'his arsehole won't go, he'll stand there no matter what.' Well, I was about to find out, wasn't I. Before the game we pulled into the car park and my mate asked me to hold this big Union Jack with Chelsea on it while he had a piss up against a wall. A little mob's come over and started fronting us and this black fella's come over to me and said "What's on the Union Jack?" I've said "Chelsea" and this geezer's had a bit of a dig at me. I remember hitting him as hard as I could and he just hasn't moved an inch. I thought 'Fuck me, I'm in trouble now' – and I was – this geezer's punched me all 'round the gaff. A little later on my eye's come up a bit and I knew I'd been involved in a scrap.

It soon got around that a few of us had got picked on and the firm at that time took great offence to it, it escalated from there and in a way I thought, 'that's nice,' because it seemed like the firm respected me. I'm not daft, I know it wasn't me personally getting a clump the firm took offence to, it was Chelsea, but it made an impression on me and I thought to myself, 'yeah, that's a bit of me, that is.'

Over the next couple of years I gradually got into it and then I started helping to organize coach trips from Twickenham for the away games. We'd be 54-handed on our coach and we'd meet up with two or three other coach loads. We'd go into a pub – boomf – we'd do the fruit machines straight away because there were no alarm bells and then go on to the next pub down the road, do the same thing there and the trip's already paid for itself. Well, I was 17 or 18 at the time and you've got no fear in you at that age, you're a scallywag, aren't you. No-one that age cares about anything because you've got no respect for society when you're younger. All you ever think about is having a laugh, getting away with it and, after you've seen Chelsea lose 6-0 to Rotherham on a rainy Saturday afternoon, trying to cop for some northern treacle to make up for it, that's all I was doing.

And let me tell you mate, we really did have a laugh because those away games were absolutely fucking blinding. Believe me, Chelsea would get on the map just for being in town, like the time we stopped off at Northampton on the way back from a Man.U. game. That's because it doesn't have to be about the football itself, does it? You stop off in a town and the local kids hear that Chelsea are there then someone chats up a bird in a pub who's already with some geezer and that's all it takes – boomf – Let me tell you, we got banned from Northampton after that night, from the whole fucking town, no Chelsea coaches were ever allowed to stop there for the next few seasons.

And it's not just your mob that can get itself a bit of a reputation, you can earn a name for yourself, too. If you can call on a firm of hundreds it's not long before you're going to come to the attention of the 'proper' people, for example my pal Dave Courtney. He's a lovely bloke, not what people who don't know him would imagine. He's no longer active but Dave would tell you himself that he earned his reputation for being 'The Yellow Pages of Crime' as he could put the right people in touch with each other for certain jobs. Dave knew I could call on any number of top kids in an instant so there were always opportunities there for some security work, whether it was on the door at a nightclub or just making sure things ran smoothly. Another example was when one of Dave's American pals was over and he needed a hand in the West End. Dave phoned me up, I got my mob and lets just say the Americans and Chelsea came out on top.

But let's face it, a toe-to-toe doesn't have to be on anything like that kind of scale as there's always the typical Curry House scenario. You know the type of thing, a few geezers cause a bit of trouble after too much booze with their bhirianis and the police are called. Yet because you're all football supporters on the way back from a game they mark it up as 'football violence' even though it could have happened on any night of the week. The next day you could get a group of rugby fans doing the same kind of thing and they'd just pass it off as 'high spirits.' Let's have it right, you and I already know there's a different set of rules off the pitch for those of us who follow John Terry rather than Johnnie Wilkinson and there always has been.

Listen, there's some staunch, hard men who follow football, don't be in any doubt about that, but being part of a firm isn't all about being hard. If you're game, your willing to have a row and stand up for your cause that can count for just as much in a toe-to-toe. And you never think twice about it when it happens because you wouldn't be with the mob you're with if you did. That, or you're lying to and cheating yourself. No, on your day you should seriously believe you can take anyone, whoever you support, or you just shouldn't be there.

For years we've had all these government ministers and intellectuals trying to find a reason behind what causes football violence. Maybe they should ask a kid who knows as it would save them a fortune on research because it's all so simple. As a young kid if you go to a school in one borough you'll end up fighting a school in another borough, if you come from one council estate you fight the lot from the other council estate, it's part and parcel of growing up and it's just the same with football. Everyone's got local rivals and they always will have. And I tell you now, it's still happening every week all around the country, your Burnleys, your Stockports, your Cardiffs, wherever. Whether they're 30-40 handed or more, it's still happening.

I don't see it going completely for years as there's something in the British breed, you can call it 'the Bulldog spirit' or call it what you want, but proper people in this country can't help but feel passionate about something they love. There are thousands of people who feel passionate about the clubs they support and they feel that way for the whole of their lives, you can never just switch off from that because it's a part of what makes you who you are. I know I'll always feel passionate about Chelsea – but the football violence has gone for me, it's a thing of the past and I'm not interested in it anymore. And that's nothing to do with the sentence I got, it's just all good things come to an end so go on the Chelsea Youth, it's your turn and have some fun.

I'll tell you something else, I even told that worm MacIntyre as much on more than one occasion because he kept bringing the subject up, it's all on his many unused tapes, like the time we were travelling through Brixton and he starts the conversation by talking about how he tries to keep fit. It's all harmless stuff at first and then he asks me what I do when I'm training so I tell him a bit about the kick-boxing I'd been doing. All of a sudden he starts getting excited as if I'm about to reveal to him all the secret moves of the football hooligan and you can hear it in his voice when he says "I bet that comes in useful during a toe-to-toe, do you use the kick-boxing much for that?" I explained that, yeah, in the past I might have used what I'd learnt through kick-boxing without really thinking about it at the time, just to swerve a punch or whatever, but I also made it clear that this was years ago and I'd stopped all that.

And MacIntyre just wasn't listening on another occasion when he was secretly filming me at his west London flat. He starts by making up some story about how his Chelsea tattoo caused a Millwall supporter to give it the large one and how he was just about to sort him out when the geezer's backed off. He probably thought his bragging about some football-related violence would start me off telling some of my own stories, but do you know what my response was? "Don't get yourself sucked into it, you'll only end up getting nicked....affray's a big charge, there's no value in it. You've got to switch off and be happy in life." I also told him, "At the end of the day, the older I have got the more I'm not interested in football violence, those days have gone, the '80s are over, it's time to get on with life." You can't live in the past and it will never be the same. As you've probably guessed, 'McInlies' comes back with more of his leading questions and he says he'll have more time for violence abroad the following year. All I can say in reply is, "My dream is to watch Chelsea play at Barcelona." Fuck it, there's just no telling some people, is there?

But there's one group though who really don't want the football violence to end and half of them will tell you as much. And that's the plain-clothes police spotters because if all the football violence ended overnight that's all their overtime gone.

Now, you go to football for years you get to learn to 'spot the spotters.' Like I've said, they know us and we know them. Some of them think we're all proper scum but there's others who come to keep an eye on us and, over a period of time, they get to know we're just normal blokes so their bosses have to keep swapping the spotters around because we can spot them and at times they try to be too matey. It's like when Chelsea were over in Norway recently, they knocked us out but there was never going to be any trouble. There were about 500 Chelsea there, by all accounts, and the Norwegians loved us but when there was a little incident these two Chelsea police out there on a 'busman's holiday' jumped at the chance to justify the cost of them being there. They started by winding up the local Old Bill by saying there might be some real trouble if they don't act now, they've got them stopping people without tickets, entering hotels and demanding to see tickets, all kinds of stuff and in the end it's the local Old Bill who've turned 'round to these two Chelsea coppers and said, "What's your problem?" because no-one who'd come to see the football was causing trouble anyway.

Do you remember at the start of the documentary when MacIntyre's in France, he's in a bar watching the England – Argentina game and a geezer in a green cap takes a fag off of him? That was my pal Ian from Kidderminster,

Well, Ian went to France on the Eurostar and when the police came through the train they started talking to him, asking him what team he supported and that kind of thing. They then told him to 'watch out for the camera' – not cameras, but 'camera' – and even at the time he thought it was a bit funny. But that's just it with the Old Bill and football, as to them it really is a game and believe me they love to play it, because they already knew MacIntyre and Atkinson were going to be there and what they were up to.

It's like when I'd go to Chelsea the Old Bill would turn up and say "Alright Jase? What's happening?" and I'd go "Not a lot, I've just parked my car as it happens and now I'm hungry so I think I'll fill my fat face with a hamburger." And they'd blatantly tell you, "We know there's a mob of 50 Sheffield United or whoever down the road." So why are they telling me that, is it to warn me for my safety? Is it fuck. it's all part of the same old mind games and they love it. Why else do you think they leave Christmas cards addressed to The Headhunters in pubs around Stamford Bridge in December.

Typical of the way the Old Bill like to make you think they know everything you're doing was the way they acted towards me soon after my pal Steve 'Hickey' Hickmott had his conviction from the Operation Own Goal trial over-turned. They pulled me and asked if I was off to see my mate and I just told them I was off to see a few mates, as it happened. They kept pushing the point that I knew Hickey had come back over to England on a visit from the Far East where he's now living and I just kept blanking their questions. But wasn't it obvious that I was on my way to see him? He's been a pal of mine for over 20 years, he's come over for a visit so of course I'm going to meet up with him. What did they expect me to do, put my head down and walk past him just because the Old Bill have fitted him up?

And anyway, their little joke backfired when Hickey turned up at the pub. Oh yeah, he was still wearing his old DMs, his combat jacket and the jeans he's had for 300 years – but he's standing up against the limousine he'd turned up in. He calls over to the cozzers, "Hello Inspector, I'm just quaffing champagne the government bought for me. Operation Own Goal. What an own goal that was, fabricated evidence, tut, tut, tut. Anyway, cheers, old boy!" That's Hickey all over he is very comical, very intelligent and fast with his mouth and I don't know why those cozzers weren't laughing because we were pissing ourselves. There's no pleasing some people is there.

Soon after I got out of prison these two Fulham Old Bill came up to me and said "How are you, Jase, what are you up to?" but I wasn't having any of it. I said, "Do you know what, my pals call me Jase and what's it to you what I'm doing?" They still tried to get a bit pally with me and replied, "You know that programme, you weren't half stitched-up," and that was more than enough for me. I told them, "Listen, just stop yourselves there, if you were so bothered about it at the time you'd have made yourselves busy, gone up to the court and told that judge and jury, 'hold on, we've known Jason for however many years and that programme was a stitch-up,' so please don't tell me after the event, after I've served my sentence. You lot couldn't give a fuck." They said "Don't be like that, of course we could," and I just turned 'round and said, "What do you mean you could, how do you work that one out? It's all a get-up and I'm not interested." And with that, I just walked off.

Even the Old Bill know they can go too far sometimes, whatever country we're in. Just ask the local cozzers in Bruges who thought they'd get heavy-handed when Chelsea were there back in the mid-90s. And once again, this all came about because British intelligence had told them to expect a lot of trouble so they already on edge and were bound to over-react.

On the back of that there were about 500 snide tickets made up for that game, so the local Old Bill thought they had good reason to get involved to do whatever they wanted to, but even those with genuine tickets were getting turned away from the ground and even though there hadn't been any trouble, the Old Bill started nicking everyone. You only had to make it into the area, walk down any street and as soon as they saw you were English, that was it, you were nicked. Out came the plastic handcuffs, everyone's got shoved straight onto a bus and then herded off to some warehouse surrounded by all these crash barriers with barbed wire on top, Families with kids, women, it didn't seem to matter they were ruthless – and that was their big mistake.

Anyway me, Muzza, Andy Cruickshank, Stuart Shooter and Brian Gowers, we've flown in to Brussels before getting a cab to Ostend and, just like everyone else, after having a few beers in Bruges we got nicked and it was a one-way ticket to the warehouse. It was a massive building, there must have been about four or five hundred of us in there. So yeah, maybe there were some of the 'naughtier' ones who'd got trawled in the net but after a good four or five hours we then spotted this old man being treated the same way and he had to have been at least 70 years old. What kind of a threat was he? There'd been no trouble prior to these arrests, nothing at all, but seeing this 70-year-old geezer in handcuffs, no, in an instant everyone thought 'fucking liberty,' you could just sense it. And that's how it always starts, there's no great plan, there never is there's just some incident which sparks it all off. A couple of our lads did have some blades on them and others had lighters so we started cutting or burning the plastic handcuffs off, but everyone was still walking around with their wrists together, pretending they were still cuffed. And then things started to get naughtier and naughtier.

Listen, let's face it, our Old Bill don't look the part do they, they're all clean-shaven 18 – 21 year-old scrawny little pricks, but this lot have got their full riot gear on, they've got a fag hanging out of their mouths and half a beard on their faces, do you know what I mean? Even so, this lot never guessed that by now everyone's got their handcuffs off and believe me, they never saw what was coming next.

You've got a few hundred football supporters being treated like shit and, you've probably been there yourself a thousand times, that's usually when a bit of a sing-song goes up.

"We are the famous, the famous Chelsea." Everyone's sung it – and then we've only all gone and joined in with the handclaps – one minute these Old Bill are bringing in herds of people and they're happy with that, they're so comfort-able being the bullies but now it's all changed, they just look and back off and in an instant we've all thought, 'this is it!' Just one incident had triggered it off but now we've turned the tables, we were like one big army all thinking "here we are, you fucking cunts, come on, let's have it." And when you see them back-peddling you know you've got the upper hand. You've been terrorised by this pack of bullies all night and then all of a sudden you see that fraction of fear. They could have got it under control but because their arseholes went straight away they've 'poured petrol on the fire' and it just escalated from there. We didn't need anymore encouragement than that, we attacked them full on.

They've gone to draw their batons but it didn't matter, people were just so up for it by now and with only about 100 of them we outnumbered them immensely. It was going to take more than batons once it started, because this was a massive buzz, this was fucking it. "You lot've been standing there with your truncheons, picking on old men, women and children and telling us to fuck off, now it's our turn."

The one major thing they did have was a big water cannon tank but the lads went 'round the back and they were trying everything to get the hoses off of them. The Old Bill were totally surprised, they'd never faced a crowd which was simply saying "I ain't having it, mate." They put the water canons on but we just attacked them and it's gone absolutely fucking berserk – crash barriers, everything and anything – we were picking them up and hurling them or using them to charge at the Old Bill. They just didn't know what to do or where to turn and we totally overpowered them, we'd ambushed them and we'd totally penned them in so they were up against the wall.

People were even doing them with their own truncheons and I remember one kid in front of the water canon going absolutely berserk, he wouldn't leave off even when it had all quietened down. So whereas the Old Bill had all been at the front of the warehouse with us in a pen at the middle, now we've all jumped over the fences. And because it's one of those warehouses with the automatic shutters my pal Stuart Glass has made it to the other end of the warehouse and simply pressed the button for the shutters to go up. The gutting thing is we could have done it hours ago. But can you imagine the conversation between this town's top cozzer and his bosses during that night. One minute it's all, "Oh yes, we have everything under control, they're all locked up in the warehouse" and then BOOM, he's got to tell his bosses 200 or so of Chelsea's main firm have just escaped and they're making their way into the town centre – "What are we going to do? What are we going to do?" – that geezer must have lost his job, eh? Oh well, better luck next time.

We got outside and I just told everyone to split up because if we'd stayed together they'd have just corralled us in and we'd have been nicked. Now it was every man for himself. They couldn't nick everyone so those who get nicked, well, they're nicked and those who don't, keep going. It was fucking blinding, I'm telling you, it was like something out of The Great Escape. Stuart Glass, he's jumped into the river to escape and he's wading his way across when the Old Bill catch up with him. They're all telling him to get out but he's not having it: "No, go get someone from the British Embassy," he's shouting at them while he's almost up to his neck in water. It was a good try, but it was back to the warehouse for Stuart.

And as for me? Well, the game's almost over by now so I thought 'Fuck it, I'm going for a booze with my pals Darren Crew and Muzza.

But silly-bollocks Scouse couldn't wait for a drink, he's gone to the nearest bar and ordered a cab and a drink. As his cab turned up so did the Old Bill. They're all there going 'You were in the warehouse' and he's trying to deny it, even though his 'runner beans' are soaking wet so it's obvious he's been soaked by the water canon and they've nicked him on the spot. I'm in the bar with Darren, Muzza and a few other pals all night, we were paralytic drunk just buzzing over what happened back there. I missed my flight home in the morning but I couldn't care less, I wouldn't have missed that for anything. It's like my mate Muzza says, life revolved around going abroad with Chelsea, it's the best and the worst thing that's ever happened in our lives because we have a right 'tin bath,' I'm telling you.

Now, there may be those who've just read about what I got up to when I was active and thought something like, "he had it coming for all the stuff he'd done in the past and got away with" about what was to happen to me next.

Well, I'd say I wasn't on trial for any of that, 'What goes around, comes around'? No, you get nicked, tried and convicted for something at the time or you don't, end of. And for anyone who still thinks 'he's done football no good,' I want to know what side of the road are you on? Because you've got the football side of it or the grass's side, MacIntyre is nothing but a grass and if you're still on his side you're on the wrong side of the road.

And I'll tell you something else, just in case you're a regular supporter who thinks none of this applies to him because you've never had a row at a game in your life. Well mate, you'd better think again. The Old Bill are filming 'normal' supporters too and if you've been going for years don't believe you're not on some film somewhere because you are, there'll be hours and hours of footage on you, just having a pint outside a pub before or after a game. So think about it, a punch is thrown in the pub or somewhere nearby and the police haven't managed to find who's responsible. They desperately need someone to nick because their boss has started giving them grief about it, so later they have a look at their footage of the regulars. If you're lucky, you'll just end up labelled as an 'associate.'

Or, just for having your regular pre-match booze with your mates you might end up serving six years, once they put their edited film in front of a jury that doesn't understand what's going on but is all too happy to think the worst. Like I said, it could happen to you.

9

THE MEET

Let's have a little re-cap here before we go on and then you try putting yourself in my shoes. Here I was just living my life, playing a bit of football and watching Chelsea, running a business, looking after my missus and the kids and generally having a laugh with my pals whenever I could. Then along come a crew of BBC undercover reporters who've decided to target me for the sole purpose of destroying my name on national television just so they could make theirs in the world of investigative journalism. They've pulled every dodgy stunt they could to worm their way into my life, they've shadowed my every move for 18 months and secretly filmed it all. So let's have it right, at some point early on they must have turned to each other and said something like, "This bloke Marriner isn't doing anything, he's not committing any crimes, he's not even involved in football violence let alone organising it – we're fucked." It was only their own arrogance then which forced them to carry on rather than cut their losses. And that's when they crossed the line.

They were desperate, they needed to catch me doing something – anything – and that was the point they, not me, became the criminals. Remember all the snide gear they offered me? And then there were all the cannabis and cocaine deals? I refused them all. You can get a serious bit of bird for supplying Class A drugs so how come they've never had to answer to the cozzers for this? They were breaking the law, weren't they? Or is it one rule for one and another for the BBC these days? As my Q.C. would later say in court, "Place in order of importance the following two ideas: What Donal MacIntyre wants or the law of the land."

So their blatant attempts at entrapment didn't go to plan and they're forced to work with scraps of film which don't show me committing a single crime and this is where they overstepped another mark, with their extensive dirty tricks method of editing. Then the programme gets broadcast and overnight I've become Public Enemy No.1. 'There's no such thing as bad publicity'? Don't you believe it, because my business went to the wall after MacIntyre's programme. My pals who are customers weren't affected by what they'd seen on the tele because they knew it was all a pack of lies but those who didn't know me personally were no longer prepared to do business with 'the ugly face of football hooliganism.'

I don't know about you but I'm not in to gossip, I hate it, it's nothing more than rumours and lies because nine times out of ten it's all bullshit. And another thing, you never get the person who starts all these 'jackanories' in the first place to stand up and admit it later. Why can't they just get on with their own lives instead of making up stories about other people's, it's all a bit sad, really. Because there's a world of difference between the harmless lies that are all part of geezers bragging down the pub – you know the thing, a six-yard tap in on a Sunday morning that's become a 25-yard screamer a few hours and a few pints later – to lies that can fuck up other people's lives.

So when the gossips get a lie to run with that's been started on BBC television, well, you can imagine all the neighbours' twitching curtains, the sly looks and hushed voices that now followed me everywhere just like the secret cameras had done before. I understand it's human nature for people to talk about other people but it's the blatant lies and rumours that people believe. Don't forget everyone adds their bit on as well and there ain't even any Queen's evidence in the first place. Oh well, I suppose it makes some people happy. I'm big enough and ugly enough to live with that, the gossips couldn't get inside my head but think what it was like for my missus and the kids my brothers, my sister, my mum, my dad, my in-laws, close friends and their families. And then just when you think the dust has settled this lie has snowballed to the point where the cozzers come and arrest you off the back of it. Think how your own life could be changed if it was you who'd gone through all of this.

I was arrested on March 22nd and having been refused bail I'd been held on remand at Wanno for the best part of a year by the time my trial finally came to court, on Monday November 13th, 2000. You think about that as well: even if me and Andy end up getting a 'not guilty' like we should have those responsible, from MacIntyre and his lot to the police, the magistrates and the C.P.S., have nicked nearly nine months of our lives off of us already.

So yeah, I've had enough of this by now, I want this sorted out as soon as possible and it was a relief to have the trial up-and-running at last, to be out of the starting blocks and even if it looks like it's all going to go boss-eyed at least you know how long you're going to prison for. But that doesn't mean I want the trial rushed so it's not run properly and yet right from day one it was all done on the 'hurry up.' This is what the presiding judge, Judge Byers (or should that read 'Judge Bias'), said on the first day: "Thursday is the start date...as far as I'm concerned, the trial is up and running and legal argument will start on Thursday at the latest."

Ok, so he wants to get things moving, fair enough. But what's his rush, has he spent the last nine months banged up on remand? Of course not. What Judge Byers wants is for this trial to be finished before Christmas regardless of what evidence may be missing, which could prove vital to mine or Andy's cases. It's fucking unbelievable, but it's true. The next day my Q.C. brought up the fact that he'd only just received two de-briefing videos of Paul Atkinson without transcripts. He explained to the judge that Atkinson played a pivotal role in 'befriending' me, so these tapes could prove crucial to our argument. This is what the judge said to that:

"This is not an open-ended calendar, I will not keep delaying matters. Get used to it. Deal with it.....I have to keep an eye on the calendar and I'm anxious not to lose more time. Already we are one week behind, but I wish to rescue this trial...I am concerned that the 11/12/00 fixture does not get lost, as it would be postponed until the Spring."

Hold on, this is mine and my co-de's liberty at stake here so let's have it done properly. If you really want to get to the truth about something should it matter how long the trial takes? The way the judge was acting you'd think he had a winter holiday booked. Remember the 40 missing tapes I told you about earlier? Well, on the third day my Q.C. pointed out that it would be an abuse to proceed with the trial as only two thirds of the material the prosecution had to make available had been served. How can I have a fair trial when the whole prosecution case is based on covert surveillance of me that has then been edited and now all this evidence has gone 'missing'? But while Judge Byers agreed there's a big difference between police footage and a BBC documentary he wasn't going to let the little matter of missing evidence hold things up. This is what he said:

"This situation is different to police covert surveillance, the police have a duty not to edit...you can comment that this is less reliable....[but] I conclude that, though regrettable not all the tapes have been served...I am also satisfied that the trial process is capable of dealing with the matter of gaps...on the big picture a fair trial is possible. It is incumbent upon me to ensure that this is so."

It's all a get-up, isn't it. The media, the police and the C.P.S. have conspired to put me in the dock so is the world-famous Great British Justice system going to treat me fairly? Well, just the way the judge was acting from the start was enough for me to lose faith in that. Talking of acting, I should have guessed that lightweight performer MacIntyre would carry on in the same way he had throughout his documentary. You won't believe what was the very first item discussed at the start of the trial. It was only an application to screen the BBC witnesses from the public gallery over concerns about identification. Well, both my counsel, Mr Michael Wolkind Q.C. and Mr Adam Budworth, and Andy's,

Mr Oliver Q.C. and Mr Whitfield, opposed this and even Judge Byers had to
agree with them as he could see how prejudicial this would be against me and
my co-de. I mean, can you imagine what effect it would have on the jury when
they find the BBC witnesses are screened to protect them from identification by
my pals or my co-de's? Even so, when MacIntyre came to court he still had two
burly minders with him for his 'protection,' which had the same sort of effect.

There are poor women out there who get raped and even they have to make
their own way to court to give evidence. But this mongrel gets escorted and all
the tax-payers have to fork out for him to have these two burly minders protect-
ing him, just because he claimed he was scared of me and my associates –
remember the supposed death threats which had nothing to do with me but
were the reason I was refused bail? – it was an absolute liberty.

Because of all the interest surrounding the case it was moved on the first day
from No.7 to the main No.1 Court at Blackfriars and, of course, all the press
were there. The first day I walked in I'd never seen anything like it, you'd have
thought I must have had two heads the way they were just staring at me. They
reported Andy and I were the two most notorious football thugs in the country,
just like the programme had tried to make us out to be, so I'd smile at them as I
stood in the dock. But you can guess what they made of the supposed danger
MacIntyre and his crew were in, there was their first headline right there.
There'd be a lot more but the Daily Mirror weren't going to pass up on that
story, even if it was the kind of reporting that was always going to be prejudicial
against me and my co-de.

The piece they ran had the headline, 'BBC Reporter Runs From Hitmen'
and claimed not only had MacIntyre received death threats which meant he'd
had to move 16 times since the programme's broadcast, but that it was costing
£250,000 to guard him, that it was an on-going risk and everyone in the documentary's production was also at risk. It was all total bollocks and even the
judge was concerned when my Q.C. brought it up in court the next day,
because the report was in contempt. But what good was the judge's concern
going to do me now because the damage had already been done hadn't it, it just
blackened my name even more before the trial had even really got going.

The only thing I had in my favour was my Q.C., Michael Wolkind, he was
mustard, he didn't miss a thing and not only is he clever – I've seen a lot of them
at work and he's definitely one of the best – he's a comical fella with it, we
clicked straight away and got quite pally. While other defendants might talk
about their cases during the intervals we'd be talking about the football.

He'd say "Who've Chelsea got at the weekend," and I'd said "It doesn't
matter does it, I'm not going am I!" or he might say "Hello Jase, how do you
think it's going?" meaning the trial of course, but I'd just laugh and say, "Well
I'll let you know when we've won the league." (by the way, we have!) I'm not
daft, I know there are times when you've got to take it seriously but for me that
was in the courtroom itself, I can't take it seriously when I'm sitting in a cell.
The way I saw it was that I'd already spent the best part of a year banged up

and I wasn't going to waste my time worrying about things while I was sat in the court cell. What's happening in the trial's happening and if you're confident in your Q.C., like I was, then you have to let them get on with it. And if you get on well with your legal team as well as I did, well, perhaps they might box that bit harder for you which was good because Michael Wolkind's like me, he wants to win. Even if I'm playing marbles I want to win.

Andy's Q.C. was shit but early on he brought up the facts about the other programmes in the 'MacIntrye Undercover' series which were just as bad as the one on us and showed even more proof that none of this should ever have come to court. They'd used the same distortion techniques in the other documentaries as well, the one big difference was we'd been arrested and charged on the back of the programme, unlike MacIntyre's targets in the rest of the series. Here's what Andy's Q.C. said about these programmes in court:

"Look at the shoddy practices of MacIntyre. Originally it was going to be six lines, one was never made and we'll never know why. One was made, about Insider Dealing and it was pulled. It may be that those with clout were able to see the programme and issue a legal threat. We don't know. But in the City the people who could take advantage of the law were able to do so. Jason Marriner and Andrew Frain did not have the money to.

"That leaves four. One concerned the world of the modelling catwalk. 'Under age models exploited with drugs and sex with older men.' The executive director of the largest agency was featured and forced to resign. After a very short inquiry by that organisation he was reinstated. They are considering proceedings against the BBC.

"Another was the Kent care home. It was closed, residents, care workers and the Social Services Department were affected. But the police investigated and found nothing much, they said the programme had effectively cheated and are considering suing for costs."

Now the Kent care home documentary was important because the prosecution knew they didn't have a case against me and Andy and they didn't want any questions being asked about the other programmes, as this would only have weakened their argument against us. Also, the BBC didn't want their entire ratings-winning series later being publicly torn to shreds so do you know what MacIntyre did about it? Let me tell you all about it.

Some people were already beginning to see through MacIntyre and his reporting methods and a couple of the papers picked up on this. The Daily Telegraph ran a piece in June, 2000, about how MacIntyre's undercover report into the Brompton House Care Home in Gillingham ended with Medway Social Services closing the place down. They told of how the police thought they'd be charging people over what had been filmed, but once they'd actually sat down and viewed the whole 205 hours of unedited tape – 205 hours not 344 like the programme on me – they decided the finished documentary had misrepresented the home and it's staff. It sounds familiar, doesn't it, so do you now see what have I been trying to tell you?

Listen, the police thought it was so misleading they made a £50,000 claim against the BBC to recover the costs of their enquiry because it had been such a waste of their time and money. And the council, too, said they wished they'd had more time to make a proper judgement yet they felt they'd had no choice but to close the home because MacIntyre had claimed on national television that the patients could have been at risk unless action was taken immediately. There'd have been a public outcry if they hadn't have closed it down.

If you think I'm making this up maybe the main points taken from the official report of Operation Oracle 99, the police investigation into MacIntyre's care home programme, will convince you. And when you read these police findings just remember 'MacInlies' and his crew filmed this during the same time as the other programmes in the series and the one on me, using the same undercover techniques and, later, the same editing methods:

"(Initial Inquiries): – A full and lengthy explanation was given into the methods used to make the programme. It was obvious at this time that Philip Clothier had not fully thought out the difficulties of using covert equipment and its subsequent use in a police enquiry...At the meeting it became apparent that the integrity of the BBC may have been in doubt...It was outlined to those present that Donal MacIntyre and Ben Anderson had visual covert equipment and audio. This could be used separately and together, meaning that the operator has full control on what he wished to film or record.

(Viewing VHS tapes): – It soon became apparent that the final programme reveals editing and dubbing that distorted the scenes being depicted and that during the editing process considerable 'journalistic licence' was used...Generally the programme was edited in such a way to give a false impression of some of the scenes depicted. Often a small part of a scenario was taken out of context without any explanation, leaving the viewer to draw their own conclusions having been primed by the narrative.

(Report of analysis of material supplied by the BBC): – Throughout our viewing and listening the enquiry team were concerned that the BBC had not given a fair appraisal of the life at Brompton...There is no doubt that the integrity of the BBC video and audio evidence is doubtful and therefore may undermine any future criminal proceedings.

(Conclusions): – From the many hours of an extremely time consuming and difficult enquiry, looking at incidents of certain behaviour in an industry not regulated by law, the Enquiry Team have reached a number of conclusions in relation to its remit...The BBC are not correct in their observations that Brompton Home is set in a 'culture of neglect at the heart of Britain's care industry'."

Yeah, of course I would have wanted this brought up in my trial as it was just further proof of what MacIntyre and his dodgy series were really all about. But just three weeks before my trial started he brought his own legal action against the Chief Constable of Kent and their media spokesman. MacIntyre had the front to claim it was to protect his name and his integrity, can you believe that? It doesn't matter what his reasons were, what happened was that it stopped us being able to question witnesses in court about the Kent care home programme because they were now part of another legal action. Coincidence?

Oh, and one more thing about the hours of tapes for the 'Care Home' programme, the police enquiry logs five cases of common assault committed by two staff members, as the total number of criminal offences caught on MacIntyre's undercover cameras. Well that's two more offences than he caught me and Andy committing in 344 hours.

As for the Elite Model Agency programme the truth about that also came out eventually, but too late to do me any good. In June, 2001, the BBC were finally forced to admit that MacIntyre had misrepresented the agency in his documentary. Before their climbdown, the BBC had insisted it would defend MacIntyre all the way but just before the libel action was about to get underway at the High Court, they issued this statement:

"The BBC acknowledges that Elite, as an organisation, warns and seeks to protect its young teenage models, whether from sexual exploitation or other potential dangers to them (such as from illegal drugs), and that this was not reflected in the programme. In this respect, Elite was therefore unfairly portrayed."

So if there was nothing wrong in MacIntyre's methods, the same ones used against me, why were the BBC now failing to back their star undercover reporter? Tricky one, that.

I'll tell you something else "MacInlies' had the front to do. Because the series was a such a ratings success, he published a book to go along with it and, guess what, that was packed with even more lies than the programmes themselves. During the one-hour documentary on me I've counted over 80 times he's lied about what's going on – that's about a lie every 45 seconds for fuck's sake – and in the book I've counted 93 different occasions, just on the chapters about football hooliganism. You'd have to ask the people from the other programmes who are featured in the book what they made of it, but you can probably guess.

But more importantly for my trial 19,000 copies were sold, so you can probably double that number for the amount of people who've read it. Add that on to the 7.4 million who watched the documentary the first time around, never mind all the repeat broadcasts and updates shown on all the BBC channels and you tell me how am I supposed to get a jury that hasn't been influenced in any way by all of that. Because I don't believe for one minute the jurors sitting in on my case didn't see the programme. Let's put it this way, I'm an average kid and nine out of ten times on a Tuesday night I'm indoors at nine o'clock watching the tele. If you've got a job and you have to be up early the next morning it's what you do, isn't it, you have your dinner, put your feet up and watch the most exciting thing on the box – and now they try and tell me none of them tuned in to the BBC's flagship series for that year? So the judge keeps banging on about how it'll be a fair trial but it absolutely fucking stinks and I really haven't even started on the jury yet.

Now, the judge claimed there would be a 'substantial jury panel available from which to select a jury,' but just because there's a number to choose from do you really think that cuts out any chance of bias? Think about it, most blokes aged between 18 and 35 would have watched that programme and thought twice, they'd at least have suspected there might not be any real evidence against me and Andy. I'm not asking for a few kids who are the worst in the world but maybe just a couple who weren't angels, who know the real world, normal people like brickies, sparkies, whatever, who might think 'hold on a minute,' and fight your corner. But you just don't get your Joe Public's anymore, they can't afford to have time off for jury service on a three-week trial so already, you've lost your fair '12 good men and true' system before you even try and select a jury. My case was originally meant to be held at the Old Bailey and when I first heard that I said 'sweet,' because there was a much better chance of getting a few proper people on the jury. Just to be eligible for the selection panel you've got to be a straight runner, a normal, level-headed person, but if they're proper just maybe they've got a son or daughter whose a bit of a Herbert, nuisance-material, and it would give them a better insight into what really goes on in the world.

But then my case got switched to Blackfriars which used to be Knightsbridge Crown Court, so where have I got people coming from now? Putney, Kensington and Chelsea, places like that, they were all upper-class. They were the kind of people who'd never had fish and chips in paper in their lives. They were the 'wine bar people' rather than 'pub people' and they live in their own little world. Yet that's the system you're now up against and all you can do is fight it the best you can. My Q.C. had a number of questions to ask the jury and if they could answer 'yes' to any of them they weren't supposed to sit on the jury. They weren't difficult questions, just whether anyone on the panel had seen the programme or read the book, if they'd worked for the BBC in the past 10 years or if they'd ever been a victim of football violence. There was one other question and that was if they had any connections with Chelsea or Leicester City Football Clubs. Like I said, not difficult to answer – if you're being truthful.

One geezer said he was a Chelsea supporter so he couldn't sit on the jury (shame really, I could have done with a bit of support in there) and another said he lived near the Fulham Dray and drank in there sometimes. My Q.C. was ok with this so he stayed. But I'll tell you something and I swear to God it's true, the moment that jury were sworn in I turned to my co-de and said, "No chance." I told my Q.C. as well that I just didn't fancy them because, for starters, the jury was made up of nine women and three geezers and one of them looked like an uphill gardener in his roll-neck and carrying his satchel, while another just looked like some old schoolteacher.

Do these lot sound like normal, everyday people, who were going to be able to tell what was real evidence and what was made up? Of course they weren't, the whole thing was a get-up from the start as I bet half of them have never even been to football let alone know anything about what really goes on in the world. I mean, we're all from different walks of life and there's nothing wrong in that, but none of those people on the jury were the type to go out and have a booze, let their hair down and shout their mouths off, they were never like I am in life. I could see when they looked at me they were amazed. And after they were amazed they were disgusted. I've got no Queen's Evidence it was a stitch-up, maybe it was just the luck of the draw, but I wouldn't want luck like that everyday. Yet like my Q.C. said, there was nothing we could do about it. And he was right, there was nothing we could do about it at the time. But not everybody answered those simple questions truthfully to see if they could sit on the jury – did they, Julia Moorcroft?

Yeah, this bird wanted to be on the jury so much she didn't mention any connection to Chelsea Football Club when she was asked (and I'll tell you what an outrageous liberty that was a bit later) but there's one other thing about Julia Moorcroft that I didn't find out for certain until the jury had to give their verdict.

This woman should never have even been allowed to sit on the jury in the first place but she had a much bigger part to play. To people who don't know about the head juror's role in the court let me tell you they have a major influence on the rest of the panel, as they are the ones who "direct the traffic." And Julia Moorcroft only ended up being the head juror.

10

LOCAL DERBY

They say a jury's only as good as the evidence presented so what happens when a jury's presented with no evidence at all, like in my case? Well, it makes them worse than useless, that's what. The jury get bombarded with so much information they can't take it all in even if they think they can. Think about it, you've got the old 'chocolate fudge' looking down his nose at everyone and the Q.C.s are all off speaking their own language whenever they take the floor. This was my freedom at stake and I was trying to take in every word but the only ones that really sunk in was when the judge finally passed his sentence – so how hard do you think the members of the jury were paying attention and how much of the proceedings did they fully understand?

And that's exactly what the prosecution were relying on because they knew they didn't have a case against either me or Andy and baffling the jury was the only hope they had of getting a guilty. The prosecution knew only too well that people can easily become tunnel-visioned in a courtroom situation like that, especially being involved in such a high-profile case. They become like a second-rate amateur winger who all he wants to do is run up and down the line. It doesn't matter how many times you shout "Lift your head, look square, look behind, look diagonal, cross the ball, have more channels." The jury would be very much like that type of player, they heard the first bit of the prosecution's case and they didn't go looking for anything else. So all the prosecution had to do was plant a seed in the jury's mind early on and keep throwing mud in the hope it sticks and it's why I say you're guilty in the dock until proven innocent, because once the prosecution have sewn that seed you're fucked. Oh yeah, you can slaughter their case at every turn like we did, but it won't make any difference if the jury's already made up it's mind.

As you'd expect the prosecution's opening speech to the jury was full of wild accusations about how football violence is pre-arranged, about how me and Andy had 'arranged' a fight up at Leicester, how we were going to attack the Bloody Sunday march and how only the police presence on both occasions stopped any trouble. He also went on to explain the reporting methods and editing techniques used for the documentary, in an attempt to give it some credibility. Yeah, I thought you'd like to read what he said about that:

"TV programmes are one thing, they are entertainment, but they would not be fun if Donal MacIntyre and Paul Atkinson played the hours and hours of film covertly taken, so they edit it, that is the programme. That is not what you will be concerned with, you will see the original tapes. We have reduced the quantity....

"I propose to show the tape, it is one hour, forty-five minutes long...it is for you to look at the entirety of the evidence and make up your own minds...the evidence is not a TV show, it is real and it is serious. The people are not actors, they are witnesses. It is for you to decide and I will assist you."

Right, so now just because they've added another 45 minutes of footage from 344 hours' worth of filming it's not TV anymore it's supposed to be evidence, is it? But evidence of what, exactly? Never mind that it's still been compiled using the same distorted editing techniques used for the programme to make me look as bad as possible, if you'd been there on the jury you'd have seen for yourself that you still don't see any crime being committed.

And the prosecution claim that the people are not actors is just laughable. Earlier in his opening speech he said about MacIntyre and Atkinson, "...they couldn't just walk in and start filming so they had to create a personality to endear themselves to the hooligans. They chose to put themselves forward as wealthy, well-to-do criminals involved in drug importing. They surrounded themselves with the props."

Well, adopting a persona is exactly was acting is, for fuck's sake. On one of the unused tapes MacIntyre was filmed taking off his shirt and putting on his under-cover recording equipment, again and again for about 30 minutes until the crew had the shot they wanted. In others he can be seen making phone calls and then pretending to make them again and again, because the camera angle wasn't quite right or he's fluffed his lines, or whatever. That's acting, end of, you can't have it both ways. Or maybe you can if the jury's not paying enough attention. So it was time for Michael Wolkind, my Q.C., to wake them up and he was absolutely brilliant. He came up to me beforehand and told me not to show any emotion, not to smirk, whatever. Then in court he goes and stands close to the jury, faces them and says, "Ladies and gentlemen of the jury, the prosecution is right, this case is about two dangerous, dangerous men," and he turns and stares at me before he continues, "they are dangerous to society, to the general public, to anyone and everyone." He then turns around sharply, bangs his hand on the counter and goes, "And their names are Donal MacIntyre and Paul Atkinson."

And he's away with this really great presentation, I'm telling ya. He explains to the jury that these two are the ones with form because of the Kent care home programme and how when the police investigated they found disreputable conduct including direct falsehood, he warns the jury this trial is not all what you might think it will be, so you've got to pay attention to the facts:

"Count the weapons – NONE. Count the episodes of violence – NONE. Count the confessions of violence – NONE."

For a moment I thought he was going to say something like "so far it's nil-nil" He went on to say how those two had wormed their way into my life through their acting, how I might have accepted them as Chelsea supporters but I found their company dull – he pretended to stifle a yawn at this point – but all the time he's building up to his punchline:

"The reporters are not objective, bear that in mind. They wanted their man at any cost. For they are not journalists – they are the Headhunters."

Philip Clothier (or 'Pip' as he's known to his colleagues and his wife Rosie Millard, who also used to be a reporter on the BBC news) was the co-producer who edited all the film into what became the MacIntyre documentary. He was up next and he even admitted in court that he did not see me commit an act of violence. And this was while he was still being questioned by the prosecution, for fuck's sake. Clothier had gone to Leicester and he'd been secretly filming from a distance while listening to what was going on in MacIntyre's rigged-up car. You remember that bit when Andy jokes about those on the bus causing trouble at a service station? Well this is what Clothier had to say about that in court:

"I went into the service station and mingled with them to see if they were the sort of people I thought they were. They just bought drinks, used the facilities and moved off."

He also secretly filmed me at the train station after the match that day and when the prosecution asked him what I was doing all he could say was 'simply going home.' It's just laughable. When my Q.C. began questioning Clothier he started by asking him if he was proud of the programme. Clothier relied, 'yes, very proud.' and my Q.C. starts laughing, he said, "No, no really, joking aside, please answer the question!"
Michael Wolkind backed Clothier into a corner very early on, like when he asked him about the BBC guidelines for filming and whether he followed them or not. Of course Clothier said he did and my Q.C.'s straight back with, "I don't think you have," as he gives him one of his looks. This fella Clothier then goes way off track with his answers so Michael simply pulls him back to the

original question with, "so, are you going to answer me about such and such?" I tell you, my Q.C. was blinding to watch.

Now, when Clothier was asked what he thought of me when he first saw me he said I was a thug and a lout. He referred to that opening shot of me when I'm supposed to be bullying a man out of a phone-box. So we showed the unedited version which is absolutely nothing like what was shown on television, it showed without any doubt that I'm just chatting to the kid after he's put the phone down and is waiting for an incoming call.

And to back up what should have been obvious to all who saw the full footage, we had the witness statement of expert Mark Buxton, a senior video consultant who's job it was to study the enhancement and analysis of video and audio tape recordings. Here's what he said in his witness statement about the phone-box scene:

"I captured both sections of video, extracts 19 and 20 and then compared the content of both extracts using a software video editing tool.

"Extract 20 shows a particular scene concentrating on a telephone box; there is a male (first male) inside the phone-box and another male (subject of interest) outside. It appears that the two males speak to each other, then the subject is allowed to use the telephone by the first male. This telephone booth scene of the extract lasts for 20 seconds.

"I understand that extract 19 is a copy of the original source material from which extract 20 was produced. The corresponding scene of the telephone box and the two males lasts for approximately 88 seconds. During this time the phone-box and the males are obscured by road traffic and passers by, both intermittently and for relatively long periods. The subject is in view for approximately 55 seconds; he is obscured for approximately 33 seconds.

"As the subject is obscured from time to time, some editing of the original material seems appropriate. However the clip of extract 20, having a duration of 20 seconds, has been extracted from 55 seconds of source material with the subject in view. This amounts to 36% of the material having been selected for presentation. In the wider context, the 20 second clip comes from 88 seconds of source material, a 23% (less than 1/4) material usage."

I mean, it's an old cliché but 'the truth, the whole truth and nothing but the truth,' with less than a quarter of the footage used and then MacIntyre's blatant lie added as the voice over. Well, do you reckon that's the whole truth?

Next during my Q.C.'s cross-examination of Clothier he focuses on the extract where they show me roaring like a maniac, going "the lads [Rah Rah] and all that," to prove to the jury that it had been lifted from elsewhere, voice-matched, enhanced and put into sequence then mixed with talk from the radio phone-in programme to make the false impression the journalists wanted to give. And I swear to God you should have seen Clothier squirming when Michael Wolkind starts grilling him about this, he just couldn't answer the question. He tries going off track again and again, it seemed like 15 minutes, but my Q.C. keeps pulling him back. Michael played the extract to the hushed courtroom and Clothier has the front to say he couldn't hear the roar. As Michael pointed out to him, "they probably heard it three courtrooms away, but never mind, let's play it again with the volume turned up even loader."

You could have heard a pin drop in there when the tape was started again, no-one was talking in the background as they concentrated fully on what they were about to see and hear. The tape was now being played at full volume and immediately the roar Clothier claimed he couldn't hear was so obvious to everyone in the courtroom that it would have been too embarrassing even for Clothier to try and deny he could hear it. But just to make sure, Michael thought he'd better check. "Did you hear it that time?" he asked with a half-smile on his face. Clothier was getting flustered, he half acknowledged that he could hear something like a roar but tried to pass it off as an irrelevant background noise, perhaps something lifted from the BBC's collection of archive noises. Clothier must have had something wrong with his hearing so Michael thought he'd put it to the test and he asked him, "You are Philip Clothier? You are the man who lifts the soundtrack and puts it into the sequence you want? You are the one who edits and puts the documentary together?"

"Yes, that's me," replied Clothier and Michael's straight back in there with "Oh, so you heard me alright that time then?"

At the end of the morning session of Michael's cross-examination he said, "OK, we'll leave it at that," but he wasn't finished with Clothier yet, he wasn't going to let him off that easily. During the lunch break Michael gets the tape couriered over to a specialist's laboratory and this is what forensic audio consultant and expert witness, Christopher Martin Mills, wrote in his official statement:

"This statement is true to the best of my knowledge and belief and I made it knowing that, if it is tendered in evidence, I shall be liable to prosecution if I have wilfully stated in it anything which I know to be false or do not believe to be true.

"I am the Director and Senior Consultant of Network Forensics, which is part of the Control Risks Group. I hold a BTEC Diploma and BTEC HNC in Electrical and Electronic Engineering. I am a Fellow of the Institute of Incorporated Engineers. I am an Associate Member of the International Association of Forensic Phonetics. From January 1982 I was employed in the Metropolitan Police Forensic Laboratory where I specialised in the Enhancement, Authentication, Transcription and Analysis of Audio of Audio and Video Tape Recordings.

"From 1986 until October 1990 I was Head of Department of the Metropolitan Police Audio Forensic Laboratory. I joined Network Forensics in October 1990. I have given evidence in Courts on these matters on many occasions, both in the UK and abroad. Prosecution and Defence in both criminal and civil actions have instructed me.

"On 28th November 2000, the Police attended this laboratory and made available for examination a mini DV cam tape and a VHS tape.

"Utilising equipment available in this laboratory, I examined and compared two extracts of sound and video information. Original recorded sound material from a mini DV cam type tape was compared with an extract of the sound track from the VHS tape of a television programme.

"The mini DV cam soundtrack contained the following words: 'the lads [Rah] [Rah] and all that,' within an extended section of speech.

"The VHS tape at the section of interest is a compilation of video images and two different sound sources. The sound sources are a mix of a radio phone-in programme and the material heard on the mini DV cam.

"The sound from the DV cam has been edited and copied onto the VHS tape in a different form. The VHS sound is 'the lads [Rah] [Rah] and all that.' The radio phone-in programme is laid over the top at varying sound levels and partially obscures the first rendition of 'the lads [Rah] [Rah] and all that.' On completion of the examination I handed the mini DV cam and VHS tape back to the police."

Michael Wolkind read the statement out to the court and then passed it around the jury and if Clothier looked like a desperate liar before he's really fucked now, because we've proved to the jury without a shred of doubt what he's done. To be honest, I would have preferred the specialist to have been there in person, a body in front of the court explaining what had been done rather than just his signed statement as I believe it would have had a greater impact on the jury. But even so, this specialist has confirmed not only that the tape has been doubled-over, enhanced etc. but more importantly that the roar has been lifted from one sequence and placed in another. So what I seriously need to know is how the people who made up that jury just dismissed this vital piece of evidence when it came to deliberating over their verdict. I need to know the answer to this and so should you.

Next up was MacIntyre and one of the first thing he says to the jury when he got into the witness box was, "Oh I'm very sorry, you've watched some videos of me and I swore quite a lot…you choose a cover that's appropriate and use language that's appropriate. This was a dangerous world." I saw straight through him from the start in there, to me he was just playing up to his audience. Even in a court of law, MacIntyre still couldn't stop acting – and lying.

And he was so arrogant as well, he'd say he was certain me and Andy were going to commit this crime or that, as if he knew what we were thinking. It was obviously a lie but he had to say it because he was trying to save his reputation as a journalist. If we walked out with a couple of not guiltys he knew his whole series was going to be shown up for the complete sham it really was, especially after the police criticism of the Kent care home programme and the fact the BBC had to settle out of court with the model agency over the lies in that programme.

But Michael Wolkind soon pulled him up on being so certain of everything, he didn't seem so sure of himself then – funny that. My Q.C. was asking him about the car trip to Leicester and MacIntrye started by saying he'd wanted to give me a lift because it would give him a chance to witness me organising violence, he goes on to say that I clearly was organising trouble during the trip and he stands by that.

So Mr. Wolkind asked him if the BBC's needs are above the law for if he and Atkinson knew a crime was going to be committed and they drove us there, that made both of them accessories. Brilliant! You should have seen MacIntyre's face, he hasn't got any choice but to make a complete backtrack and from all the cocky "I KNOW there was going to be violence" comments, MacIntyre now has to state he and Atkinson weren't sure what was going to happen in Leicester. He didn't say that on the tele, did he? No, the voice-over for the viewers was that we were all 'hardened thugs intent on organising violence.'

Michael Wolkind knew he had to play it tactically in there otherwise he might have seemed to the jury like he was belittling the witnesses. He had to 'box, box, box,' get them into a corner and then bang! Hit them with a few good punches before jabbing again and scoring some more points. And bit by bit, MacIntyre was looking more and more unsteady. I don't know if you've ever noticed this yourself but when you're nervous you drink a lot more, it's a natural reaction. Well something must have been bothering MacIntyre because I have never seen anyone drink so much water in my life, he was getting through three large jugs of the stuff at any one sitting and at one point the judge even had to halt the proceedings to let MacIntyre go to the toilet before he pissed himself. But what was MacIntyre so nervous about? He must have been coached by the prosecution on what to expect and how to act during the cross examination so all he had to do was answer the questions being put to him. It's not like he was in there fighting for his liberty like me and Andy.

From where I was standing in the dock, MacInlies' evidence didn't get any more convincing when he was questioned about the affray charge for the Bloody Sunday march. My Q.C. asked him on which tape could we hear the discussion that Jason Marriner was going to attack the march. MacIntyre said it was the "ammo and bottle" story and that gave him a clear indication, he said there clearly would be an attack and then lied in court by saying there clearly was one. He even tried to claim that me saying a bottle's ammunition is the same as me using a bottle as ammunition. Even the police didn't try that one, they admitted in court no bottle had been thrown and there were no arrests at the march because there wasn't even a fight that day, let alone an affray which is a mini-riot.

The police only later charged me with affray because the bit of cream for them was MacIntyre's film of me running around the corner. But then MacIntyre was running with me at the time and my Q.C. wasn't going to let that pass. He asked him "Did you commit affray?" and of course MacIntyre said he didn't. "So there's no offence by running towards the march?"

MacIntyre answers this by saying he had no intent to attack the march, imply-ing that in some way I had. "What did Jason Marriner do that you didn't do?" my Q.C. asked next and MacIntyre said I was trying to break through. And how exactly, according to MacIntyre testifying in a court of law, was I trying to break through?: "He was waving his hands and shouting." – Oh give me strength! Since when did someone 'waving their hands and shouting' mean they're about to commit an act of violence?

Now, when Paul Atkinson was asked about the Bloody Sunday march he didn't even bother trying to lie, the only thing he could say was that he thought I was going to cause trouble. This is the full transcript, see what you think:

My Q.C. – The "bottle" conversation, did you hear it?
Atkinson – Yes
Q. C. – Did you realise the defendant was embarrassed?
Atkinson – No, I believed he meant violence
Q.C. – Did you see him leave with it?
Atkinson – No
Q.C. – Did you see him shout threats?
Atkinson – No
Q.C. – Did you see him throw the bottle?
Atkinson – No
Q.C. – Is his 'plan of attack' on tape?
Atkinson – No, I wasn't recording

Let's face it, we were smashing the prosecution's case to pieces on their evidence all the way through. I still believe to this day my Q.C. won that trial hands down but it's the jury you've got to convince and that was a get-up from the start. I don't want to spoil it for you by giving too much away, but I reckon you've already guessed how this trial's going to end up so I might as well tell you now. I'd be banged up for nearly three years before the truth finally came out about the jury.

Remember Julia Moorcroft, the one who would later turn out to be the fore-woman of the jury? Like I told you, she really wanted to be the guv'nor, no doubt about it and the reason for that was because she didn't just have some connection with Chelsea Football Club, she was actually working for them at the time of my trial. It turns out a bloke called Johnny Helps, a friend of a good mate of mine from Millwall called John, was on jury service at Blackfriars Court on a different case running at the same time as mine. Millwall John later told me Johnny Helps has been talking to this Julia Moorcroft bird in the smoking room there and she tells him what case she's on and actually says she's seen this Jason Marriner before at Chelsea untold times.

Julia Moorcroft was working for a catering company that runs the hospitality at the club. Come on, it wasn't rocket science for the woman to realise she had to say something about this when she was asked if she had any connections with the club. And not only that, she tells John she's also seen the MacIntyre documentary and read his book. Now think about it, her position as forewoman is really important as these people take charge, they're strong and influential and they can swing the other juror's opinions. But when they're like Moorcroft they're playing with people's lives, because she had a good reason for us to get a guilty. She can then go back to Chelsea and say "I'm the one who put these two blokes away, put some business my way," do you know what I mean? By helping to send me to prison she probably thought she was keeping Chelsea's name squeaky clean to the prawn sandwich brigade mob and that in turn might get her another season or two doing the catering, that keeps her credibility up at work and it keeps her top of the table.

But it was more than that for her. She was a sharp-looking bird, very up herself (actually she looked like she needed a good meal inside of her) and looking back she loved every minute of it, this woman, I bet she couldn't wait to get herself elected as the head juror. This was her little moment, she wanted to be there, to be part of finding us guilty as this was her little 15 minutes of fame. I'm sure she's still down her poxy wine bar every now and again with the little finger up in the air going, "Do you remember that trial? Well I was the head juror."

I mean, this bird Moorcroft had taken an absolute liberty by not telling the truth just so she could sit on my jury, it stinks and it was just another lie to add to all the others that were told in my case.

▲ What an English mob in Marseilles, 1998

▼ England in Bulgaria.

◀ HMP Standford Hill – "On me head son".

▼ In my cell when I was working for our beloved Queen

▼ HMP Springhill, in the shovel with a few of the chaps.

▲ We were all in the jug together. The judge never said we couldn't do this.

▼ Me and Cass Pennant.

▲ The man himself, Ken Bates in Jablonic.

▲ Mark "Yoksi" Birch and son. Joey. Zola at the (Ranch) 2002. In the background is Zola's son No. 7.

▲ Ian Sim with Boatsy at his book launch in Nottingham.

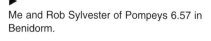
▶
Me and Rob Sylvester of Pompeys 6.57 in Benidorm.

▲ The Dog's Bollocks bar, Thailand.

▼ My pal Flynnie and his dad, Dick, when we went to Belfast for the glorious 12th.

▲ England's firm in Munich.

▼ German old bill on their toes.

▲ Brugge – the great escape.
I got out of my handcuffs
and the warehouse.

▶

A few of our lot getting excited.

▲ Us marching to Lansdowne Road before coming across a van load of Irish.

▼ Excuse me, do you know the way to the ground?

Lansdowne Road, late 80s

▲ One of the many scaps on this day.

▼ On the way to the ground.

▲ Germany.

▼ Skitzy and Tony Covelle in Denmark in 1989.

▲ Copenhagen. A few of us on the way to the ground where I got nicked.

▼ Anyone found my ticket?

▲ Me and my good pal Andy Frain, who was also my co-defendant

◄ Me and my fiancé, Julie, at Ian and Jenny Sim's wedding.

▼ Connor, Julie, Billy Boy, me, and Mason – A family holiday.

11

HOME OR AWAY

My co-de Andy didn't give any evidence at the trial but, fuck me, he was only seen twice in the whole programme so I don't think he could have given evidence about anything if he'd have wanted to. Instead he just sat silently in the dock for the whole trial which believe me, takes some doing when you're listening to all the lies being told about you for four weeks' solid. But when we were down in the cells together we'd chat about anything, about Chelsea, whatever, just catching up with how things were because we were in different prisons. I was still in Wandsworth and Andy was in the Scrubbs.

We'd chat about what was going on in the court as well, when we got the chance. Andy didn't think we'd get a guilty and listen, I don't think the prosecution thought they'd get a guilty either because their case was weaker than Darren Anderton. I suppose you've got to hang on to the hope you'll get a result all the while you're fighting your case, whatever's going on in the courtroom. I mean, if you're in the Olympics you're not there for the bronze are you, you're going for gold. And for us that gold medal was to walk.

I'd laugh with Andy and say I'd seen a pub across the road from the sweatbox, we ought to go there and have a 'light ale' – well, you live for your dreams, don't you – and Andy likes a laugh and a joke. There wasn't a day we didn't have a laugh about something that had happened in court. One of the things we did was to try and guess who the foreperson was. It was out of two of them for me, Julia Moorcroft, who it turned out to be, or the geezer who wore the glasses and looked like a typical schoolteacher.

Another time I was down in the cell I said, "Oh my God, you've got to see the geezer up in the corner," and they all asked why. "Well, I'm not being fucking funny," I said, but he must have a few quid." When they said 'how come' I told them, "because he spends fuck all on clothes, he looks like a proper 'oil lamp'!"

Like I say, it was good to meet up with Andy each day, it always is, and he remained himself. So did I and for me, that meant I was going to have my say from the witness box.

Before I took the stand my Q.C. Michael Wolkind gave me a blinding introduction speech. He started it by saying, "In a beauty contest between Donald MacIntyre and Jason Marriner, Jason Marriner comes second best (steady on, Michael!). He won't be on the front cover of the Radio Times, he was not invited to the BBC Awards Ceremony." Basically, he was telling the jury, 'don't judge a book by its cover.' He then went on to explain how the prosecution had no case and how the witnesses for the defence would prove this, including the forensic experts to show how the programme had been distorted. And he ended it by saying, "We also have one other expert – I call Mr. Marriner."

Unlike MacIntyre when he was in the witness box I was never going to put on an act. I got in there and I said, "Let me tell you something, I come from the rough side of the road, I'm Council, I've lived on a Travellers' site for years, so don't you worry about my swearing because that's just the way I am. If I'm going to apologise to anyone for it I'll apologise to my mother or my father. I'm not an actor, this is me, full stop." Well, start as you mean to go on, eh?

I'd end up being in the dock for about two-and-a-half days which is an awful long time let me tell you, most people are only in there for an hour or two. No-one really wants to go in the dock but after the first 10 minutes I was sweet and my legal team had told me I would be. I'd said to them before I went in I wasn't going to be anyone but myself and they told me that's the only way you can be.

The funny thing about being in the dock are the breaks or when you go back to prison in the evening, because you're told you're not allowed to speak to anyone about your case until you've stood down, except to answer all the questions asked of you. At lunchtime you go downstairs to a cell on your own and when you go back to prison you're not allowed to talk about your case then, either. When I got back each night I'd laugh and say, "I can't talk to you, I can't talk to you, I'm in the dock and I'm not allowed to tell you anything. The judge told me and I wouldn't want to go against the old judge now, would I – Oh alright then, I'll tell you everything that's happening!"

The best thing about taking the stand was that this was the first real chance I'd had to put my side of things across, I could tell them in my own words what a load of bollocks the programme was and the charges against me. The prosecution tried again to make out I was one of the most notorious thugs in the country and I just said it was quite laughable really, because I'd been filmed for 18 months and I haven't thrown a punch so what kind of thug does that make me?

Do you know what the prosecution said to that? "No Jason Marriner, that's because you are so clever you knew the cameras were on you, so you were the general of the generals and you got your foot-soldiers to do the fighting for you." That's how desperate they were, I'm telling you. I just said to them, "Well if I was that clever how come I didn't even know the kid living next door to me for 18 months was an undercover reporter secretly filming me?"

They also said I've been friends for years with Steven Hickmott, Chubby Chris, Ian and Dave Sim, Tony Covelle, Skitsy, and xyz, that I've got their phone numbers in my phone book, trying to make out like that was a crime or something. I just said, "Fuck me, I've been friends with my dad for years as well and I've got his phone number in my book, but you ain't mentioned him."

It is a stressful time though, because not only was I being taken to court from prison everyday, I also had to stay on my toes throughout. I'd seen how the prosecution continually tried to twist everything out of shape, just like the programme had done. It's why I said to them at one point that if I'm here in the dock then so should MacIntyre and Atkinson be, as they broke more laws than I did during those 18 months. So I just kept on answering every single question and as long as you're doing that you're 'covering every pocket on the snooker table,' aren't you, it makes it harder for them to pot a ball.

Even so, it's the jury you've got to convince, they're the only ones that count. But that wasn't going to stop me from being me, I won't do that for anyone even if my liberty's at stake. There was a Muslim on the jury and I know this because she took the oath in Islamic. At one point, when I was answering questions about the Bloody Sunday counter-demonstration, I looked her straight in the eye and said, "If you find me guilty of these charges then I will do every day in prison with my head held high, because I've been defending our country. I'm not saying those who were actually marching are blowing us up but they're supporters of that cause. If you were a Muslim, would you let Kurds march down your streets?" Enough said.

Now I was going to end up getting a guilty on this charge and for me that says it all. But as for the legal system, let me tell you this. On the back of all this they nicked three other kids, two of which were pals of mine Matthew Osbury and Will Browning. Ten months down the line and they put their hands up to a lesser charge. Their deal has seen them have affray dropped to a Public Order Section 4, which is the lowest form of public order act and they've all go off with 100 hours' community service and a £100 fine – yet they were standing shoulder to shoulder with me – you work that one out if you can because I can't. But good luck to them, I wouldn't want them put away.

Anyway, we'd already proved that MacIntyre had offered me drugs not once but twice during his investigation and I wanted to put this into real terms for the jury, to help them understand the lengths this dog went to set me up. So I told them that I go to work everyday and I work hard to earn a pound note, yet here I am being offered £100,000 by the BBC to transport 20 cars across London on my recovery trucks, so I asked the jury "Could you earn £100,000 in a day?" They didn't even blink an eyelid and I knew there and then I was going to get a guilty.

Another thing I noticed about this jury was there weren't enough notes being passed from them to the judge. There weren't enough questions being asked by any of them, it was as if they weren't paying full attention to what was going on before them and for me that's a bad, bad sign. I like to see them sitting down and writing things, something they want to bring up, good or bad, because that was the only way it was going to be discussed properly and in depth. We all forget things, don't we, but if they weren't taking notes they didn't have any prompts to trigger off any discussions when they retired to discuss points and consider their verdict.

Oh, but I do remember one note being passed from the jury to the judge and you aren't going believe what it was about. Even now it still makes me shake my head. Remember, this happened two-and-a-half weeks into my trial and there'd been talk about something from years ago, with certain people being 'tooled up.' And one juror sent a note to the judge asking what 'tooled up' meant. Fuck me, I'm on two violent charges here and he doesn't even know what 'tooled up' means, surely any kid knows that. I just smiled and shook my head thinking "whatever chance have I got here?"

Well, if you want advice who better to ask than your mum. She turned up one day at the trial so I phoned her from Wandsworth that night and asked her how she thought it was going. She said, "Sweet, we've got this geezer in the corner," so I asked her which one she meant. Now, my mum's South London, so when this old geezer took the oath he sounded just like Arthur Mullard who came out of South London. Boomf, she thinks he's with us, you know what I mean. My mum keeps going, "I'm telling you we got him," so I asked her what the signals were, why was she so sure and this was her explanation: "Well, he's got a pair of trainers on and he's wearing trousers." I laughed, here's me trying to find out if he's giving any real signs of being on my side and the only reason she can give is he's got a pair of 'Claire Raynors' on with his 'round the houses.' Fucking hell, I'd never heard anything like it....and he only later turned out to be the same geezer who sent a note to the judge asking what 'tooled up' meant!

Of course the prosecution tried to make a big deal out of me supposedly being racist and having Far Right views. When I told them I wasn't racist, I'm a Loyalist to the Queen they just called me a liar. Well, if they weren't going to listen to me maybe they'd listen to Roland Terry, a lovely geezer I've known for years who manages a local youth team. Roland looks the part, do you know what I mean, but he's really mellow and laid back, cool calm and collected about things in life. Oh yeah, and by the way, Roland's black. Here's what he said about me in his witness statement:

"I used to play a lot of football myself at the weekends and I got to know Jason Marriner as a result of playing against him, we first came into contact with each other about 10 years ago. We would talk after games in which we had played against one another and we would also bump into each other from time to time in Hampton. I mentioned to Jason during the course of one of our chats that I was involved in the running of Hampton Youth and he offered to help me out.

"We normally train on the same night and at the same place every week and Jason would always attend. He was very committed and reliable, he had the same attitude as me. We have both got a lot out of the game over the years and we want to pass on our love of the game to youngsters. We both take great satisfaction from seeing youngsters doing well and progressing. Jason is good with the children and is involved because of his love of the game, we receive no payment for our involvement.

"I know that football is Jason's life, it is mine also, although I do not support a particular team.

"I saw Mr. MacIntyre's programme and do not think that Jason was portrayed fairly at all. I have sat down with Jason over a pint down the years and we have discussed politics and race, among many other issues. Jason has made it clear when we have been discussing racial issues that he is not a racist and has said that if he was, he would not socialise with black people or help me with the team

"I was shocked at the suggestion in Mr. MacIntyre's programme that Jason is involved with the likes of the National Front, Combat 18 and the British National Party and raised this with him. He told me that he is not a member of, or involved with, any of these groups. I would make the point that if I thought Jason was involved in this kind of thing and was a racist, I would have nothing to do with him. I would describe Jason as a friend. I think Mr. MacIntyre has misrepresented his attitudes and behaviour. I have known Jason for a long time and the person I know was not the person featured on the programme."

But the jury still weren't listening were they, I'd said things on MacIntyre's film they didn't like and I tell you now, it wouldn't have mattered what I'd been up for. I could've been charged with murder and they were still going to find me guilty.

I'll tell you something else, I would love to have been in the public gallery during my trial and watched what was going on. I know I'd have thought 'wow, man.' Better still, I'd liked to have been on my own jury because when I'm adamant about something I do not buckle and there were questions being asked in there that would have got my mind doing overtime. If the other jurors had said to me 'these kids are guilty' I'd have stood my ground and said 'hold on a minute, these kids have been offered 20 kilos of cocaine and no-one's said a thing. What has this got to do with football violence and the charges against them? So slow down a minute, I think you're missing the point. Shouldn't we be asking ourselves, 'is this how the BBC should act'?' There's no way I could have let myself be bossed by the other members of the jury.

But there was no-one there to fight my corner like that so instead I'm standing in the dock after spending the best part of a year in prison on remand and I already know where this is all going, never mind that we're slaughtering the prosecution at every turn. There's still no point in letting your emotions play with you on the inside, all you can do is prepare yourself for the worst and anything better is a bonus.

And this is the view of an innocent man, so now do you wonder why I've got no faith left in the legal system? There are naïve people out there who still think it's fair in this country and if you try and point things out to them they just don't want to believe it, you'll never change their minds. But this is the truth, the reality, that the system stinks. There's no point getting bitter about it, you just have to deal with it – but you ought to know first what you're dealing with.

The prosecution started their closing speeches on December 6th, 2,000 and as you'd expect, they twisted everything and kept repeating that MacIntyre, Atkinson and the rest of them were not the ones on trial. That's because the defence had done such a blinding job of showing them up for what they really are – liars. We made our closing speeches the following day and showed once again what a load of bollocks the Crown's case had been throughout, although the defence did admit to muddling up a couple of things – and those were the names 'Donal' and 'MacIntyre.' Here's how Andy's defence closed:

"Finally, the prosecution have been confused often and now we have muddled up too! For the names 'Donal' and 'MacIntyre' should really read "Many Lined Actor" – or "Terminal Con Day."

Friday December 8th, 2000, not a day I'll ever forget. First off my sister Nikki gave birth to my niece Rosie, which was great news.

But back to business, I'll tell you now you couldn't get a fag paper in Court No.1 that day, it was packed solid. Judge Byers was still giving his summing up that morning and you couldn't shut him up, he went on for hours. He'd already spent the whole of the previous afternoon giving directions to the jury and I tell you now, some of it was every bit as twisted as anything the prosecution had come out with. One minute he's telling the jury the defence don't have to prove anything, that's up to the prosecution to prove their case, and the next he's making out there was something off-key about me and Andy exercising our right to remain silent when we were arrested.

Here's what he said about me: "When he was questioned…he was silent, but now he has given evidence…the prosecution say of those facts now relied on, he could have been expected to mention those matters then. As he did not, you may conclude it's invented or tailored to meet the prosecution's case."

And here's what he said about Andy: "Do not assume he is guilty as he did not give evidence, failure to give evidence does not equal guilt. But you can take it into account. Bear in mind there has been no evidence from Andrew Frain that undermines, contradicts or explains the prosecution evidence. If you think it right to do so, you are entitled to draw inferences from his failure to give evidence as you think proper. You may hold it against him."

So all this judge is really saying is that you're guilty if you do speak and you're guilty if you don't. It's all a game, I'm telling you and the way the cards are stacked against you, you can't win.

At half-eleven the judge ordered the jury to go and consider its verdict. They say the longer the jury's out the better your chances, because at least it means they're still discussing their decision and it's not a unanimous verdict. But someone always buckles even if they don't think they will at the start and come on, lets have it right, the whole trial had been done on a hurry up and now it was a Friday – boomf, get it done – they weren't ever going to let it spill over into the weekend, were they?

Three-and-half-hours later we're back in the court but it was a bit of a false alarm as the jury haven't come to an agreed verdict. The judge tells them he'll accept a majority verdict of 10, so for me that means another trip back down to the cells again. But this time it's only for an hour, as the jury are finally ready to deliver their verdicts. So step forward Julia Moorcroft because as the jury's forewoman, this was your moment of fame:

Count One (Conspiracy to commit violent disorder at Leicester City v. Chelsea), Jason Marriner: Guilty or Not Guilty? – "Guilty" (majority 11-1)

Count One, Andrew Frain: Guilty or Not Guilty? – "Guilty" (majority 11-1)

Count Two (Affray at anti-Bloody Sunday demonstration), Jason Marriner: Guilty or Not Guilty? – "Guilty" (majority 10-2)

Count Two, Andrew Frain: Guilty or Not Guilty?" – "Guilty" (majority 10-2)

And that was that. MacIntyre and Atkinson's 'work,' the police, the CPS and a slack jury had finally put me and my co-de in prison. The defence made a plea for mitigation before sentencing but I was already thinking anything up to a 10 because I had no faith left. It was out of my hands now, I'd been in the dock and I'd boxed clever, I'd hit them as hard as I could but there was nothing more I could do for now. Before I got sentenced the judge made a speech to the public gallery saying if he heard any outcry he'd clear the courtroom. It was all for show, he was just trying to stamp his authority on everything but it still didn't stop some friends of mine from giving him a slow hand-clap though, did it – cheers, fellas. I appreciated it.

He was really foaming at the mouth when he made his speech and when he read out my previous I spotted a couple of them on the jury nodding their heads as if they're patting themselves on the back for a job well done, thinking 'yes, I knew all along this man was guilty.'

But do you know what he said in his first two lines of sentencing – I still can't believe it and neither will you – he only goes and says, "Taking into account no evidence of actual violence." I mean, the man's just about to sentence me to six years in jail so what would he have given me if he'd seen me throw just one punch – 15 years? The old 'chocolate fudge' then goes on to say about how I've shown no remorse for what I've done, but how am I supposed to show remorse when I haven't done fuck all?

Next up he says, "I am firmly of the view that you are dangerous men, not just at football. You relish violence and will stop at nothing, with little regard for others or the law. You must be punished for what you have done. (well, let's have it right, I should have walked then, shouldn't I, but he isn't finished yet) you will go to prison for a very long time, four years for conspiracy to cause violent disorder and two years consecutive for affray. That's a total of six years."

And I just thought "So fucking what!" I turned and looked at the jury, smiled and winked and thought, "You take that to your poxy wine bar and I'll take it to my grave." They looked at me with complete disgust as if to say, "he can't do that, he can't stand there and smile at us," but oh yeah, I could, I had every right to after what they'd done. For despite everything that had happened to me I still firmly believed that good will follow bad, as even the darkest hour of your life only last for sixty minutes.

Yet then on top of my six years the judge tried to give me a 20-year ban from attending football. Now think about this. During the trial the judge remains neutral, he's there to keep order, so the only time you really get a chance to weigh him up is when it comes to the sentencing which is entirely up to him. Here's a high court judge who has been presiding over one of the most high profile cases for years and during his first opportunity to show his worth he's tried to hand me a 20-year ban when the maximum exclusion order allowed by parliament is a 10. How much faith have you got left in the system now?

After he's sentenced me he's sent this message down to the cells saying "could you please tell Jason Marriner to come back up to court because as his Q.C. has quite rightly told me the maximum ban I can impose is 10 years." I just said, "Tell the fucking judge, Up his bollocks. He's just given me six years, what does he think I'm going to do, walk up and down the stairs all day?" The judge sent yet another message down saying if I didn't come back into court I'd be in contempt. I just laughed with the warden and said, "It's very hard for me to be done for contempt of court if I'm not in the courtroom. I think the judge needs to learn about his 'contempts of courts' and his 'conspiracies.'" Well, he was getting on a bit.

12

WANDSWORTH AWAY

Prison is like a bus journey, you're stuck on board for the ride but one day you will get off, it's a simple as that. Some journeys are a lot longer than others, some like mine are six years and it's a long, long way down that road, you see a lot of kids 'reach their stops' before you do. But we all get there in the end even if it seems at times like the wheels have fallen off because whatever happens, time stops for no man. It doesn't matter who you are in life, that 'bus journey' can apply to whatever bad times we all have to get through. Meanwhile, me and Andy were just about to 'board that bus.'

It was pitch-black on a Friday night in December and it was fucking freezing. Me and Andy were split up into different sweat-boxes as I'm going back to Wanno while Andy's back off to the Scrubs. I shook his hand, gave him a hug and said, "See you later, son, stay in touch." – "Yeah," he said, "sweet."

They've handcuffed me and then boomf, I'm gone in the van. All I want to do is get back to my cell and read my paper and get my nut down, because tomorrow's another day. Listen, I'm a year into my sentence already because I'd been on remand and, to me, that was a huge lump to come off so fuck 'em. Although I still had a lump to do I now knew what I was serving.

I'm sitting in my sweat-box going to the other courts to pick people up and you can hear every story under the sun being told, stories like you've never heard, but everyone's been stitched up, haven't they. And then it comes on the news, doesn't it, "the two 'notorious Headhunters' Jason Marriner and Andy Frain have got six and seven years respectively." Someone's shouted out "fucking hell that's a liberty," and I just burst out laughing because they didn't know I was on the bus. As we sat in traffic outside a Currys or a Dixons there I am again on the six o'clock news, my face large as life on the tele. At least my remand days are over because while you're on remand you get woken up at six in the morning and you're not even due in court until half-past ten. It's not like you can have a shower or anything so when you get the shout you just think "oh fuck that, I'm going to have another five minutes." It can be freezing in your cell.

It isn't just that, if there's even the slightest chance you are going to walk you've got to pack your whole kit and take it with you, every single day, no matter what because once you've been remanded the first time, you have to be in court again within the next seven days and it just goes on and on from there until you're freed or you're sentenced.

I've got back to Wandsworth and let off the bus inside the gates, then I'm booked in as a long-term prisoner at reception. The screw tells me I've got a form telling me when my release date is. My Release date? Are you fucking mental I've just got six years, what are you giving me my release date for?

As a convicted prisoner I now have to see the doctor even though I've already been in Wanno for ages without seeing one even when I wanted to. And there didn't seem much point after what happened to a geezer called Lenny Chambers, who went to see the doctor one day about a rash. I pissed myself laughing when Lenny told me this: The doctor told him to stay out of the sun and Lenny's reply was "I haven't been out of my cell for three days." The doctor's reply was, "Well stay away from the windows, then!" That's sunny Wanno for you.

Eventually I see the doctor and he says he wants to put me in the hospital wing for the night. When I asked him what for he says it's because the sentence was probably a lot for me to take in. I said I'm not going on no hospital wing, I just wanted to get up the next morning and crack on. So I said to him straight, "If you think I'm going to hang myself over some judge giving me six years you're off-key. I've got plenty going on for me outside, thank you very much, six years won't alter my life." So I signed a form to say I'd refused to go on the hospital wing and made my way back to my own wing.

I've got my Joeys slung over my shoulder as I'm making my way back and I hear the shout "Take those bags off your shoulder" because you aren't even allowed to do that in Wandsworth – your shirt's got to be tucked in at all times, the buttons have to be done up, you're not allowed to wear a belt, there's all these annoying little things that you must or mustn't do. And prison clothes? Well, they're not easy for a kid who likes his clothes.

As I'm dragging my bags along the floor all the screws are looking at me but the lads on the hotplate have seen me walk down the landing and my mate Vince Stapleton said "It's a fucking liberty Jason, six years, it's outrageous." My cell's on the ones and as I'm making my way along the twos, another pal of mine Alan Paramasivan, said "Jase, it was a fucking outrageous liberty." I laughed and said "Why? What happened?" as if I didn't know what he was talking about and then in the same breath I've called out "Anyway, six years isn't that bad – they reckon I'll get out on a Tuesday."

The lads just pissed themselves and told me my sense of humour was blinding. And do you want to know why? Because already my attitude to the whole system was 'fuck them, they can't have me.' For months and months leading up to the trial I'd been telling everyone I was going to walk so of course the next thing I hear from the kangas when I'm unpacking my stuff is, "alright Marriner, I thought you were supposed to be getting a 'not guilty'?" They were already trying to get inside my nut but I wasn't having it, I just turned around and said, "Yeah, but I've got an appeal coming, guv, because I am innocent and one day I will get a 'not guilty,' I just never said if it would be on my first or second trial, did I?"

And after I'd put my stuff away I said to the other lads, "Well, I've unpacked for the last time for a while and I'm here to stay. Right, we're having a 'Russell Harty.'" They just looked at me, they couldn't figure out how come I wasn't fuming, so I told them, "Listen, I was Joe the Champ on remand but there's no more remand money from now on, now I'm on 15 shackers – that's a big loss in prison, because you could spend £30 a week on remand – "It's a bag of bollocks but fuck it, we're having a Riveta party tonight on me."

Let's get this right, there was no way I was going to let the system beat me just because some stranger has wormed his way into my life to set me up and another's given me six years, I wasn't going to buckle for them, I was determined to live to the best of my capabilities in prison and they cannot take that away from you, whatever else they might do. Seriously, even in a sore gaff like Wanno they cannot take away your cleanliness nor your dignity, your loyalty, morals, trust nor self-respect. They can't even take away your happiness if you don't let them and do you want to know how you start to hang on to all this while they're trying to snatch it from you? One small but important word, mate – 'hope.'

You're always living in hope and it starts very early: you get nicked, you hope you get a lesser charge. If you don't get bail, you hope you're not on remand for too long. When you're on remand, you hope to get yourself a job. You hope you get association, you hope you get a phone call, you hope you get a shower and you hope you get a cell-clean. Then you hope you get a good barrister or Q.C., you hope you get a 'not guilty,' but if it does go boss-eyed and you get sent down, you hope you'll be going to one of the better prisons.

You hope your visitors will turn up when they're supposed to, you hope you'll get a letter most days – mental things, letters, you've just got to have them, the screws even used to say to me 'just how many people do you know?' – you hope everyone's alright on the outside, you hope your canteen money gets through on time and then you hope you'll get what you ordered from the canteen. When you move prisons you hope the next one will be alright and that you meet up with someone you got on ok with at a previous gaff.

You hope you get your appeal date soon and that it goes well and that you get something off your sentence. Believe me, you lose hope and you're really fucked, because these hopes are little goals in themselves and they're vital. There's an old saying, "They can lock up your body but they can't lock up your mind."

In the prison system they call Wanno a bird killer, even though you're locked in your cell 24/7, because you know your daily routine and so once you've had your meals and you're banged up in your cell again it's another day done. That is unless you have women or drug problems, which sort of go hand in hand, as the junkies' birds are usually junkies themselves too and can't be relied upon.

Believe me, it wasn't all champagne and skittles for me either, I even had rows with my missus Julie sometimes and she's as good as gold. She is a million-per-cent, she was there for me before all of this, she was there all the way through it and she's there for me now. But some days it's just hard not to think or say the wrong thing.

And as for drug problems, this'll give you a clue as to how fucked-up some of them are: one day when I was going to court there was this 'fraggle' with a right problem who was going to get discharged. Every day you do in prison over your sentence you can get £90 and this kid was in the discharge box saying, "I wish they'd keep me in for another day, because then I could pick up an extra £90 and go and get myself a good few rocks." I just shook my head and thought, 'what a prick, what chance has he got?' But I'll tell you something that is shocking, a lot of proper people who didn't touch drugs on the outside end up with a drug problem in jail and it's the prison system itself which encourages this.

The reason for this is that unlike pot, which stays in your system for 28 days and there's nothing you can do about it, Class A drugs like heroine, ecstasy and cocaine only stay in your system for about 48 hours and you can flush that out even quicker if you drink enough water. The only time I've ever seen anyone drink as much water as someone with a habit was when 'MacInlies' took the stand in court. So some of the proper people on long term sentences don't have a puff, they get on to the 'Fleetwood Mac' instead because with smack, they're out of their heads, another day's gone off their sentence before the stuff wears off and, if they drink enough water afterwards, there's less chance they'll end up getting stung by a Mandatory Drugs Test. The only drawback, of course, is that they wind up with a 'roger rabbit.'

But anyway, if you're in the right frame of mind all you care about then is chipping away at your sentence so you're behind your door, you're reading and already the time is passing, you get up and have your breakfast, you go back and you do a little bit of this and that and before you know it, you go and get your lunch, come back to your cell and you have a little siesta. Then maybe you'll write a letter, go and have your tea and then, if you're lucky enough to have a radio because that's your main vice in prison, you might hear an old time favourite song to bring back good memories or wait for the football to come on – I can't tell you how good it is that there's a game going on somewhere nearly every day now – and when that finishes it's another day over and done, another day less to do.

Even so, you cannot tick your days off like I've seen some people try to do, I've heard a kid saying "I've been here six weeks and five days now," and I've

said, "What? Leave off, how did you ever get through that?" and he hasn't even
realised I'm winding him up. Well, me being me, I've got to take it a bit further
haven't I so I go, "Well, that isn't too bad, you're probably going to get eight
years at least, aren't you and all of that six weeks will come off as well." You
should have seen this geezer's face, it was a picture. "I'm not getting eight
years," he said, so I told him, "Well, I know someone who got an eight for that,
if you're lucky you might get a seven but I can't see it, can you?" and he's finally
twigged and gone, "Oh leave me alone Jason, will you," but you know, you will
drive yourself mad like that, trying to tick the days off one by one.

Wanno's a 23-and-a-half hour a day bang up and that can be soul destroying
– just think how you'd cope banged up nearly all day, every day, week in, week
out – I've seen grown men buckle in places like Wanno because you're only
getting out of your cell for those three meals and, more often than not, the affray
button goes when you're eating followed by all the screws on their whistles.
They go steaming in and all of a sudden their friends come out of the woodwork
when there's an altercation. Fuck me, I've never seen a place that's supposed to
be so short-staffed have so many workers as when those whistles blow. But then
there's never enough around for us to get any exercise, funny that.

I remember one day I said to this kanga, "Any chance of some exercise,
guv?" and he went up on his heels and down again like an old cozzer, before
telling me, "Exercise, Marriner? No chance." They're supposed to give you an
hour a day exercise but don't worry about that, there are no rules they have to
stick to. I mean, I get on with people, I'm not one of those kids who are always
in their faces shouting so I took the piss and said: "C'mon guv, I heard it
stopped raining in China three days ago," and he all he said was, "Marriner,
What's the word on the street?" and I said "I couldn't give a fuck about that I
just want to know if I'm going to get any exercise." He totally blanked that and
said, "You wouldn't know what the word on the street is because you're in
here!" – which still makes me laugh to this day.

Listen, you've got to laugh at them and with them, you've got to do the
prison system with happiness. If they see a weakness in somebody and they see
them struggling they will try and break you.

Wandsworth is the only prison which is still run by the P.O.A, which is the
Prison Officers Association. It's so behind the times the screws don't want it to
move forward because all the time you're banged up they don't have to work.
One day we see the governor for the first time in ages and everyone's on to him,
telling him we're being denied all our basic rights and we've called for a
meeting. He gave us a time for the following day for a number of us who had
genuine complaints.

One of us, Dave Roryson, a nice bloke I'd known at Chelsea, had just done a
nine out of a 12 and he knew the governor from Gartree. Dave was in patches
because he was an e-man, you know an escapee, and he'd seen a few different
nicks so he knew how things worked. He said to the governor "Right guv, we're
human beings, if you were a dog you wouldn't get treated as bad as this, Wanno

has got to be the worst nick in the country. I'm going to tell you something, tomorrow I've got an adjudication and I'll be put down the block." Dave's smiling at the governor all the while which has him puzzled as he can't work out why Dave's so happy about being put into segregation.

So Dave tells him straight, "I'll be put down there, I'll get a phone call, a cell-clean, a shower and exercise every day and that's four more things than I'd be getting on the landing." And that's Wandsworth for you, it has a rule of its own and you have to learn how to bend it. Every day was a task and you have to wipe your mouth with a lot of things when you're inside but whenever I looked at a screw I used to say, "I'm doing six years and you're doing life and that's a big difference, so you just crack on guv."

So even while I was still on remand I knew I didn't want to be banged up in my cell all day if I could help it. I mean, in Wandsworth you're banged-up bottle-handed and even with a good pad mate you're bound to get on each others' nerves at some point over a 23-hour bang-up. I'm not being funny but you try and live with your wife for that long in one room, every day, seven days a week – and you can fuck your wife – no, I had to get out and the only way out was to get a job.

Now, I didn't like them much but I got on alright with the kangas, because if you show any signs that you've got an attitude with them then you've got no chance. So you say to yourself 'what am I going to do that's best for me long-term?' Am I going to be one of those short-tempered kids who are always going up to the screws and shouting "you're a fucking prick" and this, that and the other, or am I going to do my sentence my way. I believe the first one past the post is the winner. If you're a bit of a character and an easy kid they half-like you, but you've still got to work your ticket with all the 'yes sir, no sir, three bags full sir' bit. Now, if someone wants to call you a cunt for that, fine, but let me ask you, who's the fool? I got enhanced while I was still on remand and for that I got an extra visit, up from three to four a week, and now I wanted a job.

Half of your applications will always end up in 'File 13,' they don't make it past the bin because it's one of the ways the screws are testing you. Everything's always 'tomorrow,' or 'wait and see' with them. Some days it's funny and some days it's shocking but one thing you soon learn is that you need one of them to speak up for you. They're not complete fools, they're not your pals and they're quick to tell you as much. But after work, whether it's morning, lunchtime or at night, the first thing all the kangas from Wandsworth do is go and have a drink round their clubhouse.

This is where all the times I've spent giving it the 'alright guv, how are you doing' to this screw called Shadbolt is finally going to pay off. He's down the club talking with the others and he happens to mention something like, "he ain't a bad kid, you know, that Marriner, I might give him half a chance." Lovely, after three or four months I've put in an application for a job and the kangas have backed it. Security run the prison so they have to clear me but they get talking to the other kangas and then you've got a chance.

My application gets mentioned to the Senior Officer, then the Privilege Officer and once they know you're not on the 'Chinese rugs' you're in with a chance because they know you're not going to be interested in contraband and serving up. Obviously this was important to them, because I was going to be working on the hotplate and that would give me contact with the whole wing.

Talking of drugs, whether people like to hear it or not most of the serving up goes on in church – they've go no respect, these smackheads, but what do you expect – because if you can't get out of your cell during the week for some other reason the one place they can't stop you going to on a Sunday is church. Now, I don't take drugs and I don't serve them up and I certainly never went to church on a Sunday on the outside, so I'm not going to start on the inside. No, you didn't see me in the pews at Wanno on a Sunday.

But I don't know if it was the drugs that made them do it or not, yet some of these kids thought they'd tactually taken up religion for real. On my life, you've never seen so many kids, especially when they're about to go to court, walking around with their bibles and praying, they didn't leave off. So neither did I. I'd go "What you praying for?" – "oh God will help me," they'd say. I couldn't help myself, I'd come back with, "Well God didn't help you when you got nicked, did he. What are you talking about God to me for, go and have a lay down you nutter."

Anyway, because the kangas knew I wasn't on drugs I'd have a V.D.T. – a voluntary drugs test – every month. But an M.D.T. is a mandatory when you just get swagged, strip-searched and you're made to have a piss, you have to go. Well, my wing got dawn-raided one morning and we're all standing outside our cells at 7 o'clock, freezing our bollocks off. This drug dog jumps up on my bed and I called out to the screw, "get that fucking dog off my bed, guv, it's a fucking liberty, I've got to sleep on that." They don't find anything, of course, because like I've told you me and the gear don't mix, but as I've gone back in there's all my stuff all over the gaff – "Oh lovely, I hope you don't leave your front room at home like this. And by the way, that's a really clever dog you've got there as he's even managed to open a box of matches."

I'd always have a cheeky comment for the screws, just something to get their nuts working, because a bit of clever sarcasm has more of an impact than a string of verbal abuse. I'm lucky, it's something I've done all of my life so it was easy for me and even more so because I knew from day one there could only ever be one winner while you're inside and that's the system. All you can do is bide your time until you have the last say (which is what I'm doing now) but to try and do that in prison would have been nothing more than fighting a losing battle, one million per cent.

However, just because you can't win that doesn't mean you have to lose, either. It doesn't matter what it is you need to do to make sure the system doesn't beat you – it can be any little thing at all – but you have to do it, you cannot give an inch to them in there and you have to be prepared for a hard-fought 'away draw,' because that's all you can get. In Wandsworth I had a thing about the lock-up and it didn't matter whether it was two minutes or 20 seconds before the kanga came around to shut and lock my cell door, I always made sure I slammed it shut myself.

I'm big enough, fat enough and ugly enough to shut my own door without anyone else's help, thank you very much. And by not letting them bang me up it gave me a little bit of self-satisfaction. It was only a little thing but it meant a lot to me.

13

IN THE AWAY END

Some people inside don't like the idea of working for the kangas, the Guv'nor, or whoever it is that they see as being in charge but let me tell you they're not thinking long-term, you're working for yourself. If you work, it goes down on your CV and that can help you when you're sentenced, or when you're progressing through the system and you want to move to a different prison. You have to learn quickly to start thinking about tomorrow even when you're on remand, because what happens if you don't walk and you end up getting a lump of bird what you are you going to do then?

The following day after being sentenced I was straight back on the hotplate, by which time I was No1. It didn't mean much to me but the beauty of it was it meant I got a single cell. I liked serving the lads and having a laugh as they come along the counter, nicking trays of chickens from the kitchen which meant I could look after my own, that kind of thing, I just wanted to get straight back into it. If I hadn't have had that I'd have been stuck in my cell thinking about my sentence and everything else that's gone on over the past year.

Yet every now and again, the same ones who refuse to work or just want to give the screws grief are now going, 'fuck me, how did he get that job, guv?' about anyone who had a job. I'd earned mine, I'd been in that gaff for the best part of a year by the time my trial started and once you've been there a few months the screws know you well enough to make up their own minds.

Like I said, one of the main reasons I wanted a job in Wandsworth was to get me out of my cell but we also used to call it 'money up front' and that was for the simple reason you were also working for the right to a shower and a phone call every day. Believe me, when you're behind your door you aren't even getting to make a phone call once a week. And of course, just like any other job on the inside or outside, there's the other perks. Not only did I now get a cell to myself I was also allowed to keep all the things I needed for the job in there and believe me, there's plenty of little bonuses in that, mate, I'm telling you. It meant you could live clean, which you couldn't on the minimum you get from the prison service, you could clean your cell every day, you could wash the floor. These things are like gold dust to you, just being able to wash your plates in a different sink to the one you wash your face in and most important of all it meant you could keep your self-respect.

With all the supplies at hand it meant I could also keep other people happy, like with the little reflective sheets we used as mirrors I could make sure they all got one and I could get them enough razor blades as well as I've got as many as I need. It's always good to be able to look after your own. Inside, proper people don't forget.

Talking of those mirrors, I had my pal Mark Wotton in the cell above me, nice bloke, a 'penny chew,' you know, a Tottenham supporter. After the bang-up he'd put his mirror at the cell window, I'd get mine and we'd angle them so we could see each other: "How you doing, partner?" and we'd have a bit of a chat. Like I said, he was a good kid and we had the same sense of humour – in other words we were always winding each other up. I'd say stuff like, "Do you know what I like about you Mark?" – "No Jase, what's that then?" – "Fuck all, Mark, that's what." Or, "Who have Tottenham got on Saturday? Well I hope you get turned over," and he'd come back with "Fuck off, you fat Chelsea bastard."

We got sentenced at the same time and I remember laughing at him, saying "I got a six and you got an eight, so you were here before me and I'll be out before you, you fucking wanker!" Yeah, I know, it all sounds a bit close to the bone doesn't it, but it was all a laugh and a joke between pals and that's how you've got to be. Most times when we were having a chat you'd start to hear the others calling their mates, asking if they had any bacca or whatever. They'd start swinging these lines made mostly out of bed sheets or laces tied together, with a sock or a pillow case stuck on the end of them. Back and forth, back and forth passing stuff and all you'd hear all night long was 'swing us a line, swing us a line,' it would drive you fucking mad after a while. So I'd nick their lines, catch hold of them and I wouldn't let them go for a couple of minutes. Once I'd got hold of one it was all, "Let go of it, let go you bastard," and I'd shout up, "Go and get your head down, can't you do your bird?" I suppose for some it was a bit of a bird-killer, a half-hour chat at the end of the day.

I remember this big black American geezer who was in for a bit of fraud. I used to dish him up two extra portions of rice each day from the hotplate and he'd give me a half-ounce of tobacco at the end of each week which I used to trade for phone cards or bars of chocolate. If you didn't feel like eating them there and then you could always use them to gamble with, "I'll bet you a Mars Bar Chelsea beat Arsenal tonight," that kind of thing. But football could be a bit of a problem if it was a wind up. Football's a passionate thing for anyone who supports a club and the thing is with me everyone knew I supported Chelsea.

Yeah, you've guessed it, every single time Chelsea lost some joker or other would want to come and tell me all about it. I'd say to them, "What, do you think I'm stupid or something, do you think I don't know the score, what are you telling me for?" or I'd say something like, "Listen, I've been going to Chelsea all my life and I've seen them lose more times than I've seen them win, so don't you worry about it."

The one thing I knew I couldn't get into trouble over was football, no way, that would have been like a thief getting caught stealing in there, or a drug dealer serving up gear. You've got to box clever when you're inside, so if someone on a wind-up came up to me and said, "Did you see that Chelsea lost again last night?" I might say something like, "One, I didn't see it because I haven't seen a tele for eight months now and two, I thought it was just the batteries in my radio running out but it wasn't, it was Chelsea passing the ball very slowly. I knew they'd finally run out when Chelsea couldn't get over the half-way line." Humour will always be my best self defence and it just lets them know they can't ever get in my nut that easily.

It's like when I was having a chat with this kid one night, he was a bit street-wise and told me he'd seen the MacIntyre programme and thought straight away it was a bit patchy. I turned to him and said, "A bit patchy? They edited and put together more clips than Jeremy Beadle."

When there was football on the radio, which was most nights, it was just like New Year's Eve each time someone scored, you'd hear all these doors getting kicked and banged and on New Year's Eve itself, well, it was all the banging of the doors, cups against the railings and the shouts of 'Happy New Year,' the lot – it was almost 'naughty.' Of course you'd always get someone acting miserable who'd go "Happy New Year? Fuck off, I've got another three of these to do so tell me what's happy about it?" But I'd always say to them, "Don't worry about it, it's the start of another day, another month and another year. We're already chipping away at the next one, we're getting there because they cannot stop time, it stops for no man," and I'd always remind them of that.

That's not to say I didn't have low days myself (you wouldn't be human in a gaff like that if you didn't) but you just have to snap yourself out of it even if it means having to look at another kid and thinking he's worse off than you are. He may be looking at a lump of bird, this geezer, or maybe he's just got a lump.

Before I got a cell to myself I was banged up with this kid called Paul Gowans, he was a nice kid from Wandsworth, but he had a bit of a crack problem. What he'd done is phone for a local pizza delivery man and then with his mate they'd ironed this geezer out before grabbing £40 off of him. That was enough for Paul and his mate to get a rock each so it was easy money for them and they did it all again a couple of nights later. But this time they've gone too far, they've really hurt the geezer. Paul was a fiery character and this time the geezer he's ironed out has ended up with brain damage. Paul gets nicked and he's now looking at a lump of bird from a GBH Section 18, which is only one down from an attempted murder but I'll never forget this, he was genuinely remorseful. I'm not lying to you, you can tell when someone's just making out like they're sorry for what they've done, but not this time, Paul really meant it.

I read the note he wrote to the judges and it was good, it was honest and because he'd now been moved over to another wing from me I was made up for him when he got a message to me saying "tell the General I've got an eight, sweet," because he was quite happy with that, getting eight years. I mean, I knew he had a habit and I don't like drugs but he's done what he's done, this geezer's genuinely sorry for it and that's life. During that same week I got my first visit to Wandsworth's gym – it's only taken about nine or ten months to get this – and as I'm walking through I pass his landing so I ask him how he's doing. "It's not good, Jase," he said, "the kid died." It turns out Paul got sentenced on the Friday and the kid's died the next day. They've recharged Paul with murder and he ends up getting life. A proper shame, a waste of two lives.

Yet I'll tell you one thing about being inside, just in case you don't already know this, you've got to keep your friends close but you've got to keep your enemies even closer. They say you shouldn't judge a book by it's cover – even if it's a cover as good as this book's, if I do say so myself – but that's all they do inside, all the time.

People are on edge, this isn't normal living so all the time you hear stuff like, "I'm not sure about him, he's a plant, he's Old Bill." Wandsworth's a horrible old Victorian building with enough real filth on its walls and floors already so when kids start flinging mud more of it sticks. With no evidence at all, no quiet words, nothing, two kids will go, "Fuck that, who's he? What's he been nicked for?" and the other'll go "How should I know, I haven't spoken to him yet." You can sort of see what's coming next, can't you, because all the first bloke's got to say is, "Well I'm not going to speak to him then, he must be a plant," and that's all it takes, some quiet kid minding his own business has just been labelled as a grass. There will be many who aren't, they're just not right for prison they're like a fish out of water and don't realise the way they act and hold themselves draws suspicion from others around them. And then again, of course, there's others in there who really aren't what they seem and that's why the people are wary. What do you reckon the 'proper' people inside would make of someone like MacIntyre? Well, here's hoping we all find out one fine day and I would fucking love to be a fly on the wall for that one mate, I'm telling you.

Like I've said, there are a lot in there who aren't proper people and I'm not talking about those with a serious habit or some piece of scum who thinks mugging an old lady's normal. There's still the 'bacons' as well who all do the laundry jobs as it's the only one they can have. These lot give me the fucking hump. What happened was that we used to have to pick up our clean kit from them and bring them the old stuff, but because of the kangas being there you've got no real chance of getting at them. That's why it was more frustrating in the visiting hall because when you walked in there they'd all be there on the left hand side, there was no real segregation apart from them being brought in and taken out before you.

Oh believe me, when they walked past everyone would scream at them for being fucking nonces: "Sex case, sex case, hang 'im, hang 'im, hang 'im," wall to wall, it's all you could hear but even with scum like these you've got to be careful – can you believe that? – because they're quick to scream to their solicitors and the B.O.V., the board of visitors. More times than not the bacons would end up being wrapped in even more cotton wool, being given proper treatment and privileges that were denied to the rest of us. It's one thing being normal and working your ticket, but to most of us it seemed like these scum only had to squeal a bit louder each time and they'd get upgraded to first class.

14

USING YOUR FULL SQUAD

Like I told you, you have to know how to work the kangas because most of them have been doing this job for a long time and whatever else you might think of them, don't kid yourself they're all fools. You're in Wandsworth, one of the hardest nicks so you've got to graft them and get them on your side. Why slag them off and have them hate you, so you end up slammed behind your door all day? All you're doing then is making problems for yourself.

And some of them weren't all bad, like this old screw Mr. Stewart he just wasn't as evil as he seemed to some of the lads, even if they may take some convincing of this. Just ask one geezer I knew by the name of Errol Watson, a nice geezer and I ended up in a few nicks with him as it happened. Errol's up on the 'threes,' the three landing in Wanno, and whenever I bumped into him it was always, "W'happnin' Jason, Whah gwan?" This one time I just said "How you doing, Errol, I'm not up to much myself so I'm just going to use the phone." We go down to the phones together and there's Mr Stewart. Now this old kanga, he really pretended to be racist but he wasn't at all, he just loved winding people up. Some of course would take real offence, but those who knew him would just say, "Don't worry 'bout that, breddren, it's sweet."

Now there's a queue as long as a milk-round all waiting to get on the phone and when it finally comes to Errol's turn the number he's rung is engaged. He tells Mr Stewart this and says he has to come back later and try again. You've got to understand that Mr. Stewart liked Errol, but this is what he said in reply: "You've had your phone call, Watson, don't start all your excuses with me, you've had your turn and that's your lot, now go on and fuck off." What else can Errol do, so he goes away and comes back a bit later asking if there's any chance of making that call now. Again, it's "No, fuck off." Yet later that same evening, Mr Stewart's gone over to Errol's cell and told him, "Watson, phone call." Errol's still really fuming and asks him "Why are you playing with my mind like that, Mr Stewart, why do you do these t'ings to me? I've been left seething behind my door." So Stewart told him, "You asked me if you could make a phone call and I said no. If I'd said yes in front of everyone they'd all expect to make a phone call later, or whenever it suited them. But by saying 'no' to you and then coming to your door later you'll think 'Mr Stewart can be a right bastard, but he isn't a bad bloke all the time' – now go and make your phone call, hurry up about it and then fuck off." That was what Mr. Stewart was all about, he was 'Old School' and you could either take it or you couldn't.

"Canteen – Cunt." Those were the first words he ever spoke to me and when I got to the canteen he's still at my shoulder. He said, "Were you ready when I opened the door?" and so I told him, "Of course I was, you saw I was already on my feet, didn't you." Stewart said, "Good, because if you hadn't have been ready, I'd have slammed that door shut on you and you wouldn't have had canteen for another week." I just looked at him and said, "What? Do you really think I'm really that bothered about getting hold of some poxy tuna and noodles?" He reckons he's got me and replies, "Oh you'd have been bothered alright because you wouldn't have been able to buy fags." Well that was easy, I just told him I didn't smoke yet he's straight back in there with, "But you must buy fags like everyone else, even if it's just to serve them up to someone later for extra phone cards?" And I told him straight, "No, I've got plenty of other tricks for that" and because I'd given him an answer for everything he'd thrown at me he liked that, he respected it – some people are just made that way.

But I'll never forget the sight of him on Christmas Eve when he's come in absolutely lagging drunk with this big red nose stuck on his face and he's wearing those joke dreadlocks as well – he was totally ruthless, I'm telling you! – he's come marching straight up to my cell door and shouted, "Marriner." Instead of jumping out of my skin I've turned to face him slowly as I was reading my paper and lazily said, "What is it guv?" and he just screams, "you're a cunt" at me before slamming the peephole shut. Listen, prison is all mind games and he loved playing his mind games with you. I've seen people fuming about him and I've had to tell them, "No, he loves all that but he's sweet, he's alright, just play along with it" and he honestly never got under my skin. I remember one time he came up to me and said, "Marriner, have you got any phone cards?" I thought I'd have a bit of a jolly up with him so I said, "What do you want one for, can't you use the public phone? No guv, I haven't got one" and he gave me one of his phone cards, just like that. I'm telling you, he was all right for a screw.

But don't think there weren't screws I absolutely hated because believe me, there were and sometimes, like any other scumbag, it can take a while before they show their true colours. Me, I've always hated bullies and there was this one kanga I thought was alright – that was until I saw him take a right liberty with someone and then he went right down in my estimation. I was working on the hotplate at the time talking to Ray May and Vince Stapleton. Near us there was this Geordie screw who was a Senior Officer but he was a right piss-head, too. As we were talking this kid comes through and I know him to be a smack-head, but he's said to the screw, "Guv'nor, I'm not being funny, but I've had three nights on the trot where I can't sleep because of savage toothache" and the kanga just dismisses him. "You can't sleep because you're on the gear again and you're clucking," he just didn't listen to the kid at all. Now I don't know if this kid's lying but he might be telling the truth and this screw's in authority, he's got to show some concern because at the end of the day the screws are there to provide a service, to look out for your well-being and make sure you fit back into society when you eventually get out. Now this kid's still standing there, holding his tray and he carries on until the kanga snaps "Fuck off" at him.

"Who you fucking talking to," the kid said, "you can't talk to me like that," but the screw's having none of it, "I can do what I want, now fuck off before I smack you in the mouth and you'll have no tooth." I could see it was never going to end there and the moment this kid said something else – crack – the screw's chinned him, the tray's gone up in the air, another screw's seen this and, of course, he blows his whistle. The kid gets nicked, he's on a charge and now he's down the karaoke while nothing happens to the screw because they never go over on their own, do they. No, from then on I saw that screw in a different light, he was just another bully with a mean temper after all who thought nothing of taking liberties because he was in a position of authority.

So you have to make sure you look after your own because no-one else will. You look at people coming in when you're already seven or eight months down the line into your remand and you don't wish it on them, because it's a struggle, I really have seen grown men buckle badly in there. You need to be more mentally strong than physically strong to survive in prison.

One incident which sticks in my mind was when I was coming back from a good visit with Julie – I made sure they were all good visits and my pals would often write to me later to say they'd come there to make me laugh and it had been the other way around – but as I'm walking down the landing with that extra bounce in my step I saw this Moroccan, or Algerian, well, he was a 'Peter Lorrimer,' a foreigner of some sort and from what he'd told me before I knew he was up for a bit of fraud.

He'd been up on trial but they'd adjourned it for three months and a three-month lay down is an awful long time, especially for this geezer as he really believed he was innocent and things like that can take their toll. He was only a small, thin, middle-aged fella and I could see him as I came along, still bouncing off the walls from my sweet visit. All of a sudden he's crouched down into a ball, half screaming and crying, he was really in tears and I ran over to him, saying "Whoa, whoa, whoa, what are you doing, chav?" and he's all "I just can't take this anymore." Now I'd been in Wandsworth nearly a year by then and I think about eight people had hung themselves during that time and I can see he's about to buckle so I said, "Don't tell me you can't take it, just get a grip of yourself son, you've got to take it."

It turned out he'd just got back from a bit of a bad visit, then he'd had an argument with one of the kangas and it had done him, it was the straw that broke the camel's back. But what I really needed to get through to him was, "Listen, please don't let them see you like this, because they'll love seeing you like this." Oh yeah, they might have shown a bit of concern to his face but believe me, deep down they'd have loved it. I grabbed hold of him and said, "You can't let them know you've been broken even if you are. Please, just pull yourself together and learn to smile at them."

He starts wailing "No, no, leave me alone," and all of a sudden the whistle's gone so I'm out of there. But I think he was alright in the end, I reckon he must have got the sympathy vote from some kanga because he got a bit of cleaning work to do just to get him out of his cell a bit more. Like for a lot of people, prison just wasn't for him, but he must have learnt how to cope with it at some point because I ran into him again two prisons down the line so I guess he must have got a few years, innocent or not. When I saw him again I said to him, "Have you got a grip of yourself now, son?" and he was bouncing, he was sweet, he was in an open prison and just four months from going home so he knew he'd broken the back of it.

I did get some self-satisfaction knowing I'd helped him and others like him, knowing I'd shown them you can't let the system get you down. Because despite of all these hurdles you face everyday you just have to find a way to get over them, you haven't got any choice. I hadn't been inside before, I'd had no experience and I had no idea what to expect but I learnt very quickly that you have to grin and bear it and not only for yourself but for when your family comes to visit. You must always let them see that you're alright, because they'll be going away crying their eyes out if you don't and you really don't want that.

Now like I said, letters are blinding but nothing beats a visit, although they can be a bit tough on your family because at Wandsworth they've got the door wide open as you come through and the visitors can see through there, into the prison itself. They can see for themselves how dark, cold and Victorian this place is, with all its bars and meshing. It's a dark, horrible coldness that stays with all your visitors and it gives them a better idea of the kind of conditions you're living in, which is not easy on your missus or your kids.

But for me a visit was everything and you didn't know if you were getting one or not until first thing in the morning. Whoever's coming to see you would have had to have phoned up the prison the day before, so if a little chit came under your cell door in the morning and you're sharing a cell you're up like a greyhound out of a trap to see if it's your name on it or your pad mate's.

Already you've got a spring in your step as you're starting to get ready a couple of hours before. You've only got £15 a week to spend in prison and shaving balm costs a fiver so you only use a little bit and you have to shave carefully because those prison razor's give you all the rashes. But you know, you're making an effort and that gives you a bit of self-respect back, especially while you're still on remand as you're allowed to wear your own clothes.

What happens then at visiting time is that you get out into this box and every kid going on a visit goes in there first, it's full of all the wings except the Rule 43s. Everyone's smoking which isn't easy if, like me, you don't smoke, but you're so pleased to have a visit you don't really care too much. You don't know who your visitor will be until they turn up so you're guessing who it is and hoping they make it, because anything might have cropped up since they phoned the prison so you couldn't know for certain if you'd see someone until they actually arrived.

And then if you've had a good visit – I made sure all of mine were good visits – you go back to the wing with a real spring in your step. I've seen it go the other way when people have had a proper row and it's left them gutted, but for me it was never disappointing whoever turned up. I was just happy someone had taken the time and effort to come and see me and also, if it wasn't the person I thought it was going to be it meant there was a good chance they'd be on the next visit which, if I was lucky, might even be the next day.

But I could always feel the eyes on me in the visiting hall, the sideways glance that said "Do you know who that is, it's Jason Marriner, the one from the MacIntyre programme," but it wasn't really too much of a problem because most of those who did that were already a bit pally with me. It also gave me the chance to show their visitors that I am human after all, despite what they might have seen on the television. I'd go up and have a chat with them – "Alright? How's it going?"

Oh, but I was terrible. Like I said, I cannot and will not pass up the chance for a piss-take wherever I am. If this geezer's got a few visitors there with him I'd say, "Is that your lovely lady?" and of course they go "yeah," so I'm straight in there with, "that's funny, because the picture of the bird you've got on your cell wall doesn't look like her, she's got ginger hair, that's not the same bird at all." You could see the jaws dropping and this geezer's pleading innocence to his bird as she doesn't know it's just a wind up and to me it's all "Oh drop me out Jase!" But I'm not that much of a trouble-maker, I'd always tell her "No, I'm only joking sweetheart" before I walked off laughing.

Now, although I said you could never be totally sure your visitor would turn up until they're sat in front of you, I was very lucky, my friends and family always turned up and I really appreciate the effort every single one of them made for me. If someone wasn't going to turn up, they'd have to have a really good reason. Well, how about this as an excuse.

My mates Chonker and Silbo were supposed to be coming to see me one Friday and they didn't turn up, I can't get hold of them and that's that. And if your visitor doesn't turn up you still have to sit in this fucking box for however long it takes for all the other visitors to have gone, so you can imagine just how bad that makes you feel. I'd been in Wanno seven or eight months by then so I got hold of my kanga while I'm sitting there in the box and asked him to check on the name-sheet outside in the visiting hall, to see who it was who was supposed to have come and visited me. When he came back and told me I thought, "No, surely not, that's not like them to let me down."

The worst thing is walking back onto the wing, as everyone's going, "Alright Jase? Good visit?" and you have to tell them, "No, they didn't turn up," there really is nothing worse, you're totally gutted. I've got the zig for about 10 minutes and I feel really let down, because these are really good pals of mine and I swore blind to myself there and then that I will never let anyone down on a visit when I'm on the out. But whatever, there's nothing I can do and while it is a wasted visit by the time the weekend's done it's forgotten.

So I'm back out on the hotplate first thing in the morning and you aren't going to believe this but all of a sudden, they've all walked through the hotplate on the other side, Butch, Clive, Big Alan and Chonker. They'd only gone and got themselves nicked, hadn't they. I tell you my jaw just dropped. As Chonk walked through I said to him, "I know you were meant to come and visit me but you don't have to stay with me this long." He said he thought it would be good to come and see me in person, rather than just in visiting hours.

Actually, they fell on their feet a bit there because I was in a position to say to them, "listen lads, tell me what you need and I'll sort you out for you," I could get whatever they needed until they could get to the canteen because they've come in there with nothing, they haven't even got a fag paper between them. I bet they must have thought, "We've fallen out of a window and gone upwards" and that's what it's like when you get your own good little school in there. Fortunately for them, they all wound up getting bail about two or three weeks later.

As for me, it had already got back to me from a kanga that the Governor wanted me out of Wandsworth lively because I was too high-profile and he didn't want to be seen with egg on his face if everything goes boss-eyed with me, because if that had happened it was bound to have hit the papers and it would make the prison look bad. I told the kanga, "look guv, look after me, I've done a job here, I've played the game." I was trying to go to Coldingly prison in Woking but it didn't happen, I ended up in Elmley in Kent. Even so I'd had enough of Wanno, it really is a fucking sore gaff, if animals were kept in the same kind of conditions the R.S.P.C.A. would be up in arms about it and that kind of living takes its toll. I'd had a co-de but he isn't with me now and I've come in to prison on my own so I'll go on my own. You can still keep in contact with pals from previous prisons if you want to and to this day I still do with some of them, but only a few.

I've got enough friends out here on the outside to not run around making new ones. It's nice if you can meet nice people because it's 'nice to be nice,' isn't it, but you know, that's past now, onwards and upwards – "See you later, Jase" – "Yeah. See ya later."

15

MOVING TO A BETTER CLUB

It'll seem strange to anyone who's never been to prison but a lot of people inside don't want to go to open prisons, because they're too open – can you believe that? – they reckon the temptation of not having your door locked, being given the key and the trust that goes with it, would be too much. They say the time goes slower that way but fuck that, let me tell you. I used to say let me be the judge of that because I want my town visits and everything else and the only way to get that was to work my way through the system. So I took my first step towards this when I got shipped out to Elmley prison in Kent, a couple of months after sentencing. It was a progressive move for me, as I was going to a working prison.

For anyone who doesn't know the system this is how it works: there are different categories of prison, double A-Cat; A-Cat; B-Cat; C-Cat and D-Cat. At a double A-Cat you've got two screws going with at all times,everywhere you go they're at your shoulder and an A-Cat's the same sort of set up. A B-Cat like Wandsworth's a local prison but I'd been there for a year now and when they've done their paperwork they can see I've played the game and I'm eligible for a C-Cat. Elmley's a B-Cat local with a C-Cat unit and while I started off in the B-Cat local I want to progress. This looks good for me as there's such a massive turn-over there's nothing I can see stopping me getting on to that C-Cat wing as soon as possible. And the longer I'm on there the nearer I am to being transferred to a D-Cat and an open prison.

When I first got to Elmley I was told I wouldn't like it there much because it's a 23-hour bang up and I just said, "well, that's a half-hour more than you get in Wanno" and anyway, that turned out to be a lie because when I walked on to my spur – it wasn't wings at Elmley, it was spurs – everyone's still out of their cells. People were playing table tennis, people were on the phone or just hanging around having a chat and this was at about 6.30 in the evening. It's just a bang up in Wanno so I was already impressed and even more so when I found out it was a 7.45pm bang-up. It took some getting used to after nearly a year in Wanno and I was looking around me thinking, "What's going on here?"

There was also hot water available on tap so now I could fill my flask up when I wanted to and that's important, because if I got hungry or wanted a drink I could make some pot noodles or whatever. At Wanno you could buy a flask but they'd only let you fill it with one cup of hot water, somehow that's supposed to last you the whole night but it never did and let me tell you, there's nothing worse than being in your cell feeling cold and hungry. But now here I am in my cell and it's warm, it's alright, I'm not hungry because the food is so much better than Wanno's, there's proper chips and proper portions – there was even an menu, it was unbelievable – so just having the option made Elmley a major boost and I hadn't even made it on to the C-Cat section yet.

Each spur had a houseblock and the idea was to progress from the first one to No.5, missing out Houseblock 4 which was for Rule 43. I told a kanga I'd come there as a C-Cat prisoner but he said it didn't matter, I still had to progress through the B-Cat wing. One of the reasons I made it clear I'd come as a C-Cat prisoner was because in Houseblock No.1 it looked at first like I was going to be in a three-man bang-up. I said, "Come on guv, we're bottle-handed as it is, that's enough isn't it?" He asked where I got 'bottle-handed' from and I explained it was 'bottle of glue,' as in two, which made him laugh.

I knew by now that even when you try and have a laugh with them they're still going to test you, there's nothing you can do about it, you just have to get on with it. Yet this kanga did say that because of the high turnover you usually only stayed on each Houseblock a couple of days until you got to No.3, when it would probably take a few weeks to get on to Houseblock 5. And anyway, after what I'd seen of the place in just the first 30 seconds I knew I didn't want to go back to Wandsworth, I can assure you. We even had electricity in our cells and can you imagine what a bonus that is when you've had to live without it for so long? During the football season, I'd bang myself up!

Another bonus with moving is that it takes you a few months to get into a new regime. Yeah, you adapt to the new surroundings quickly enough (you'd be surprised at how quick) but the time you have to spend getting to know what's going on and how things work it's helped you chip away at another three or four months of your sentence without you realising. Even so, a nick's a nick, isn't it and you've got to put your stamp down straight away. The first thing one geezer asked me as I've come on to the spur is if I've got any batteries and when I told him no I haven't got any he doesn't believe me. Pointing at my bag, he said, "You've got to have some in there," What did he think I was going to do, just hand them over so I told him straight, "What are you? A Cozzer? They're my batteries mate, I'm doing a six and these won't last me six months let alone six years, so ask the next customer, ok?" There's plenty of triers in there and more often than not they will get it so you have to let them know straight off.

There's another kind of prisoner you'll find in every nick and that's the smackhead. They're a very good reason when you're serving a long sentence – and six years is a long sentence – why it's good to move on. You get them in every prison and you hear the same old stories out of them every single day, because all they exist for is wanting or waiting for their next parcel and there's only so many times you can hear that story. When I first arrived at Elmley and I'm in the holding cells as they start to fill up, I heard all those same old stories about how everyone was stitched up – I could have told them my own story but I thought I'd save it until now – yet it was the junkies' stories which sickened me.

I remember years ago people wouldn't talk about these things but they all think it's big and clever nowadays, the mouthy smackheads boasting about how the Old Bill told them that, if they put their hands up to two, they'd do the other 14 as T.I.C.'s. They're talking about burglaries like it was normal and also hand-bag snatches, how when the Old Bill found the bag they couldn't find anything on them because they'd been wearing gloves. And I just thought, "You fucking scumbag, you've nicked some woman's handbag and you're proud of getting away with it."

This'll give you an idea of how low a person can be: I'd only been in Elmley for under a week when I heard about this kid who owed out about a tenner's worth of canteen. He only went and nicked his pad mate's bacca to pay off his debt and then put himself on the Numbers rather than have to face his former cell mate. The way I book it, that's typical of a smackhead as they've got no morals as any real man would rather take one on the chin than be locked up with the nonces. The screws might think all prisoners are the same but the proper people inside don't see it that way.

It's why when you go to a new prison you have to let people know what you're in for because you're going to get asked anyway and the last thing you want to say is, "I don't want to tell you." You do that and you've got the biggest question mark hanging over you from the start: "Is he a grass? A nonce?" So you declare, even the smackheads do and the burglars. People don't like them much do they, so they pass it off by saying it was a commercial burglary like a warehouse or an office. I didn't need to declare though as everyone remembered me from the MacIntyre programme.

It's also a way of finding out who might make a good pad-mate, which is so important as one of your biggest nightmares is sharing a cell with some geezer who's going to make things in here even worse. I mean, you start thinking, "Am I going to end up with a smackhead who'll be clucking all night, sweating and turning because he's hot one minute then getting up and shivering the next – "Just go back to sleep, will you" – will I end up with some smelly geezer or some religious nut who prays all night long. I got banged up with one geezer and believe me, the bloke never stopped praying. I doubt if I need to tell you just how much that could drive you up the wall.

That's why when a good pad mate leaves you, once you've got as far as a

C-Cat, you get a real fucking lump in your throat. Because listen, if you go to prison and you've got yourself a nice little 'school' – top whack half a dozen, that's plenty, you don't need any more than that – and you're having a bit of a laugh then all of a sudden time's being chipped away without you even noticing it too much. And another week, another month, maybe even another year has gone by if you all stay together, because if you don't let the rest of it get to you, you can still have a bit of a laugh in there. Although don't get me wrong, I wouldn't swap it for being out.

One of my pad mates at Elmley was a kid called Mick Collins, he was a staunch Left Wing kid who got done on the May Day riots and he was alright, as it happens, he was actually a right mellow, laid-back geezer so it was easy to get along with him. Like me, his case was another example of 'one rule for one and not for another,' as he got the longest sentence handed out for the May Day riots, two years for violent disorder and another two for arson. Another kid called Darrel Walker got 18 months for violent disorder – and then there was another May Day rioter, Matthew MacDonald.

MacDonald had professional parents and he went to Eaton, so what sentence does he get for the same conviction? Just six months and he was let out after two. It stinks, doesn't it. But like I said, even though me and Mick may not have had much in common on the outside, in there we could wind each other up a bit just for a laugh and we got on alright.

So when someone like that leaves it's one of those times it pays if you've been using your initiative, if you've been thinking ahead and have been playing the system. You know what I mean, speaking to the screws when you want something and keeping them at arms' length at other times. I know when one pad mate Grant Griffin left the first thing I did was have a chat with another bloke called Mick, an Arsenal geezer and I said "Listen, do you want to bang up with me?" He says, "yeah, sweet," so I'm straight off to speak to a kanga about it and get it sorted.

It's good if you and your pad mate have got the same sort of interests, this, that and the other, you can generally have a chat with each other no problem and help pass the time easier. Now Mick was a smoker but because we got on he'd open up the cell window and make an effort to blow the smoke out, because you do have to give and take in there.

Another thing about having a laugh with your pad mate is that sometimes you can use that to your advantage, because if your laughing and joking in front of the screws it might give you the chance to ask something off of them by passing it off as a joke. The night screws were auxiliaries, just 'wannabe' screws, so me and my pad mate would wait for them and when we knew they were coming we'd quickly put some music on. I'd start dancing like a lunatic, while my pad mate Grant's standing on his top-bunk, doing the Hawaii Five-O surfing board routine. You should have seen these fake screws' faces when they got to the cell door.

I walked up to them as if everything's normal and say "Alright guv, how are you doing? Now listen, I'm not being funny but I'm doing six years, right – and that isn't half as bad as it sounds because I'm getting out on a Tuesday – but is there any chance of a little drop of something?" The night screw had to say "Oh I can't do that," so I just laughed and said, "Are you sure, because everyone's got their price?"

Saying something like that could have gone badly boss-eyed if they'd taken offence and complained to the officers but if you're laughing when you say it, they can't take it seriously. And anyway if you don't ask you don't get, do you, so it was always worth a try. Having said that, when we mucked about like that the screws would spin us the next morning because they thought we must be on something, dancing around our cells like madmen. They thought we were proper off-key, they'd be scratching their heads saying "What are you doing?" and of course I'd reply "Six years, guv."

But the real reason a good pad mate counts for so much is because it helps keep you switched off from the outside world. That, I'm telling you now, is an absolute must, it's the whole thing about coping with your time as you have to learn to forget about the outside world because you aren't seeing it for a while. If you want to sit there in your cell and think "I bet so-and-so's having a barbeque on a day like today" you will only drive yourself mad, it's just no good for you thinking that way. What you have to do is teach yourself to think, "If they're having a barbeque fucking good luck to them, because I'll be out there having a barbeque of my own one day, it just isn't going to be today that's all." My pad mate Grant said that it had been hotter here today in Elmley than it was Hawaii, so I said 'Well thank fuck we're here then than in Hawaii!'

Yet just because you aren't seeing those on the outside and you're having to switch off from your normal life that doesn't mean you want everyone on the out to switch off from you, not at all.

The people I know through football have been my pals for years and years, it's like a family to us. All the way through while I was in prison they were in general contact with me, whether it was letters or visits and I can't thank them enough. Quite a few times they sent me and my co-de Andy Frain a couple of hundred quid and let me tell you, you're on £15 a week in the nick so that's a nice few quid. But more than that, it was good to know they were all in the pub still raising their glasses, they hadn't forgotten about us whatever other people might think. Wherever my mate Trav went, like one trip he did to Hamburg just to watch Man. City play in a friendly, he'd automatically send me a post-card and listen to this, my mate Peter McBeath came all the way down from Newcastle to visit me in Elmley, which is in Kent. That's a long, long way and he had to be there for half-eleven in the morning. Be honest with yourself, would you be willing to make that kind of effort for someone else? I hope you would. Everyone, from London to Newcastle and beyond, they never forgot me. Top mates.

What happens is that over years and years you start meeting up at England away games, you get to know them and they become pals. It doesn't matter who you support or where you come from, if you get on well and you've got a good bond you're pals, it's as simple as that. Talking of pals, do you remember I mentioned Hickey, Steve Hickmot, my mate who served four years because of Operation Own Goal but then ended up getting £96,000 in compensation when the Court of Appeal finally threw out his conviction?

Well Hickey lives in the Philippines now and he flew over especially to see me when I was inside. He was still wearing the same old combat jacket and jeans and he was as funny as ever. I asked him why he didn't spend a bit of his compensation on some better gear but he told me he wanted to spend it all on whores with sores. He said, "I've just flown over 9,000 miles to see you, don't they know me, do they really not know who I am? I've just had to wait outside in a queue!" I said, "What do you want, special treatment?" and he said "YES! I deserve special treatment, I've had enough of these piss-holes myself – anyway, how are you Jason?" – seriously, he's funny as fuck Hickey, he really is and not only that he's a living legend at football. Also, what with him already having been through the same sort of stitch-up as me I've learnt to expect the kinds of rumours and lies that will follow me around in the future. For example, I read in the press that Hickey got deported from Japan just before the World Cup and I know for a fact he never went there, so I know I'll have all of that 10 years down the line. Because the press have to fill their papers with something and what's the best thing that sells papers – CRAP.

16

MOVING THE GOALPOSTS

Like I said, Elmley was a working prison and personally I don't think that's such a bad thing. Or it wouldn't have been if they'd actually let me do some work. They said I couldn't work in seven parts of the prison because I was too high profile but setbacks and knockbacks? Fucking hell, I've been knocked back more times than George Best from his local and it was a constant struggle against the system – but I never gave up

I got on well with the gym screws and by the time I'd made it onto Houseblock 5 I'd got a job as a gym orderly. This really was the cream of the jobs for me because you did your cleaning, you worked with the handicapped or whatever and then in your free time you could train when you liked. You didn't have to queue up in the morning and put your name down for training like the others did and I tell you now, Elmley's got the best gym in the whole prison system it's as good as any on the outside, it's even got an 11-a-side Astroturf football pitch on the outside which was great because I got picked for the team.

I tell you, if I didn't get to the gym it used to drive me mad but it was ok, I was getting to the gym Monday to Friday, so now I'm doing my training, playing my football and I'm losing a bit of weight, I'm getting my sharpness back. This was very important to me because one of those goals I'd set myself in prison was to lose a bit of weight, to come out looking sweet. It's not that easy when the authorities have only got 90p a day to feed you on, so you're getting a lot of bread, potatoes and rice, which isn't much good to you when you're banged up for hours without getting the chance to burn it off. Also, if you've eaten at about 5.45pm and you're getting banged up two hours later, by about 9 or 10pm you start getting a bit peckish. You can see how it would be easy to put weight on, not lose it, but because I had the gym training I managed to lose over two stone.

When I finally did get out everyone said, "Fuck me, you ain't half looking well Jase," and I'd just smile and say, "See, things aren't so bad."

The only drawback I could see with the gym orderly job was it was one where you might be tempted to cause a bit of trouble, as you've got to give the vest, shorts etc to the nonces, the rapists and the child molesters, the grasses, the fucking internet paedophiles. They were segregated from us at all other times, except when they came down to the gym, which would only be in the evenings. As it happens, in the end even that didn't affect me because I never had to work with them myself, you'd only run into them if you worked late at night in the gym which I didn't do.

And just as it's going well, I got swagged off the gym job by the head of security. Like I said, they run the prisons, it's security who have the final say. The gym S.O. who's pulled me this lunchtime actually said they were all gutted for me and that they'd try and fight my corner but I knew there was nothing they could do up against their bosses. It didn't stop me trying though did it, because this was an absolute liberty, there was no proper reason for me losing this job.

I don't mind anyone doing their job if they're doing it fair and square but the head of security didn't even know me, he was judging me by what he may have heard and yet I hadn't done anything wrong. There was no excuse for it because I'd earned that job, it was the best one and I only got to keep it for a couple of weeks. So yeah, I had the hump and when I got the chance I was going to let him know all about it. I was told I could request a complaint form and see if I could be reinstated. I knew it was just a formality, that nothing would come of it but I went ahead with it anyway.

One day soon after I'd put my complaint in the head of security came up to me while I'm outside playing football. He said he's sorry about the gym orderly job but there's been a ricket and the bottom line of it was that I was just too high profile to keep the job. But then for some reason he starts getting a bit saucy and I just thought 'I'm not having that,' so I told him straight, "I'll see you about this in your time, not mine, because at the moment this is my time. I'm only playing football because I made the effort to get up at 7.45am and put my name down for it. And I'm not playing on my own either, there are 21 others out there on the pitch, so it's not like I'm getting some special privilege, is it." He said I had a bad attitude so I just laughed and said "Oh, have I?" as I turned and walked away from him, yet he did write at the bottom of the request for complaint form that I was taken off the gym orderly job for no other reason than due to my notoriety because of the MacIntyre programme. But adversity brings me great strength, it always has and it always will. All you can do is take it on the chin and smile, like I did with one probation officer who started to kick up a fuss.

What I'd done was to work my way around losing the gym job by putting myself on a referee's course, which I passed. But probation went mad about it because – and listen to this for an excuse, because it's a peach – they actually said it had something to do with my crime! I went to see the probation officer about it and to see why she had the hump with me. She tells me about how, as far as the authorities were concerned, the referee's course coincided with my offence so I calmly tried to explain to the woman that I thought it would let me see the game from a different point of view, learning what it's like to be the man who takes the flak rather than one on the terraces giving it.

But she just wasn't having any of it so to show what bollocks the authorities' view was I asked her if a man who's been convicted of fraud would be stopped from taking a computer course and she said no, not if she thought it was relevant to his case. Ok, fair point, so then I asked her, "What if someone's nicked for drugs, can he then not go to the gym?" and she looked a bit puzzled when she said what's that got to do with it?

"Well, he might have got done for shifting 50 kilos of cannabis," I said, "and if he's in the gym and he goes on the weights, what if he starts pulling 50 kilos on the bar?" The probation officer starts getting all snotty and says, "Oh you're being pathetic, that's just stupid," so I replied, "Oh, it's me being stupid, is it?" and then I just smiled at her. Well, a referee's course coinciding with my crime? You've got to see the funny side, haven't you. Anyway, after the fuss about the ref's course I put myself on the Community Sports Legal Awards course and passed that too, and this time with no fuss from probation. I wonder why that was?

Like I said, no-one wants high-profile prisoners because if anything goes wrong and the newspapers get hold of it, it fucks the whole prison, well, the ones who run it anyway. So it seemed like no prison officer would put pen to paper with me although every now and again you'd get one who would fight your corner and I had one in Lesley Hazel, because she took her responsibilities personally and she was totally professional about her work.

I did an Enhanced Thinking Skills course with her, the only Home Office course in prison and it carried a lot of weight. During my time on the course she saw for herself that I wasn't a fool. Oh yeah, she knew I was a laugh and a joke and this, that and the other, but she also understood that I was sensible when I had to be. And Lesley was a prison officer who, if she saw you weren't a nuisance, if she could spot some potential in you, then she would do all she could to help you.

What she was doing, unlike too many of the other screws, was actually doing her job properly because a major part of their job is to reform you as a character, so when you return to society you fit back in. That's what she wanted to see, she took a pride in her work and satisfaction from doing what she could to achieve this.

Now, I may have lost the gym orderly job but there's another good one in prison and that's in the laundry. It was a shame I didn't get that one in Elmley, as my mate Kevin Cressey already had that, because everyone wants their laundry done quickly as you can wear your own clothes in a C-Cat. And because Kev could only do x-amount of washes a day he knew exactly what that could mean. Sometimes you'd go to him, "Listen Kev, I've got a visit coming up, any chance you could get this done?" He'd lift the laundry bag, drop it again and say, "Oh, I don't know about that, it seems a bit light to me. Isn't there a tin of tuna or a packet of biscuits in there for me?" and then of course, if there's a little 'payment' in the washbag for him, all of a sudden he reckons he might be able to get it done after all.

Now with me, because he was my pal he'd make sure I had a clean bit of gear whenever I needed it, but one day I thought I'd leave him a 'prize' in the bag, just as a favour. "Sweet Kev, you'll do alright with that laundry today because there's a nice bit of salmon in there for you," I told him, only it wasn't salmon, it was poxy tuna. He just laughed and said, "Oi Jase, this is a ringed motor," and because he never usually took anything off me I said, "Well aren't you going to give me that back then?" Kev turned 'round and laughed, "Not me, cousin, once it's in there and it's hit the pad, it's mine!" He was funny like that so I just laughed back, "I don't believe you, Kev, I can't believe you're actually keeping it." But I got my own back soon afterwards when we were walking around the exercise block one day.

This traveller Dave comes up to us, asks us how we're doing and we told him "yeah, not too bad." Dave knows that on the outside Kev's got a nice house with a nice big drive so he thought he'd try his luck and says, "Listen Kev, I've got my old bit of trailer and it's on the side of the road at the minute. I'm not out for another year and I need somewhere to put it, I couldn't whack it up your drive, my old cousin, could I?" Kev looked at me, I looked at him and he's raised his eyebrows as if to say, "What do you reckon to that, Jase?'" So I told him, didn't I: "Come on Kev, help a man when he's down can't you, he's out of luck, the kid." He just looked at me as if to say "you cunt" but we laughed about it later. Obviously, you can see how doing the laundry was such a good job for Kev, because the coup for him was that he didn't have to spend his canteen, he was getting everything he needed already. He was doing laundry for 120 people on that wing and with all the biscuits and chocolate bars he was getting he could then do a trade back for a phone card, or whatever it was he might be short of. He knew you've got to be a character to get by in prison, you've got to be able to do the deals.

Yeah, 'it's not what you know, but who you know' eh? And one day when I got a craving for beans on toast like you would never believe it sort of helped that I had a pal who worked in the officers' mess. Now, I never did get that beans on toast but I did get something a whole lot better instead.

My pad mate Grant could see something was up and he asked what was the matter. "What's the matter with me? What do you think's the matter pal, I haven't had beans on toast for a fucking two-stretch that's what's the matter with me." I went to go and see my pal at the officers' mess and told him what I wanted but he said he couldn't help. Well, I like proper uncut ham so I asked him if he could do me a proper ham sandwich instead. Now you've got to remember that these sandwiches may seem like simple, normal little things to you on the outside but in prison they were like gold-dust. And my mate's only come back with a triple fucking decker; prawns, ham, salad cream, tomatoes, lettuce, onion and thick slices of the best ham, it really was a proper sandwich.

I hid it in my cell and a bit later on I said to Grant "do you want a cup of 'sticky toffee'?" There's a bit of football on, I'm feeling sweet and Grant's happy himself because he's ordered a nice bit of chocolate from the canteen for tomorrow. "No, I don't want chocolate," I told him as I pulled out the sandwich and said, "just take a look at that! – see, when the judge gave me six years, he didn't say I couldn't have that, did he." My pad mate's just laughed and asked how I got hold of it. "Oh, this is a regular thing, Grant, you just stick with me, son, you just stick with me."

Spontaneous cravings like my one for beans on toast were always good for a wind-up, Grant would say something like "Jase, how would you like Cantonese style tonight?" and I'd go, "I'm not being funny, but I think I'd rather have Tracy from Bermondsey, I'll stick with the English bird." But later I'd throw it back at him, "How do you fancy aromatic duck then, partner, I bet you could do with that right now couldn't you? Think about it, smothered in a nice bit of 'rocking horse,' you know, the plum sauce, and all the onions, all this and all that, I bet you can almost taste it can't you?"

Now it's one thing having a laugh with your pad mate or a chat with your pals, but it takes a bit more than that to become the talk of the entire prison. Did you ever see the episode of 'Porridge,' (why don't the BBC make programmes like this anymore instead of wasting our money on the shit they're now churning out?) with Ronnie Barker and Richard Beckinsale and do you remember the excitement the football match at 'Slade' prison stirred up? Well at Elmley it happened for real.

For at least two weeks before the kick-off it was all the talk – it was still all the fucking talk two weeks after – because we were playing a charity match against the screws. We, the kids who spent day in, day out getting treated worse than dogs, the ones who had been cut off (unjustly in my case) from our friends, family and society in general, we were now going to be playing the fucking kangas and believe me mate, this side of it was never going to be for charity.

One of the gym screws, Gary 'Lambo' Lambert, was a quality player but he was injured which was blinding for us because he really could have made all the difference for them. Instead, he was now our manager. Fortunately, I can have a game and from out of nearly 1,000 in the prison I get picked to play. In the weeks leading up to the game the screws would come up to me and say, "I'm marking you Jason," and I'd just laugh and tell them straight, "You've got that right because I'll be attacking all the time."

Now the screws know things like this game help the prison to run more smoothly because anyone who's been picked to play isn't going to get involved in any sort of incident leading up to the game. They'll half wipe their mouths instead because they don't want to risk getting in to trouble and missing their chance to play in a game like this. Only 50-odd prisoners were allowed out to watch the game itself, which is a liberty really, because this was a C-Cat prison and it is supposed to be for charity. But once the game got underway the kangas got untold grief, fuck me did they ever, although I'm not sure what side one of the linesmen was on.

Did you see Frank Lampard's 'first' goal for England against Slovakia, disallowed by a dodgy linesman? I scored early on and it was disallowed – yet it wasn't a screw who'd raised his flag but one of our lot, a con, who gave the offside. To be fair I might have been off-side but at the end of the day the bottom line was it was us versus them. I couldn't believe it when he gave it and his brother's on the line as well shouting at him, "you fucking wanker."

But we did score later on and oh, mate, let me tell you, everyone's gone absolutely mental, it lasted right up until the screws have equalised. Everyone was gutted then, those of us on the pitch and the 50 or so cheering us on. But then with something like four minutes to go I've threaded a sweet ball through to this kid who's come on as a sub and he's got the legs to latch on to it. Everyone's just willing the kid to score – well, the cons that is – and he only goes and does it. Ahhh, man, I'm telling you, you would not believe what it was like once the ball hit the back of the net and then, on the final whistle, the pitch got invaded, everyone's jumping on the screws and the cons alike as this was such a massive win for us. It was a hard-fought game and as I came off a screw said to me, "Fair play Jase, you played well there, son." I said to this screw, "I'm not being funny, but I played like Paul Gascoigne yet that kid next to me played more like Bamber Gascoigne, he had a touch like Harold Shipman. How did he ever get picked?"

Anyway, everyone was buzzing afterwards and it's things like winning that game which helps you get through because all the while you're still on a high from that you're feeling sweet and you're chipping away at your time that bit easier and all the while you're not getting nicked because of this, you're one step closer to your D-Cat. You have to stay adjudication-free for six months to have any chance of passing your FLED, which is your Facility Licence Eligibility Date and it's a lot easier to do if you're feeling sweet. And don't forget, your FLED's your key to a D-Cat prison, so this was important if, like me, you wanted to progress.

That doesn't mean I wasn't going to face more knockbacks, fuck me no, like when I put in a request to go to Blantyre House on a progressive move. All of a sudden, I'm told they've changed the criteria so that no-one convicted of football violence could go there which was an outrageous liberty when you consider some murderers and Section 18s could still go there.

And this is the excuse Chris Bartlett, the Governor of Blantyre House gave to me in his knockback letter:

"As we are now taking more long-term prisoners our turnover is not so great. We therefore have to consider not only the individual merits of each application but also prioritise those applicants who have the greatest need for our resettlement regime. After a thorough and sympathetic consideration of your application, we are regretfully unable to offer you a placement at HMP Blantyre House. We wish you good luck for the future."

Do you believe a single word of that? No, I didn't neither when I first read it. What it boiled down to again was me supposedly being high profile because no-one high profile was allowed to go there. The excuse for my first request being knocked back was because they reckoned I hadn't served a fifth of my sentence, then, when the notice about 'no football violence' goes up they back date it from May to February 1st – and guess what, I'd put in my first request in February. Funny that, isn't it.

No, it isn't funny at all, but you've got to keep laughing at them. There was this one screw who said to me, "Why are you always happy, Marriner?" and so I told him, "Well why not, guv? I'm living, I'm breathing, I'm healthy, I'm sweet and I'll get out eventually (unlike you). What do you want me to do, walk around moping and being miserable every day?" And even if they won't admit it to your face that's exactly how they want you to be, yet they just couldn't have me like that. I'll tell you another thing I held on to which, if you're ever unlucky enough to end up in prison you should never forget: whatever happens, you always have the last laugh and the last word, even if you're doing life.

When you pack your gear on that final morning and you walk through those gates, hold your head up, because that is you having the very last word on the matter. And however much that gets up their noses there is absolutely nothing they can do about that – so you make sure you enjoy the moment.

17

INJURY TIME

I must have seen nigh on 1,000 people go home during my time inside, some you know, some you don't. If it's a good pad mate I've just lost then it might take a little bit of time to adjust. But if I've heard Jimmy from another landing got a 'not guilty,' or Steve's got a 'no evidence' I was genuinely pleased for them even if I didn't know them. As I've said before times stops for no man. KEEP THE FAITH.

All you can do until then is keep trying to progress. After nine months at Elmley I went for my D-Cat again and this time I got it. I was off to Standford Hill which was literally across the road – but it was like I'd stepped into a different world. When I got there I was sort of half-told by the prison staff, "If you want to fuck off, then fuck off, because no-one's going to come looking for you, that's the Old Bill's job, not ours" And when I came out of reception all I'd been given were the directions to my wing, there were no screws to escort me there. I'm telling you, after 18 months / two years inside it was such a shock to be treated this way.

I'd also got a single cell for the first time since I'd been No.1 on the hotplate at Wanno and not only that but one of my old pad mates from Elmley was there, Grant Griffin, a Charlton supporter. I liked him and we got on well so that was a bonus. He was already a lifeguard there – yeah, Standford Hill even had its own swimming pool – and the next thing you know he tells me about this screw who loves football.

This screw played against me when we played Standford Hill and so I laughed with him and said, "Did I run the show?" But behind the banter I'd planted the seed that I wasn't such a bad kid, that he could let me get involved with the sports without it all going boss-eyed for him and he did end up making me captain of the football team. After induction I mentioned to him that that there was a lifeguard course coming up. "Oh, I'd like to do that," I told him, "that's a bit of me, that is." It was a really hard course, as it happens, but I passed it and got myself a job as a lifeguard.

That was great, I worked with the handicapped and the old people but the best thing was I could get some proper training in again. I can't see how people don't train in prison, I mean, it might take a lot out of you and you do have to force yourself to get back into it but once you've completed that first training session you feel better for it straight away and you sleep better afterwards. Otherwise you just get lethargic, doing nothing all day every day and that makes it very easy to fall into the trap of letting yourself go.

It wasn't long before I was running the football team on B-wing and we'd play A-wing on a Saturday morning. There was a big board in the foyer where the screws' office was, right in the middle of the wings and as the football manager it wasn't unusual for me to ask for a bit of chalk to write up the team sheet. One day, just after we'd lost the Queen Mother, I put a big notice up on the chalk board saying, 'Due to the sad sudden death of our beloved Queen Mother at the age of 101, the Home Office has decided that any long-term prisoners serving paroled sentences are now entitled to 101 days back off their sentences. Please ask for an application form from the office.' Everyone's read the chalk board and I'm not joking, within minutes there was a queue as long as the milk round. I went up to a screw half-laughing and said, "Allo guv, have you got any of them apps left?" I was almost pissing myself but I still don't think he guessed. The whole thing was just one of my little mind games with the screws and why shouldn't I, as they were playing them all the time so it's good to get your own back once in a while.

Now while I was away I met a bundle of people who claimed to have been set up by the Old Bill, everyone's innocent, it's all a stitch-up. Some you believe and some you don't, some you feel sorry for and some, like the smackheads, you really couldn't care less about. Yeah, of course there are more guilty prisoners behind bars than there are innocent ones but they do exist. See what you make of this.

I met my pal Gary Mills at the open prison through training and he told me he'd already done 13 years for murder but he could have been out five years before if he'd admitted to being guilty. But Gary flatly refused to admit to his guilt because he just did not commit the murder he'd been convicted of.

My pal's never denied he had a fight with the kid who died but he's always maintained it was self-defence and he wasn't responsible for the injuries which actually killed him. There's scientific proof that when this other man first went to hospital he had a few bruises but he was taken back to hospital four hours later after being in the police station and in this time Gary, who was also locked up, has heard him get a kicking in the cell next door to his. When this other geezer goes to hospital a second time he's got now a broken leg and there's no way the doctors would have missed an injury like that when they examined him on his first visit. But more importantly, this man's later died of internal injuries, also missed in the first examination and other experts have since said the doctors just couldn't have missed these either, he had to have suffered these injuries some time after the first hospital visit. So my mate Gary's not had another row with him, has he, because he's been locked up in his cell.

These things do happen, Gary's had his life taken away from him, he's in his mid-forties now and he's got two kids he's not seen growing up during those 13 years. But he is staunch, Gary, and he's got a great sense of humour, he's good as gold. That's why I cannot begin to tell you how good it was to hear he'd been released in June, 2003, after the Court of Appeal finally overturned his and his co-de's convictions on the grounds that they were unsafe. It's only taken 13 years but they got there in the end, eh? What do you mean you didn't hear about it? Well maybe that's because David Beckham's transfer to Real Madrid was splashed all over the front, back and middle pages of the papers at the time of Gary's release and real news doesn't sell papers, unlike gossip about Posh and Becks. That's the world we live in and editors, just like documentary makers, give the public what they want.

You know what I told you about knockbacks well, just because I've now made it to a D-Cat prison that doesn't mean they've stopped, far from it. I tried to get into Latchmere House which is an open prison, a resettlement one, and I got knocked back from there because they said I was high-risk. Fuck me, not that same old song again. I mean, I'm a D-Cat prisoner by this point, which means even by their own rules I'm not a high-risk, so it was just another of their cover-ups.

And even when I was accepted at my next gaff, Springhill Prison in Aylesbury, it was still an uphill battle to get the privileges I'd earned as my right like the town visits and the community work outside the prison. I'd already been on a number of town visits from Standford Hill before I faced a Risk Assessment Board about a visit to spend some time with my missus Julie when I got turned down for no good reason – the World Cup finals in South Korea and Japan. Fuck me, I've travelled some countries but to get there and back, watch a game, have a fight and all within an eight-hour licence? And I didn't even have my passport, the police had that. I'd struggle to do that even if I had my own plane.

Anyway, this is a bit of the letter I wrote, dated 24th June, 2002, just to let the powers that be know they were off-key, yet again :

"Following my conversation with Governor Mr. Boulter regarding my town visits, I was of the impression that, providing I passed a Risk Assessment Board, I may be allowed the privilege of a town visit to spend with my fiancée and children. I was risk assessed on June 21st and was passed….but was then denied the visit. Up to this point, I have made 13 successful town visits and have been working on licence in the community. I also came to Springhill on licence and have conducted myself in a proper fashion since my arrival…I feel very disheartened and my fiancée and children feel the same. Please could you look at my case, as I am willing to comply with any restrictions you may put on me....Thank you for your time and consideration."

Even when you've progressed this far through the system you still have to keep wiping your mouth, don't you, because if you read between the lines of this letter I think you can see what I'm really saying here – yeah, even when you comply with their rules it's an unfair struggle. Anyway, I finally got permission for the home visits I was entitled to and to work outside the prison. First off I ended working at an Oxfam shop in Oxford, I'd get taken down there in a prison van then picked up again in the evening. I was there for about three or four months and listen to what the shop manager said about me in my reference:

"...his interpersonal skills have excelled and he has developed strong customer relations...Mr Marriner is friendly, reliable, trustworthy and a pleasure to work with. We will be extremely sorry to lose him."

Well, it was very nice of her to say that about me and I do appreciate it – but after dealing with screws and smackheads for nearly three years it was going to have to be one awkward customer who came in the shop and got under my skin. After the Oxfam job I got myself a job as a transport co-ordinator in London for which I would like to thank Vaughn Jackson for giving me the chance and I was driving myself there and back everyday, working on licence six days a week. Now that was a funny thing to do, having to hand yourself back in to prison at the end of every day but the temptation not to bother was never there for me.

You can't have a drink but you are allowed to go out for a meal at unlicensed premises or whatever, so when you're at home on a Sunday evening and you're starting to get comfortable you have to really force yourself to leave and get back. That isn't easy, but you have to do it because if you didn't go back you're bound to get caught at some point and once that's happened you'd be shipped straight out of a D-Cat back to a bang-up. Even if you didn't get into any trouble again for the rest of your sentence, you'll never get back to a D-Cat prison.

But that wasn't what got me back there. It was Julie, my kids, my family, the friends I've known for years and their families; the very people it was hard to leave on a Sunday evening, funnily enough. It's because they're the ones who've really suffered through all of this, not me and they were staunch they stood by me for three years, all their visits and letters and now I'm at Springhill I can finally visit them on a day out. So what am I going to do now, am I going to be the selfish one who has it on his toes, so all these friends and family have to come back to some place like Elmley for a visit, where they'd had to turn up by 11.30am just to be turned away for an hour then come back and be searched so they can finally see me between two and four in the afternoon? That's a fucking long day out for them and there was no way I was prepared to put them all through that again, because you've got to think of the effect your actions will have on the people you care most about. And also, not only that, doing a runner just wasn't the way forward and taking a backward step just wasn't the way I'd batted from Day One.

I'm not denying it was hard to go back on certain days but, then again, as prisons go Springhill was blinding, it was unbelievable. There were 24 of us in a hut, it was all double-cells and at the end of each hut you've got a TV room, there was running hot water, your own sink and showers. It was a bit like trailer living back on the travellers' site. And I'm telling you, because of the other good people in there, the best I'd met in the nick and I hadn't known any of them before I went there, it was absolutely mental. There were so many of the lads there in the hut, so many of the chaps all doing a bit of bird, not 18 months or whatever, you just knew the authorities were thinking 'we've got to do something about this,' because on a Saturday evening we were there with our feet up, watching Match of the Day and it was as if no-one could touch us. There were just too many proper people in there and we were the guv'nors!

There was Simon Brown, Jay Usher, Lol Aherne, Billy Whiteley, Lenny Hagland, Johnny Matthews, UK, Dean Lingham, Del Goody, Mark Dimbleby, Pops, Martin Ward, John Mortimer, Dale Thomasson, Steffan Bauldof, Marcus Fuller and Chris Whalley to name a few.

Me and John Matthews, who we nicknamed Uncle Buck after the geezer in the film were the window cleaners for all the huts and it was as funny as anything. Well, the World Cup was on at the time so how many windows do you think I cleaned? Yeah, exactly. Yet when a screw came around it was a quick wipe with the shammy and a 'just about to do the inside now, guv.' Of course he'd ask why the tele had been left switched on and I'd just shake my head and say, "I don't know, guv, I just can't believe it."

Uncle Buck was a character and the pair of us walking about with the bucket was a coup in itself. The windows did get really dirty and they don't clean themselves, so if you wanted yours done more than once you had to weigh-on, a packet of biscuits or whatever, just like Kev with his laundry job back in Elmley and I'm a business-minded kid so this all came as second-nature to me.

One time this kid comes up to us and reckons he could get the job done in two days. Me and Uncle Buck looked at each other and said, "You can't do all that in two days, what's up with you?" knowing all the while that he could (we could) if he put his back into it. I looked at Uncle Buck, winked at him and challenged the kid, "I'll give you 100 black jacks if you can do all that in just two days every week," and he's gone for it. So for just 50p a week each me and Uncle Buck are now sat back for the whole time, drinking tea and coffee, eating toast and watching the World Cup while this kid scrubs the windows just to prove his point – while we're also picking up our prison wages. It worked like a dream for us because the screws weren't always on our case, what with it being an open prison, and even when they did come to check up you'd either hear their shoes outside (because you got to know their walk) or their keys jangling. Then, it was off with the tele, grab a spare bucket and cloth and pretend to make a start on the windows, with a "Hello guv, it's 'taters' out there this morning," as he comes through the door.

Yet while the screws weren't always on our cases, they weren't complete fools. They knew we only had so much for canteen funds and, let's face it, if you can pick up your deodorant, your biscuits or whatever, for a few pound cheaper at the local store near where you worked on your town visits, well, you aren't going to lose £3 at the canteen buying it there.

The only problem here was, of course, that you weren't allowed to bring stuff back inside so if security were doing their job properly your car and your bags would get spun every time you returned. Then it was all "Oh sorry guv, how did that get in there?" as you lost your stuff but you had to try, didn't you. I'd come too far to trip over on a serious charge, but this was just part of the game.

I was out with some pals recently and they said to me "Do you regret what's happened to you?" I just said, "There's no point in regretting it, it's happened," but what I don't regret is meeting all the proper people I met in there and we still have a laugh about some of the good times we had (although I can't tell you all the coups because that would ruin it for the next man).

I know it sounds like it was all champagne and skittles but believe me, there were still ways you could get tripped up and I don't just mean by the screws, either. I remember this geezer coming up to me one day and saying, "That bloke who works in the library, he's Old Bill." I turned to him and said, "How do you know?" Talk is cheap and money buys houses so I just laughed as I knew he wanted me to do his dirty work for him. I said, "Anyway, you're only doing nine months, you cut that in half straight away to four-and-a-half moons, you get your tag and you're only doing two moons, so please don't drive me mad about this cozzer because at the end of the day, if he is Old Bill and I back-hand him it's me that's back behind the door. Go get a nut-nut to do it.

"And not only that, you must think differently to me, I've got to get in to him." The kid looked puzzled and asked me why, so I explained it to him, "If he's Old Bill he must be bent, that's why he's in prison. That's who you want on your side, isn't it, a bent Old Bill, a bent solicitor and a bent judge." I hadn't come all that way just to trip over for a prick like that, no way.

Because even in Springhill the screws are still waiting to pounce as my pal Lol Aherne found out. He's gone out on a weekend town visit on the Saturday, just before his scheduled release the following Monday and, let's face it, he's got a bit 'Man. Utd.' Well, wouldn't you be excited too, just two days away from going home from a five-stretch? So he's had a cheeky 'light ale' before returning back to prison. And by doing that he's made the big mistake of thinking he was 'home before he was home.' I got back from work at the same time he's returned and I've heard security ordered him to walk in a straight line, but Lol's had just one too many for that and he's failed the test. Now the prison officer who's doing this already knows Lol's less than 48 hours away from going home to his wife and kids, all he really had to do was give Lol a squeeze, tell him "Get in your cell, I don't want to see you come out of there all night and I'll be checking up on you every half an hour. If you're out of your cell, you're nicked. Now there's your yellow card, so fuck off." And I do know a few screws there who would have done this, they would have taken into account he was about to go home, that he hadn't committed some other offence on his town visit and despite the fact that being 'given enough rope to see if you hang yourself' is part of the rehabilitation, they would have handled in differently.

But not this one, he was known for being a dog and he's nicked him on the spot. Hearn gets stuck in the bang-up nick across the road on an eight-week lay down, to find out if the parole board are going to revoke his licence and of course, he was absolutely gutted. He's just about to walk through the gates and all because of a cheeky beer and one vindictive screw he ends up doing another eight weeks. It's another reason I didn't do the same thing myself because I wasn't prepared to give the screws the satisfaction of seeing me trip up like that.

And then, of course, the rumours start which is probably worse in prison because you're in a confined space so the latest bit of news is all some people have to live for. A few good pals saw Lol and believe me they swear blind he wasn't that drunk. But within day if you listened to the stories you'd have thought he was totally lagging. They were spread by the same sort of slack tongues which would have made some people believe a rift had developed between me and co-de, Andy Frain. I'd go to one prison, then another and all I'd hear was 'are you and Andy still falling out?' But think about it, we were long-term pals, we'd been going to football and having a drink together for years, we'd been seen in the documentary together and then we got nicked together. We were always going to be too high-profile for the authorities to keep us together without buckling their system so they spilt us up right from the start. But all the way through we spoke to each other and stood by each other, we're still pals and we're still loyal to each other. When I first came out of prison Andy still had a couple of months left to do, so what did I do? Yeah, I went to visit him because we're pals, end of. Where do these rumours start? I couldn't tell you, I couldn't tell you who adds to them and I don't think those who start this bollocks even hope to gain anything from it, they just enjoy it – and people like MacIntyre make their careers out of feeding off the kind of craving too many people have for idle gossip.

Some of us have got better things to do, for while the goals you achieve and the battles you win inside on a day-to-day basis are really important – they're more than that, each little victory is vital – I've had another even more important battle going on throughout my time in prison: my appeal against my conviction.

Anyone like me who's been stitched up and sent down is going to appeal against their sentence and if you are going to launch an appeal you have to get your application in within the first 28 days. Believe me, you never give up from that day on, you try to do whatever you can and you don't stop thinking about anything at all which might just help your case. Looking back now I realise it was out of my hands, all I could do was relay whatever messages I felt were important to my solicitors and I tell you now, in the death I drove my briefs mad because I wouldn't let any of it go, I'd get in touch with them over anything and everything I could think of.

But that's only because the Court of Appeal really did take the piss with the amount of time it took to get a hearing. 'Files were missing' was one excuse – I'd heard that one before from the prosecution during my trial, hadn't I – but some of these files were missing for a whole year, do you think that might just have happened on purpose? It's not really a tricky one to answer, is it..

Ahh, but I still had one card left to play and this one was an ace. Do you remember I told you about Johnny Helps, he was the kid on jury service at Blackfriars Court at the same time my case was running and the one who met my head juror Julia Moorcroft in the smoking room. It was about time my luck changed and thankfully Johnny's told another pal of mine, a Millwall supporter from South London also called John, about his meeting with Julia Moorcroft at the court. When Millwall John's heard about my sentence he gets in touch with me while I'm still at Wanno and says, "I'm gutted for you Jase, it's a fucking liberty – but what about that head juror, didn't you get the message about her?"

He tells me all about Johnny's chats with this bird and while I couldn't prove it right then, I get straight on to my legal team because I just knew that despite other major points to be brought up at my appeal hearing, like the entrapment argument regarding MacIntyre and his crews' filming methods, Julia Moorcroft's connection to Chelsea through the catering work she did for the club would be the key to me getting a successful result. I phoned my solicitor Huw Jones with the news and he e-mailed my Q.C Michael Wolkind the same day. I didn't know it at the time but the recorded dates on those e-mails would prove important.

I knew I'd need more than just Johnny's word to prove that Moorcroft should never have been allowed to sit on my jury as it's like I keep telling you, when you're innocent you've got to prove it even before you're convicted. But afterwards? Well, it's an even bigger uphill struggle just to get your appeal heard, never mind getting your conviction overturned.

Yet at the end of my trial I'd said how I believed 'good will always follow bad' and after all I'd done to make it happen it seemed it was finally going to.

It's now May, 2002, and my mate Muzza's at the F.A. Cup Final in Cardiff – I would have been there myself, if I'd had the chance – and after the game he's gone back to the hotel to drown his sorrows a bit with Darren Rowe. Suddenly Muzzer spots this woman he half recognises. He can't quite put his finger on what it is about this woman first of all but then the penny drops. It's the head juror from my trial, Julia Moorcroft.

Muzza remembered there was something to do with a juror connected to my appeal but he wasn't sure exactly what it was about. Even so, he thinks it might just come in handy to get a photograph of her and believe me, he wasn't wrong there – because Julia Moorcroft is only working for Chelsea's hospitality on the day of the F.A. Cup Final.

Fair play to Muzza and Darren, they've got Darren's sister to go over to the juror and say, "You look like so-and-so off the tele, do you mind if I have my photo taken with you?" and Darren's sister has her picture taken with Moorcroft. It being Cup Final day there were a few people about in high spirits despite the score, so it was easy to get chatting with strangers and Muzza asked this other bird a few questions about the woman he's now sure was connected to my case. This woman tells him that Julia Moorcroft isn't just working as a caterer for the club but that she's actually the corporate manageress for the day.

Muzza didn't know the significance of this at the time, which is probably why it took him another three months to send me the photos of Moorcroft (typical Muzza) but when he was talking to another mate that summer he was told it didn't look like the juror part of my appeal was going to come to anything and it was then he remembered to ask Darren to give the photos to him so he could send them on to me in prison.

The very same day I received them I also got a letter from my legal team saying there is no matter to pursue with the juror, the Appeals Court wasn't interested one iota and the judge had had enough of the matter. I'd read the solicitors' letter first and what did I say about good following bad? Well, I opened Muzza's letter next. I didn't look at the 'dolly mixtures' first of all, I'm just reading this letter saying, "Dear J. Please don't get your hopes up, but I saw this bird at the Chelsea – Arsenal game." It was then I saw the pictures and thought "blinding, get in there!"

First off, I'm on the phone to Muzza to half-jokingly give him grief about holding on to the pictures for so long. "I've been trying to find out about this juror bird for ages." It's typical Muzza-style because he's so layed back but I was laughing because I know he's come up trumps for me there. We still laugh about the fact he could have got me out three months earlier and he now says he hung on to the photos to give me extra time to lose some more weight!

As soon as I came off the phone I'm straight back in my peter writing to my legal team again, saying 'tell the judges up their bollocks about this jury business being closed.' I sent them one of the photos with a staunch letter saying 'do you recognise her? if she's Arsenal there's nothing I can do about it, but if she's a Chelsea supporter, or is working for them, then she should never have been allowed to sit on the jury.' My legal team do their bit to confirm what Muzza's told me and bingo, it turns out she really does work for a hospitality company connected to the club.

Despite this new evidence we still have to fight for a hearing date at the Court of Appeal and when we finally got one, my Q.C. pointed out how unusual it was to be allowed to launch an appeal involving a juror. In fact, a member of a jury has only later been cross-examined at the Court of Appeal a handful of times before, so what does that suggest about the juror now being questioned about my case?

Also, if you so much as mention a juror in your appeal, the Appeals Court shit themselves, they back-peddle and start to get nasty with you. You get bombarded with questions like 'What do you know about her, do you know where she lives?' that kind of thing, but we do eventually get to court where Johnny Helps was called by the prosecution.

I tell you now, he was staunch and when they asked him why it took him seven or eight months after my trial to tell what he thought he knew about this woman, trying to make out he was just doing a favour for me, he did not move. He told them straight that he hadn't taken anything like as long as that, that it was within the first month of my conviction and that was when the e-mails from my solicitor became so important, because they were all dated and showed that Johnny was telling the truth.

When it was Julia Moorcroft's turn to take the stand, my Q.C Michael Wolkind could easily have paralysed her in there with his questions but, because there's no jury at an appeal hearing just three beaks whose decision is final, he had to be tactful as he knew they were bound to be more sympathetic to her than would be to us. But like I told you, Michael knows what he's doing and when he stepped up for his turn, he trod lightly. He began by asking her "Was that the highest profile case at the time?" and she replied, "I believe so." Still keeping it sweet he asks her, "So you would have wanted to sit on this one, wouldn't you?" and it goes on like this for a while but all the time my Q.C's getting the measure of the woman and he knows what buttons to push to get a reaction. I swear, when he mentioned the word 'catering' you could see this woman flinch because she hated the word so much, she wasn't into catering, she was into 'hospitality.' She was an almighty snob this woman, to her the word 'catering' made it seem she came from 'Council,' just like me, and whereas I'm happy to accept we all come from different walks of life her own prejudices couldn't stomach that.

Moorcroft still tried to deny the company she worked for had any real connections with Chelsea and she even told the Criminal Cases Review Commission just before my appeal that she'd only worked for Chelsea twice. So slowly but surely, my Q.C. gets the truth out of her and it turns out it wasn't twice, it wasn't three times either. That's when Michael Wolkind said, "It may not have been twice or three times and, while the number may not seem impor- tant to you, it is very important to my client. So please answer, were you involved in hospitality work for Chelsea Football Club four times?"

"Oh no," she said, "definitely not four times." – and in her own way, perhaps just this once she was telling the truth. As the next person we got in was someone who worked for the same company holding a record of how many times Julia Moorcroft had been involved in corporate hospitality work at Stamford Bridge. It was nine times.

Not only that, this was a big firm she worked for and to have been corporate manageress for Cup Final day, well, lets have it right, she wasn't new to the job.

Me and Andy should have walked there and then but the appeal was referred for judgement so I'm off back to prison while they reach their decision . I've still got my job as a transport co-ordinator and about four weeks after the Appeal hearing I get a phone call from my Q.C. who told me I got two years knocked off and I'm due to go home right away. I really didn't know what to think at the time, I just said "Alright Michael, thank-you very much."

I'd done my bird and I was only about six weeks from my parole date anyway so the way I see it I didn't get a four, I got a six and I did it all. That's because I'd already served two years and 10 months and if I'd got a four at the original trial I'd have only had to do two years to be eligible for parole. Non-parole would have only meant serving two years and eight months, so I spent eight months more in prison than I should have.

It was a great feeling to be released and it was good timing, too, as it was just before Christmas so it was lovely for Julie and kids but don't try and tell me justice had finally been done. I'm not being bitter about this, I'm just telling you how it is. We'd slaughtered the prosecution at my trial and we slaughtered them again in the Court of Appeal so all the authorities have done is to give me just a big enough sweetener in return so I can't claim I've had a knockback and take my case to the European Court of Law. The Appeal Court couldn't admit Julia Moorcroft should never have sat on the jury because then they would have had to have quashed my conviction, so instead they decided I'd been given an excessive sentence.

Were they having a laugh? Of course it was an excessive sentence even if I'd actually been guilty of something. I got a six in total for conspiracy to commit violent disorder and affray and after my sentence, when I was in Wandsworth, I heard about some rapist who's held a girl captive for two days while he's abused her and he's only got seven years, so he'll only serve six months more than me for doing something like that. There were many more. I was banged away with a kid serving five years for manslaughter and alright, he may not have meant to do it, I fully accept that and I'm not saying he deserved to get more. But he's killed a geezer – did I really deserve a year more than him for what I'd been (wrongfully) convicted of? Then of course you get the likes of Graham Rix, he only did a year in Wanno on the cucumbers for having sex with an underage girl and don't try and tell me he didn't know how old the girl was, because she was his mate's daughter. What gets me is this man was in for rape but they still kept his job open for him at Chelsea when he got out. I've done absolutely nothing at all and yet I've had to serve a longer sentence than him and I'm still banned from attending football.

I'll tell you another thing, I would rather have served the extra two or three months of my sentence so I could have fought the case at a higher court because I'd just lost three years of my life in prison, so what's giving me a couple of months about? I'd waited longer than that in a canteen queue.

All these things are important, they go to show you how it is still one rule for some and another rule for the rest, it's something none of us should ever forget.

But even so, I'll always find something in every situation to have a laugh about and there is one more thing I haven't told you yet, which to this day still makes me smile just to think about it. What happened was that my Q.C. finally got the official say-so that I was to be released on a Friday, only for one reason or another he couldn't get the message to me for a couple of days. Oh and by the way, how's my luck, I only got let out on a Tuesday.

18

HOME WIN

Have you seen much of MacIntyre on the tele lately? No me neither, funny that isn't it. It seems like he's crawled out from under his stone, made his name through that one series – mostly off the back of me – and now people have finally got wise to what he's done he's had no choice but to crawl back under the stone from where he came. I mean let's have it right, 'MacInlies' has gone from a prime-time 'flag-ship' tele series on BBC1 to late-night slots on (supposedly) lesser channels that no-one is watching. For example, on Tuesday April 6th, 2004, millions of viewers tuned in to ITV 1 to watch Chelsea beat Arsenal 2-1 at Highbury, in the quarter-final second-leg of the UEFA Champions League. The other channels know they're on to a loser when a game as big as that's being shown live so they'll fill that time-slot with any old bollocks. Channel 5 showed MacIntyre's latest sad little undercover programme, which just about says it all. Face it, 'MacInlies,' you're 15 minutes of fame are up.

But along the way he's managed to slaughter my tyre and recovery business because no-one wanted to know after they saw the programme (like I said, who says there's no such thing as bad publicity), he's got me banned from attending football for 10 years and, to top it all, he's even got me serving a six-stretch for doing absolutely nothing wrong.

Yet just because 'MacInlies'' career is on the slide, don't kid yourself he's the last of a dodgy breed. No, there are plenty of other shifty undercover journalists out there keen to fill his shoes, whose minds are every bit as warped with the 'anything goes and sod the consequences, the end justifies the means' mentality. Believe me they're out there lurking around right now, stalking their next prey. Could it be you?

I'll tell you why I'm so sure. I was having a chat recently with my pal Eoin McSorely. He works at Maxim magazine now but while he was editor of Front he told me about some journalist who'd come looking for a job there. This happens all the time to Eoin but he's easy-going and he agreed to meet the kid. It was a loose interview, they've met in the pub and the bloke's claimed he's a good investigative journalist who can do this, that, and the other for the magazine. But right from the start Eoin's not happy in his company, not only is the fella unlikeable, he's being very vague and not offering any real ideas, not saying anything that couldn't have been said over the phone yet he was the one who's made the point of meeting up.

At one point this stranger lets on that he's worked on the MacIntyre series, including the football hooliganism one and Eoin's thought 'Bingo.' He lets him chat and the kid starts giving it the big one, painting a picture of how 'scary' it all was (Eoin's biting his tongue, because he knows by now it's all bullshit). They go their separate ways and the next day Eoin gets a courier-delivered envelope, there's no note, no explanation, nothing. He puts the tape in the video and there it is – their whole conversation, secretly filmed on a camera hidden in the bloke's car-key fob. The journalist probably thought it made him look clever but to Eoin all it showed was how underhand he was. Well there's one job interview that's gone boss-eyed, yet I bet this bloke's still out there, doing the same sort of thing. You've been warned.

As for MacIntyre and the rest of his crew who were involved in that sham of a programme on me, well fuck them. Because, despite it all, everything in my life now is back to 'normality.'

And just like 'hope' is the one word you cling to while you're inside, 'normality' is the one which means more than anything once you've finally packed your gear and walked through those gates for the last time.

Anyone who's ever been inside already knows this but when you're in Wandsworth and all the other places like that, it's the simple, normal things you just can't have that you now really want the most, like the beans on toast I wanted so badly that time in Elmley. You want to be part of all the everyday stuff, like throwing your clothes down in the corner of the bedroom last thing at night and then hearing your missus nagging you because you haven't put it in the wash basket, do you know what I mean? You want to be able to ask your kids if they've done their homework yet and when they try and give you some excuse you used yourself 25 years ago, have a go at them because they're trying to kid a kidder. You just want that 'beans on toast,' or whatever it is you miss the most back in your life.

And when I finally got back there I fitted straight back into it all like a glove within about three seconds, give or take a second or two. I know a lot of people so of course there were a lot of pals who wanted me to go out the same night, but no, I stayed in with Julie, because she's done every single day with me, it was the least I could do and I tell you now not only was it easy to stay in, it was lovely, too. Then in the morning I woke up and I'm in my own bed, Julie's taken the day off work and I'm feeling cushty.

The only weird things that took some getting used to when I first came out was that everything seems to be at 100mph on the outside, which makes your head spin a bit, and then there's the changes that have gone on in your neighbourhood while you've been away. I was at a wedding reception at Stamford Bridge recently and I was going to nip down the road to get Julie something to eat from the local Kentucky, except when I got there, it wasn't! I didn't know it had closed down because I haven't been a round for a few years.

But just the following week after getting out two football teams get in touch saying they want me to play for them, so I'm straight back into the football again, the old routine and there's only one thing now which sometimes makes me think of prison. I've still got pals of mine doing a lump of bird and when I look at the clock, I might think something like, "Oh It's 12 o'clock, they'll all be having their dinner now," because I know exactly what they're doing at any time of the day.

I'll tell you something that makes me laugh nowadays, people keep asking 'haven't you changed because of all this?' How was I meant to change, was I meant to buckle, was all this meant to destroy me? Am I now going to stop bragging and telling stories when I'm down the pub with my pals? – no of course I'm not. Some people have conspired to set me up for a six-stretch. I will never change who I am for people like that and anyway, what's done is done. I can't turn the clock back and it's one of the things I learnt in prison, you deal with what you can do something about. If things are out of your hands then there's nothing you can do, nothing at all, so just get on with it.

People still ask me about the programme and that's one of the main reasons I've written this book, so at last the truth can be told. For the next few years I have to go to a police station every time England or Chelsea play abroad and hand my passport in the week before. When the game's over I then have to go back and pick it up afterwards – I reckon it's just because they miss my happy smiling face. Even though I've done my sentence I'll continue to hand my passport in because I have to, but this is shocking when you think about it compared to say some Rule 43 paedophile. So he – or she – will be on the sex register for as little as three or four years. Shouldn't they have to contact a police station every time they walk past a school or a park where children will be? Otherwise they're free to nonce themselves up looking at little children and there's no-one trying to stop them. That's the way I book it and it really annoys me.

The authorities ought to be directing their regulations towards more important matters like this instead of targeting 'football hooligans.' I know of people whenever Chelsea are playing at home who are not allowed within a three mile radius of the ground. It doesn't matter how ridiculous this is, it's the law and forget about civil liberties, because no-one's going to fight your corner as a football supporter.

Yet while none of this has changed me, who I am and what I do, prison did teach me to have different outlook on life. I did learn to appreciate what really matters a lot more and I'll give you an example.

I'm a short-tempered kid, I wish I wasn't sometimes but that's just how I am.

We had some bad snow when I first got out, the worst we've had in years and it took me eight hours to get home one night, bumper to bumper all the way. I sat there because the traffic just wasn't moving at all and I called Julie. I said, "Listen babe, I'm stuck in traffic, but are you alright, are the kids still playing in the snow?"

Julie said, "Where are you?" and I laughed and told her, "Don't ask, babe, but I'm not behind the door. Whatever happens I'll be coming home tonight darling, whether it takes me until four in the morning or whatever, I'm coming home. So it doesn't matter how long it takes, does it?"

She was a bit surprised and said, "That isn't like you," because in the past I'd have driven all the way home down the hard shoulder rather than got stuck in a traffic jam. But it was something which had struck me while I was sat there waiting for the cars in front to clear: "there's more to life than getting the hump over the weather and the traffic." I pointed out to Julie that there's thousands of people all over the country not able to come home tonight because they're stuck in prison – yet I'm no longer one of them.

19

PREMIERSHIP *V.* MACINTYRE

Document 1: The cross-examination of Donal MacIntyre, Friday November 24th, 2000.

BLACKFRIARS CROWN COURT   No.T20000418

Pocock Street
London SE1 0BJ

Friday, 24th November 2000
Before:

HIS HONOUR JUDGE BYERS

R E G I N A

-v-

JASON MARRINER
ANDREW FRAIN

MR C VAUDIN and MR O GIBBONS appeared on behalf of the prosecution

MR M WOLKIND and MR A BUDWORTH appeared on behalf of the defendant MARRINER

MR M OLIVER and MR J WHITFIELD appeared on behalf of the defendant FRAIN

CROSS-EXAMINATION OF DONAL MACINTYRE

Computerised transcript of Smith Bernal Reporting Ltd (Official Shorthand Writers to the Court)

Friday, 24th November 2000

Cross-examination by Mr Wolkind

Q. May it please your honour. I suppose it is just as well you did not want to make a programme with footage of Jason Marriner being violent because you didn't get any, did you?

A. Well, Mr Marriner on several occasions admitted to me that he had been violent and I remember one particular incident when he said that he had just escaped being nicked by the police in an incident in 1998 when a number of his colleagues had been arrested and convicted for football violence.

Q. Sorry, were you about to tell us about any violence that happened in the period the jury are interested in or do you want to repeat something you said yesterday about violence outside the period? Would you like to say it again for the third time? What is the month you are talking about, outside the period the jury are considering?

A. Pardon?

Q. What is the month you are talking about which is outside the jury —

A. Mr Marriner told me about that when we were in, I think, December 1998.

Q. So popping back to the period we are considering and your comment that the TV programme was not to include violence from Jason Marriner, specifically, I suggest to you it is just as well because you do not have, actually, any footage?

A. No, we don't have specific footage at all of Mr Marriner beating up anybody.

Q. Or any physical involvement involving violence from him?

A. No

Q. (extract is played back in court). We know the clip continues with you flushing away the cocaine.

A. I think that was given to Mr Clothier.

Q. Is that not you? That is somebody else destroying it. So either the drug is looked at and flushed away or it is taken elsewhere to be analysed?

A. I think it is — the reason why I brought it in there was to show and demonstrate in front of my body camera that I had the cocaine. I opened it up — because I am obviously doing this for the film — put it back in, closed it up, put it back into my hand, I think I must have put it back into my pocket. Before I left the toilet I obviously have to flush because otherwise people would wonder why I've gone into the toilet. So I flushed, came out, and sometime after we left the bar we gave the substance to Mr Clothier who got it tested and I understand it was confirmed to be cocaine.

Q. Cocaine which you had got not directly from Danny Walford but a friend of his?

A. Yes.

Q. His friend possessed a class A drug, therefore, did he not?

A. Yes, he did.

Q. It had nothing to do with you, he had it?

A. Yes, he did.

Q. He was, therefore, in possession of it which I am sure you know is a criminal offence?

A. Yes, I do.

Q. Supplying cocaine is another criminal offence which is more serious still, is it not?

A. Yes, it is

Q. How did he come to supply that drug to you, please, and commit the more serious offence?

A. Well, it was quite clear to me that some of the people there present at that meeting had consumed cocaine. I think one of them had said to me they are off their head. In order to demonstrate that cocaine is a recreational drug for many of these hooligans then I thought to buy cocaine to confirm the fact that they were using cocaine and handed that substance to Mr Clothier for testing.

Q. Do we know the name of that man who supplied it to you?

A. The name escapes me at the moment.

Q. Do you not mind for dramatic purposes but to simply refer to him as X. It is obviously Walford's friend. Do you know what X was going to do with that cocaine but for your asking him to supply it?

A. I have no idea

Q. So what we do know is, he, X, was committing the offence of possession of a class A drug. Thanks to you he committed the offence that evening, did he not, at that place of supplying a class A drug to Donal MacIntyre?

A. He handed to me over a substance of cocaine. Yes, that's correct..

Q. The 'yes' is what? The 'yes' is an agreement to my suggestion?

A. Yes, is the — we were not seeking to paint him as a drug dealer. Merely I wanted to confirm that he was using cocaine and that he was — that a substance was as he said it was.

Q. Using cocaine and that it truly was cocaine would be proved by his mere possession of it, that you got him to supply it, did you not?

A. I asked him to sell me some cocaine, yes.

Q. Why did you encourage X to do something that as far as you knew he would not otherwise have done if you had not been there?

A. Because I wanted to demonstrate that these hooligans were using cocaine and that this is often part of their behaviour.

Q. So your desire to make a point in a television film is more important than the fact that you encouraged him to do something that he would not otherwise have done if you had not been there; and that was a criminal offence that you encouraged him to do, is that it?

A. I understand that — I cannot speak for Mr X and I do not know whether he had ever supplied anyone else, but I did ask him if he had the substance and I handed over £20 for that.

Q. But what you do know is he would not have committed the particular offence at that night at that public house of supplying drugs to you but for you asking. He did not offer it, did he, you asked?

A. My recollection of the events was that there was, er, that I had asked him for cocaine and that there was cocaine about on the table.

Q. He did not offer it to you, did he?

A. I can't recall.

Q. You saw the clip just now.

A. I really have to see the full context but I can't recall.

Q. The full context. Is there more between — we are talking about this man committing a criminal offence because of your intervention — is there any more context beyond the start where you ask Danny Walford if he directs you to this man and the end where you flush the toilet? Is there any more context or do you want to see that part again?

A. I think that you've got to see the full context in the demonstration that football hooligans use cocaine and it is important to recognise and it was demonstrable because we prove the substance indeed was cocaine.

Q. Let us see if you follow this. Imagine if he supplies drugs on Monday, Tuesday, Wednesday, Thursday and Friday, are you saying it is all right then for you a journalist to make him commit the offence on Saturday as well by you asking him for drugs, is that your point?

A. No. I am sorry, I do not understand the question?

Q. Imagine he does supply drugs, you do not know that individual, do you?

A. We had some contact with him but I don't know him specifically, no.

Q. You do not know whether he has ever in his life before supplied drugs, do you, that man?

A. I am not aware of that, no.

Q. But just imagine that you did know that that man supplied drugs on other days, does that mean that it is all right for you to encourage him to commit the offence on this day, is that all right?

A. I really can't speak for that gentleman.

Q. No, is it all right for your actions in encouraging him to commit that offence, that particular offence supplying to you?

A. It was clear that I wanted to have and confirmed that these hooligans were on cocaine and that was to me the mere nature of the event.

Q. So is it what Donal MacIntyre wants that is the golden rule, because you wanted it that is good enough?

A. No, it is not.

Q. Is there, for example, a different sort of rule that you must never encourage anyone to do anything they would not otherwise have done if you had not been there? Is that also a rule?

A. Yes, out of character.

Q. Out of character did you say?

A. Yes.

Q. Really? So you can encourage someone to kill a person if they have done it before, you can encourage someone to beat someone up if they have done it before, supplied drugs if they have done it before? Where is the out of character condition, please, where did you find that?

I have a copy of your book. Just so to explain so there is no misunderstanding, I cannot improve yourselves during the trial because the jury are not forbidden to read it. Certain excerpts we will look at together but they cannot have the book in all. Go to page 8 please it is within your preface and we are going to read what Donal MacIntyre says is the golden rule and we will look for your extra condition.

The golden rule is this: "As an undercover reporter you must never encourage anyone to do or say anything that they will not otherwise do if you have not been there. All the more so, of course, if there was a criminal offence." That is obvious, is it not?

A Well, in the —

Q. No, is that obvious? All the more so if the thing you are encouraging them to do is a criminal offence?

A. In the context of the use, the criminal use of cocaine by football hooligans, I was keen to demonstrate that, in fact, they use cocaine and had it in their possession.

Q. But why did it matter what you are keen to do, what happened to the golden rule? If you had gone off that golden rule, Mr MacIntyre, what about the law that you are inciting someone to supply a class A drug. Did you care about that?

A. I was aware of the law.

Q. Thank you. Then share your awareness. You were committing the criminal offence, obviously, of inciting someone to supply a class A drug, were you not?

A. No, I wasn't.

Q. Because?

A. Because I was merely demonstrating that football hooligans use cocaine and the only way that we could demonstrate that was to have that substance in our possession and get it tested.

Q. So the law lies down before Donal MacIntrye's desire to prove a point?

A. No, it doesn't.

Q. But you tell me, please, why you have not committed the offence of incitement of X to supply a class A drug, tell us your defence?

A. The offence was possession. The hooligans had it in their possession and I merely wanted it to get to prove that it was in their possession. I think that we demonstrated that.

Q. Mr MacIntyre, that is a silly answer, is it not? If the offence is just possession then it is seeing him possess the drug would be enough; you got him to supply it, did you not?

A. There is no confirmation that somebody hands you a sugar lump or somebody hands that it is confirmed to be cocaine. And I think it is important for us to demonstrate that when the hooligans were mentioning cocaine they were off their heads. And that this may be a factor sometimes in their behaviour because it was important for me to try and demonstrate that when they have said they were off their heads they had cocaine, that in fact they had had cocaine.

Q. You continue to emphasise what is important for you. See whether perhaps you can put in order the following concepts. What is important for Donal MacIntyre and the law of this country? Which order would you like to put those two in?

A. I think there is no doubt the law of the country.

Q. You mentioned the offence is possession. You did agree, did you not, that you knew that supplying a class A drug was also an offence and indeed a more serious one than mere possession?

A. Supply, yes, it is a more serious offence.

Q. So going back to my question, please, what is your defence to the suggestion that I make that you committed the crime of inciting another person to supply a class A drug? Bearing in mind, Mr MacIntyre, mitigation may be that it was very important for you. What is your defence? Did you incite him to supply it?

A. The football hooligan in question had the drug in his possession, that was the first step of my enquiry as to whether it was, in fact, cocaine he was talking about.

Q. Did you incite him to supply?

A. I asked him — supply — did he have any cocaine and he said yes.

Q. But he had not mentioned it before? He had not approached you before, had he?

A. No. There was some suggestion, I think, that there was cocaine on offer.

Q. Yes, him, that man. Do not generalise, please, that man, that cocaine, had he offered to supply it for you?

A. Directly no, but there was some suggestion that there was cocaine on offer and I was seeking to find out who had it on offer.

Q. For all you know but for your intervention that would have been his personal piece of cocaine.

A. For all I know he may have in the past supplied cocaine or this may just have been his personal stash of cocaine. But what we did demonstrate clearly that football hooligans use cocaine. We had heard this on a number of occasions before and it was perhaps the first occasion in which we could actually confirm it.

Q. Did you incite him to supply that amount of cocaine to you?

A. No, I wouldn't say that.

Q. Why? You said you asked him to, why?

A. Because in order to incite, I mean, I would have had to have given the cocaine in the first place. This man had the cocaine in his hand and I asked him — and there was cocaine apparently on offer. That was the suggestion.

Q. Why do you say that you would have had to have given him the cocaine before you could incite him to give it back to you? What are you talking about?

A. Because I think the initial crime is possession and I was keen to demonstrate that football hooligans use cocaine. The only way we could demonstrate that, without a shadow of doubt, with this new generation of hooligans, where cocaine had become a drug of choice, was to buy the cocaine off him.

Q. Are you able, just for a moment, to leave aside the important TV programme you were making and come back to my question about the laws of the land, did you incite him (that means, for example, I asked if you had encouraged him to —

A. No, I did not.

Q. If he is sitting there and you go up to him and say, "Can you give me some cocaine?" Do you think to any ordinary person that would be an encouragement?

A. No. My general, from the course of the entire day was that they were happy to talk about cocaine and there was a suggestion that cocaine was on offer. I asked Mr Walford, he did not have it, and then I asked Mr X. I am sure if Mr X is happy, is available —

Q. It does not matter whether he is happy but for you asking there was absolutely no evidence you can give us that he was to supply to you?

A. I think you would have to ask Mr X. But it was clear the suggestions —

Q. Oh please, whilst you were there was there any hint that he wanted to supply you with cocaine until you asked him?

A. The suggestion, there was a suggestion that their openness and there was cocaine around that was on offer.

Q. No, that man?

A. I asked a number of them which person had it and I asked him if he had

— and he knows candy (?) (which is their phrase, and some quarters for cocaine) and he said yes he had.

Q. Do you have any evidence that that man intended to give you cocaine but for your asking?

A. I think you've got to ask him.

Q. Do you have any evidence?

A. My suggestion was —

Q. Did he say, "Mac, come over here, I want to give you some cocaine?"

A. No, he did not.

Q. Did he say, "I want to show you some cocaine because you look like the sort of person who would use it"?

A. No. It was clear to me that there was a suggestion of cocaine on offer. I did not know specifically who carried the cocaine. For me to ask that many questions would put my undercover guise at risk.

Q. A number of times in the book you talk about the courage that you needed to act undercover in this way, do you not?

A. It is not just me but I think other members of my team.

Q. Maybe it is not but you need to actually acknowledge my question first before you praise the rest of the team, you need to acknowledge my question first. During the book you talk about your own bravery? Carry on to add them in if you want.

A. I think it is a difficult and a dangerous world.

Q. Do you talk about it because I might have it wrong, you see, that is why you have to say, yes, you are right or no, I am wrong. Do you talk about your own bravery in the book?

A. I think I — it may have been mentioned. I also talk about my own fears.

Q. I will give you all the list of page references if you really want them. But you would probably agree that you talk of in certain places about your own bravery in doing this, your courage. So going back to Walford and hopefully leaving it with this question, do you have the courage and decency now to admit that you incited him to commit the criminal offence of supplying you with that amount of cocaine on that occasion, therefore ignoring all the generalities that you keep raising?

A. I do not accept the defence counsel's submission.

Q. Did you supply Mr Clothier with the information that a leading member of the headhunters is a major dealer of class A drugs including cocaine and steroids as well as soft drugs such as cannabis, did you supply him with that information at one stage?

A. I recall back that my information was that actually the cocaine which was supplied to me that day had come from Mr Frain.

Q. Oh it was Mr Frain? When you supplied that information did you actually tell Mr Clothier who you had in mind? You may not have wanted to put it down in correspondence, I can accept that, but did you actually put a name to it so that he does not come in front of a court and say the name Marriner to them?

A. I can't recall the conversation.

Q. Who would you have described in this way, "A leading member of the headhunters is a major dealer of class A drugs including cocaine and steroids as well as soft drugs such as cannabis." I am going to jog your memory even further. You said, "This man is somebody we formed a close relationship with. We believe he may within a short time offer to sell any or all of these types of drugs to members of the team, the BBC team." Who was that?

A. Well, I was aware that Mr Frain supplied drugs and that I was also aware that Mr Marriner had friends who were drug suppliers.

Q. Do you recognise Jason Marriner there?

A. Yes, I do.

Q. Tell me, please, is he a major dealer of class A drugs including cocaine and steroids or did you ever believe him to be such a major dealer?

A. No, I did not.

Q. Did you believe he or anyone within a short time was going to offer to sell class A drugs to the members of your team?

A. I was aware that there were some members of Chelsea headhunters who were involved in drugs.

Q. What was my question, interesting thought that answer is, what was my question?

A. Could you repeat it?

Q. Of course. Did you believe that any member of the gang, the headhunters, was within a short time going to offer to sell class A drugs to you or any members of your team?

A. Yes, I believe that, yes.

Q. What did you say then?

A. I would believe that — and my information was from a member of the Reading gang and an associate of Mr Frain was that he sold drugs.

Q. No, I did not ask you if he sold drugs. I asked you whether you believed that within a short time a member of the gang was going to offer to sell class A to you or to any member of your team, did you believe that?

A. Yes.

Q. Why?

A. Well, because we were beginning to form a close relationship with the Reading hooligans associated with Mr Frain.

Q. But Mr MacIntyre your own guise were that you were major drug dealers?

A. Yes.

Q. Did you think that some member of a Reading football hooligan gang was going to offer to sell class A drugs to you, the older successful drug dealers, did you believe that?

A. Well, the thing about our guise was that if we're serious drug criminals, you would not carry small amounts of cocaine for your personal use. It would be ludicrous for you to take in our undercover guise to be carrying small amounts of cocaine which would give a window apparently in our undercover guise to the police on our cover, so if we're picked up on a small amount of cocaine would be ludicrous, so our undercover guise did not allow for us to have possession of small amounts of cocaine. So it might sound a bit odd but that was our thinking.

Q. That may be your problem as a major drug dealer, but what leads you to think and to tell anyone that a member of the gang within a short time was going to offer to sell class A drugs to you? Did they tell you they were going to?

A. We had conversations about — we were aware that Mr Frain supplied drugs and we were getting closer —

Q. Sorry, Mr Frain supplied drugs not his friend, Mr Frain himself?

A. Yes.

Q. He told you, did he?

A. His friends told me.

Q. Someone else told you something about Mr Frain and did that someone else or anyone directly say, "Within a short time we are going to offer to sell drugs to you"?

A. No, they did not but that was, er, we thought a reasonable assumption.

Q. You also thought that if you could feed such lies to anyone else at the BBC they would continue to fund and have faith in your programme, did you not?

A. This is a long and difficult investigation and the lies within the BBC had no part of it.

Q. Is this an accurate account of the information you passed on to Mr Clothier? Did you pass on that a leading member of the gang is a major dealer of class A drugs, including cocaine and steroids as well as soft drugs such as cannabis and that this man is somebody you formed a close relationship with and we believe he may within a short time offer to sell any or all of these types of drugs to members of the BBC team? Did you pass that on?

A. I can't recall that specific conversation.

Q. Had you formed a close relationship with Mr Frain?

A. No, but we were forming a close relationship after Bloody Sunday. There is no doubt that after the events of Bloody Sunday when people coalesce together apparently on a —

Q. Shall I just stop you so that you do not mislead anyone, not unintentionally of course. If that information came on 13th November '98 it is unlikely to be influenced by events that were three months in the future. So bearing in mind 13th November '98 is the date of information, had you then formed a close relationship with Mr Frain?

A. No, I had not.

Q. But you are aware of how the TV programme was put together but I think you explained to us Mr Clothier is a man who really produced it?

A. That's right.

Q. Meaning he works the material and he edits it?

A. Mr Clothier receives the tapes, logs and then puts it together for a television programme.

Q. You must have been very disappointed with Mr Clothier's work, were you not?

A. Absolutely not.

Q. Well surely you were disappointed with some of his work on that programme, were you not?

A. No.

Q. What about his inclusion of a part that was meaningless, irrelevant, of no significance that one could barely hear? Was that not a great disappointment to you?

A. I am not aware, if you could explain?

Q. Forgive me, surely you know that on that TV documentary there is a part that is meaningless, it is irrelevant, it has no significance, one can hardly hear it, do you not know that? I will play it to you and you will tell me if that description is accurate.

The documentary itself opens with these words, as you remember. You introduce yourself: "My name is Donal MacIntyre and I am a BBC reporter. I worked undercover for the last 18 months," do you remember saying that?

A Yes, I do.

Q. "and I've lived five different lives." You said that, did you not?

A. Yes, I did.

Q. Five, I suppose, because four disguises and when you had the time you had your ordinary life as well?

A. That too is worth five lives but we did investigate another world but the programme wasn't broadcast.

Q. Oh five is the introduction we hear to the football programme which was the first one transmitted, because at that stage you still thought you had a fifth programme to show, did you not?

A. No, there was potential for a fifth programme.

Q. It was a little bit more than potential, you would not be saying an introduction to the first programme that you have lived five different lives unless you still expected at that stage you were going to broadcast five episodes, is that right?

A. Well, we do our best.

Q. Perhaps you do. But at the stage when you said I lived five different lives that was because you thought you had a first, second, third and fourth and fifth portrayal of you acting undercover?

A. I think it may have been ambiguous but there was an expectation at that time that there would be a fifth programme, that did not come to pass.

Q. The one on insider trading stock market, that failed, did it not?

A. Yes, it did.

Q. The book — if you remind yourself, if you like, it is page 7 of the preface — that talks about how you had lived four different lives?

A. Yes.

MR WOLKIND: "Imagine your life," you say to the reader, "being divided between four cities and four different apartments." I suppose you did not really want to put in brackets, (actually it was five cities and five different apartments but one flopped). Then you continue, "In the course of a day...."

JUDGE BYERS: Wait for him. Do not make comments unless they are part of a question.

MR WOLKIND: When I said I suppose you did not want to say it, I felt sure you would agree readily, you did not want to say five because you do not have to put in brackets that one flopped and you are not going to read about it?

A Well, I am happy to say, you know sometimes our undercover guise works and sometimes they fail. That is the nature of the work.

Q. Then you go on, "In the course of a day I've assumed four different personalities." But we really know it is five, do we not?

A. Well, actually we started the — which is part of the problem to be frank — undercover investigation into the city and financial trading and insider dealing very late on and to be frank that was probably the primary reason why the film did not work and my undercover guise was a bit thin.

Q. Forgive me, you must have been close to transmitting it because your programmes went out weekly and on the day of the football one going out to the public they were still told that your name was Donal MacIntyre and you had worked undercover for the last 18 months. "I've lived five different lives." You are only at that stage a month away from broadcasting the fifth one?

A. I think the court would grant us hope in terms of expectation. It just did not come to pass.

Q. The preface continues, "In the course of a day I've assumed four different personalities, worn four different wardrobes, spoken four different street dialects and left a little bit of me behind in each of those worlds." I do not know if you got a little bit back from the stock market, but you would not want to tell them in the preface, would you, that the fifth one had flopped? It would not be a nice introduction to a book.

A. Well, it doesn't matter. I still got my tattoo from the football world that I (inaudible)

Q. As long as it makes up for it for you.

(extract of video is played back) Part of that, of course, you now remember was meaningless, irrelevant and of no significance. You accept that I am sure, do you not?

A. I am sorry, I am not too sure about the phrase and where you have got it from.

Q. You have watched the clip, it did not last too long, I am sure you can remember it. Part of that clip did you not then recognise as being meaningless, irrelevant and of no significance if you managed just about to hear it at all?

A. I do not understand the meaningless?

Q. You say you do not understand it, do you mean you understand it but you disagree with that description?

A. I can't recall it now. I am not sure of the context.

Q. The context is, did you spot within our 30 seconds viewing just now a part which was meaningless, irrelevant and of no significance? Did you spot such a part?

A. No, I can't recall. Can I see it again? (extract of video is played back)

Q. Have you spotted it yet?

A. I am not too sure of the context, meaning in reference to what?

Q. What context do you want? Somewhere within that clip I am asking you whether you spotted something that can be fairly described by a sensible adult as meaningless, irrelevant and of no significance? Did you spot such a part matching that description?

A. I am sorry, I can't help you.

Q. What was happening in that clip then, explain it to us?

A. I recall Mr Marriner as talking about the violence after the game in Leicester. I think he said it went berserk twice is my recollection. I think also in that clip you saw my tattoo. And he asked me what I had been doing recently and I think I told him I had been filming.

Q. Yes, carry on, what else happened in that clip?

A. Erm, that's my recollection.

Q. You heard the radio, did you not then, the radio played over?

A. Yes, I did.

Q. Tell us what is that about?

A. That's a clipping from David Mellor's radio programme.

Q. 606 on Five Live on Saturdays, yes? And the clip ends? How does the clip end?

A. Um, can I see it again?

Q. Certainly. You only need go back just enough to show the end of this clip (extract is shown again). Stop quick before it fades. How did that just end?

A. It ended with an edit with Mr Marriner and sound and the radio being run at the same time.

Q. What sort of sound was coming — you could hear it — from Mr Marriner?

A. Mr Marriner was, um, being Mr Marriner as he is sometimes. He was making....

Q. We have heard he talks as well, you see, I do not know how often he grunts or roars. But what was the context of his making that noise being Mr Marriner?

A. I'd have to — I can't recall the context, I am sorry.

Q. What was the context as it happened to the viewer? Just imagine you are involved in a production and you just viewed it as we all could if we were in front of the television, what was the apparent context of the roar, please?

A. I suppose in the context of his demeanour related to it going berserk as a football hooligan in Leicester.

Q. So the impression to any ordinary viewer would be that here was a man roaring in the context of violence, things going berserk in Leicester, so in that sort of context?

A. I think there is a back ref. to that but I think that, you know, I don't think — people take their own views on that. I mean, I am not too sure that is terribly significant at the end, particularly in view of the context of it going berserk in Leicester.

Q. We started with a description of violence serious enough for it to be called twice berserk. We then heard a pretty bad story of a child so scared of what happened that he never wants to go to football again. So things fairly serious, are they not?

A. Well, I think that is part of the reason why we did the programme.

Q. Thank you very much for sharing that. The sound at the end in that context would it come over, do you think, as something scary or frightening? It is pretty unattractive, is it not, in the context we have just heard?

A. It did not — I mean that's Jason being Jason, but I did not find it scary and people will take their own view.

Q. You see, you may know him, you may know he is a cuddly bear rather than scary, but the context or the impression it would give to the viewer, do you not think, having just heard about violence going berserk and a child scared away forever from football, do you not think it is there as an illustration of something nasty, nasty face of football and the nasty sound of football?

A. Not necessarily.

Q. What is it there for otherwise?

A. I think you would have to ask Mr Clothier.

Q. No, we have asked him now it is your chance. What is it there for?

A. Mr Clothier edited the programme and I think it is difficult for — it is sometimes — people not to understand that my role was for enough evidence gathered to present and then to voice-over the programme and not to put the programme together.

Q. Where is the roar lifted from?

A. Pardon?

Q. Where has is been lifted from, you talk about an edit?

A. I have no idea.

Q. Do you not? I shall remind you. Extract 12 please. As we get ready to watch extract 12, tell me if you agree with this bold claim: for the first time ever your show would be an honest and detailed portrait of football violence?

A. I think it shows exactly how football violence is organised. Yes, I accept that.

Q. You recognise that claim? It is at page 13 of your book.

A. I do.

Q. "The first time ever we wanted to paint an honest and detailed television portrait for who they were and what they were about." Meaning there had not been an honest one before, that is the inference?

A. No, I think — I do not think the organisation of football violence have been portrayed as it was as we did it close-up and personal before.

Q. The first time ever honest and detailed. Let us watch (extract 12 is played back in court) Does it come back to you where the passage shown on the TV documentary was in fact lifted from?

A. If you say it is lifted from there and that is confirmed by the producer then it is lifted from there.

Q. At 01.22.04 You come up with the witty suggestion that Jason had red card the ref. You heard that, did you not?

A. I did.

Q. — and you smile in pleasure. The story Jason told you was a great story, was it not, truly witty?

A. I mean —

Q. But was it not, the referee says to him, "What's your name Jason?" That is not a bad story, is it not?

A. Jason can be funny sometimes, yes, absolutely.

Q. It may be that the referee is being funny, "What's your name Jason"? In any event it is not a berserk or particularly violent occasion when he tells you this old story, is it?

A. No, it is not.

Q. After he tells the referee how to spell his surname he gets sent off and the fans roar as he tries to demonstrate?

A. Yes, they do.

Q. Do you think in that part being lifted and added onto this story of berserk violence at Leicester and a child being put off forever supporting football, do you think that is an example for the first time ever a TV portrayal being honest on this subject, do you think that is a good example?

A. I think this is an honest programme and this is an honest portrayal of football hooligans for the first time on television back at the car organising football violence.

Q. If Mr Clothier edited in this courtroom he would take out the word "not" from the plea of not guilty, would he not, and you would say it is honest. How do you suggest it is an example of an honest — for the first time ever — TV portrait when roaring in the context of a funny story is lifted and placed immediately at the end of a description of berserk violence, how honest is that by your standards, Mr MacIntyre?

A. Basically they produce and edit the programme.

Q. Judge it for me? How honest is it by your standards? You have seen it, you want to be honest, tell us if it meets your requirements?

A. I think it was just Jason being Jason. If there is another interpretation I can see people may take the other interpretation, but erm…

Q. I can barely hear you, I am sorry? You are acknowledging, I suppose, that those who do not know Jason are being sold him in a certain way and that roar would add to the picture of his being a violent thug?

A. I think people who know Jason know he is a violent thug.

Q. Thank you for the character reference but I asked you about the viewers, not people who know Jason Marriner, do you see, because what you are doing is slip in as many criticisms of him as you can, are you not? So going back to the question about the viewers. When they watch that editing is it honest or will it lead them to think there is a violent thug roaring in the context of berserk violence?

A. I think it was — that comes after the Leicester — the trip where they organised football violence. And I think they had every ample opportunity to know who Jason was having seen that and my view was that it was Jason being Jason, though other people may have a different interpretation and that's reasonable.

Q. In Copenhagen both you and he got beaten up by the Danish supporters, did you not? Who got it worse?

A. I am not too sure. Jason certainly got beaten up and I got beaten up. I got beaten up but it wasn't too bad afterwards, no broken bones.

Q. Did you get revenge?

A. No. When I was beaten up and when you are beaten up you've just got to curl up and you can't fight back and, you know, so you go to – –

Q. But a bit later on. I did not say did you fight back, did you get revenge, I suggest after the event, did you get revenge later?

A. No.

Q. Did you see Jason getting revenge?

A. No, but Jason told me he went about, grabbed some guys from the pub afterwards and hit anyone that he saw, words to that effect.

MR WOLKIND: Can we see extract 1 please. (Extract 1 is played back)

JUDGE BYERS: Mr Wolkind, when we have these extracts I wonder if somebody could tell us, because I know it comes up on the bottom part, but the date and the time and the place?

MR WOLKIND: Yes, I will try on each occasion.

JUDGE BYERS: It would be helpful I think for the note.

MR WOLKIND: We cannot always be certain but it may assist your Honour if I hand up after the break a schedule we have just so you can use the column that has the date on it.

JUDGE BYERS: That will certainly be helpful to me. But I think it is useful not only for the note but also to the jury to know the sequence in which these extracts occurred and then they can perhaps compare some of them with the ones that have been placed before the Court by the Crown.

MR WOLKIND: It is 5th November '98 for Copenhagen. You may remember, Mr MacIntyre. This is extract 1. (extract 1 is played back in court). In that clip is Jason Marriner looking for trouble?

A. I understand he is going to, er, the game.

Q. Sorry?

A. I think we are waiting for a taxi to go to the game but I can't recall.

Q. Did you hear Jason Marriner say this: "I'd like to lie down, put my feet up and watch the highlights"?

A. In that?

Q. Yes.

A. I did not hear him say that.

Q. All right, we will play it again after the break if we may.

A. Sure.

JUDGE BYERS: Mr MacIntyre, you must not talk to anyone about your evidence and do not let anybody talk to you about it. Yes, you are free to leave the court. Members of the jury, 11.55 please.

(Brief discussion re Danny Walford and pending trial) (the court adjourned)

Q. I am sorry, you wanted to see extract 1 again. There is no transcript available (extract 1 is shown). Did you see him yawning?

A. I did

Q. Did you hear him say these words? "I'd like to lie down and put my feet up and watch the highlights."

A. Erm, I find it difficult to hear but if that's your transcript then I am happy with that.

Q. I have remembered but you have forgotten already, can you speak up please?

A. Sorry.

Q. You say that some time after the match he spoke to you again, explaining that he had been beaten up?

A. About he had been beaten up. The full description which he'd given to me which we had recorded was when we were turned back to Britain and he explained how he had been beaten up and then having gone back to an English pub and grabbed some people and beaten up some other people.

Q. Describing it sounds like revenge, not self-defence, but revenge afterwards.

A. I think that's for Mr Marriner to say.

Q. No, it is for you to explain so we are clear. He did not try to defend himself and attack them back, this was later, was it, having got other people he went back and looked for them?

A. Yes, after he had been beaten up he went back to the pub and took some other men, were his words, and went up to beat some other people up.

Q. It, therefore, was a fine example for you of organisation of football violence. Sometimes one team wins the other team organises and comes back and they win.

A. Well, I think when people — is my voice loud enough — go abroad, I mean hooligans go abroad, there are obviously two distinct forces and they often clash in the streets and it is not quite as organised as it is in England, for example, and the Leicester journey when there were phone calls being discussed between the rival parties. It is just a different dynamic.

Q. Tell me where, please, in any of your witness statements I can find you dealing with Jason's confession that he rounded up people in order to beat up the Copenhagen fans? Do you have your witness statements available?

A. I do not believe that in the course of the statements we discussed Copenhagen.

Q. I will give you the references for where you discussed Copenhagen.

A. Sure.

JUDGE BYERS: May we have, please, the statements. They will be in original form there. Are they typed, the originals?

MR VAUDIN: Yes, they are.

JUDGE BYERS: Thank you.

MR WOLKIND: Looking in particular, please, at page 9 which is the third page of your statement, 5th May this year. It is the last paragraph, Mr MacIntyre. Do you list the four matches you went to with Jason Marriner in the '98/'99 season and you include Copenhagen?

A. Yes, I do.

Q. Do you comment there about the events in Copenhagen, including Jason saying that he went back getting revenge?

A. No, I do not.

Q. At page 19 of the bundle, which is the 13th page of that same statement, do you refer to an occasion in March when you are in the flat with Mr Marriner you continue to talk in general about being arrested and how you are both attacked in Copenhagen?

A. Yes.

Q. Does he as he describes how he was attacked in Copenhagen go on to describe the revenge that he got?

A. No, he doesn't but —

MR WOLKIND: Is it not odd?

MR VAUDIN: I am sorry, your Honour, but I wonder if the witness could be allowed to answer the question?

A. I mean, it is quite clear because the tape is recorded where Mr Marriner says that he went back to the pub and grabbed some English supporters and beat up some people they found — any old person I think or any person, I am not too sure of the exact words.

Q. Forgive me, I am a little lost on what you said. The occasion in March and I can identify for you your Honour, this is the same occasion where Mr Clothier gave evidence it was in June, the prosecution may now agree it was actually in March; so there is no filming in the flat in June, was there?

A. I can't recall.

Q. We will sort it out and have an admission before the jury so that it is all agreed. But in March, as I suggest, you have a conversation which turns to the subject of you both being arrested and how you were both attacked in Copenhagen?

A. Yes.

Q. Were you suggesting that on tape in that conversation he describes getting people to go and beat up the Danish fans?

A. Absolutely not. On the way home from Copenhagen Mr Marriner said — I think he gave a description about how he went back to the pub, grabbed some people and went about to beat up any old — any person he could find, which seem to me they were his words more or less.

Q. Where was that?

A. That was coming from Copenhagen in a car going back to drop Mr Marriner off at his business.

Q. You mean from the airport in London?

A. Yes, I recall that, yes.

Q. Who was in the car?

A. Mr. Atkinson

Q. Is it taped?

A. — and myself. Yes, it is.

Q. It is taped and he talks about going back and getting (inaudible)?

A. I think that is my recollection, yes.

Q. You have it on tape, excellent. Will you find it for us over the short adjournment, the tapes, you are given access to the tapes by the prosecution?

A. I will certainly be happy to look for it.

MR WOLKIND: Thank you very much.

JUDGE BYERS: As long as you are happy for him to talk to the prosecution team.

MR WOLKIND: Yes, certainly. How many people suffered injuries as you understood from Jason's confession?

A. I don't think numbers were mentioned but…

Q. Who was with him?

A. He said, what he said was, "I went back to the pub. I grabbed a number of other English," words to that effect.

Q. Do you have one name for us at least, did he mention one name?

A. I don't think he mentioned any names.

Q. Did you ask?

A. I don't think I did.

Q. Tell me, please, why you did not mention this in a witness statement having heard him confess to rounding up people to beat up the Danish fans?

A. Well, I mean, we spent a long time with Mr Marriner. These offences were not subject to British law because they happened in — if they are offences — because they happened in another country and I am not too sure whether I was asked about it or whether it occurred to me.

Q. What about notes so that you would not forget the details and you would allow us to test it, what about notes of what he said?

A. Well, I think there was a tape of what he said so the tape represents our notes. That's my understanding there is a tape of that conversation.

MR WOLKIND: Have a look at page 98 of your book, please, and shall we see how you describe it there.

JUDGE BYERS: Mr Wolkind, do you have a copy of the book for me.

MR WOLKIND: I have given our second copy to the witness.

JUDGE BYERS: Because it is only that it may be helpful if I have it just as I have a witness statement.

MR WOLKIND: Yes, certainly.

JUDGE BYERS: I am very grateful.

MR WOLKIND: Do you see that he is explaining that he too had been beaten up and he gives his description of that?

A. Yes, I do.

Q. Then you say he told you this: "I just went home, got hold of my lot and said 'Come on, we're going to fucking work here'." Do you have that?

A. Yes.

Q. Every single word of that is made up by you, is it not?

A. Erm, no it is not.

Q. Did you enquire whether he caught them, these words were in quotations in your book? "Did you catch them, did you see them, I enquire?"

A. It's there but my recollection is that it is on the tape.

Q. "Once you start, fucking any cunt was going to get it now, weren't they, you know what I mean?" Please tell me what did inhibit you form asking what injury he had caused or how many people he hurt, what stopped you asking for details?

A. Because when you go undercover investigating people who you believe to be dangerous if you ask too many questions and the wrong question, if you ask questions like that, then you could blow your cover which would not be a very sensible or safe thing to do.

Q. Of course you can ask too many questions but are you suggesting that if Jason Marriner had genuinely, truly — if you are telling the truth, imagine, for a moment — said that, "Once you start, fucking any cunt was going to get it now," are you suggesting that if you had asked him whether he had managed to get any good blows in that would have been a question too many, do you think so?

A. Well, I mean that was my impression at the time.

Q. Do you think that was the last question you could ask; did you catch them, did you see them?

A. Erm, you know, when you are working undercover you say things to protect yourself and your identity, so it is very dangerous to ask too many questions. They would either think you are either a barrister or a policeman.

Q. Or dangerous to ask too few otherwise they think you are a dummy or a fake.

A. Well that's for Mr Marriner to say, it is not for me to say.

Q. No, you were helping me and helping the jury about the difficulties in asking questions because you do not want your cover to be exposed. So I am asking you, once again as the undercover reporter, you would be in equal danger if you showed no interest, they would think what an odd chap, he comes to Copenhagen, he comes to matches, he runs with us but he does not seem interested in us. You have got to show enough interest as well, have you not?

A. I really cannot speculate about Mr Marriner's reactions to my questions or otherwise, that's for him to say.

Q. Go back to your explanation, please that your cover would be in danger if you ask too many questions. Do you see I am asking about you, not Mr Marriner? Do you not agree your cover would be in equal danger if you did not ask the obvious questions and show a certain level of interest? I am asking you not Mr Marriner.

A. Erm, absolutely not. I mean it is a very dangerous environment and I don't think there is anything more need be said. We have to be very careful about what you say, less we expose undue interest in his activities and that would raise questions in his mind and therefore put me or anybody in my company in danger.

Q. Can we see the extract, please, from the flat filming. This is what I have suggested is 3rd March. There is no transcript available from the prosecution. (3rd March extract is played back) Stop there please and what we are looking for, Mr MacIntyre, what you say about Copenhagen and what he says about Copenhagen. Did you realise we came in as you raised the subject of Copenhagen?

A. Yes, we realised.

Q. Thank you. So you heard him say right at the end, whilst it is fresh in our mind, he has never been a bully. But you described 20 people and him, putting may be exaggerating but I am just asking you whether you heard it, described 20 people and him?

A. I just heard it, yes.

Q. That he went to the floor, put his hands up. You, however, boasted a bit more, did you not, explaining that you gave your best?

A. Yes, I did.

Q. His response to that was well he came off second best. So you are comparing, I suppose, yours a little boast and his just a resignation that he came off second best?

A. I mean that may be the case. But what is absolutely certain is that what he told me he did afterwards on our way back from the airport.

Q. No, we are discussing this for now. You can come back to that if you want. Does he mention anywhere during your recollections of Copenhagen that he went and got revenge?

A. Not there, no.

Q. Then do tell me, please, if you are claiming that he said in the car he had rounded up people and got revenge, it would have been absolutely safe for you to have asked one more question than in the flat without arousing any suspicion. You could have said, "Well at least you got a bit of your own back or at least you went out afterwards," could you not?

A. Well, it did not occur to me at the time and working undercover, you know, it is a fluid environment, you ask questions as they occur to you. It is a nervous environment and you can't ask too many questions.

Q. We are back to that then? Is at least you got revenge one too many questions in that context that we heard, is that what you are telling us?

A. No. I am just saying is that when you are working undercover you cannot have a clear note or a list of questions to ask, you know, you are prepared when you go into the field, you discuss it with your producer and then you try and ask as many of them as possible within, you know, constraints, conversation and safety because often the conversation, obviously, if you are working undercover would not run to any particular pattern.

JUDGE BYERS: Mr Wolkind, every advocate knows that sometimes you do not know whether it is one question too many until you have asked it.

MR WOLKIND: That is interesting, I do not disagree, but I do not accept for one moment that applies to this situation, with respect. For you in this context to have made a comment that at least you did something afterwards would not in any sensible view have been one too many questions, would it?

A. Well, that may be your opinion but I think when you are undercover – –

Q. I want yours?

A. I think, you know, it is a very difficult environment, you are investigating very difficult and dangerous people, you can't — and have a script, except that is genuinely prepared before you go into the field and you try and get as much information as you can and you do the best and, you know, perhaps if Mr Wolkind had been undercover with Combat 18 he would do better, I cannot answer for that.

Q. Who brought up the subject of Copenhagen?

A. From that clip there I take it that I did.

Q. It was something that you had prepared to raise with him, was it not?

A. It could have been, yes.

Q. For your purposes for the programme you wanted, what would be more interesting for your purposes, the fact that Jason Marriner had been beaten up or the fact that Jason Marriner had got a group of people for revenge. Just choose, please, which would have been more interesting?

A I was keen to hear a lot of what Mr Marriner said and I was keen to bring up the subject of Copenhagen, which I did.

Q. Having brought up the subject of Copenhagen and just popping back to my question, which would be more helpful to you, your TV programme, a description of Mr Marriner being beaten up or a description of Mr Marriner getting people to get revenge, choose?

A. I think as I say myself in the television programme that when you are in the company of football hooligans sometimes other football hooligans regard you as a target which they did in Mr Marriner's case and which they did in mine.

Q. I did not hear, which did you choose?

A. Sorry, there is no choice. Because Mr Marriner did not say it at the time but, erm.

Q. But which would you aim for? Imagine that the difficulties of being an undercover reporter and the dangers as his Honour has said of asking one too many questions, limited to just a minute or just one topic, what would you go for Marriner being beaten up of Marriner getting people to get revenge, violently, which would you go for, go on choose?

A. I think that in a situation where I was undercover with Mr Marriner I wasn't in a position always to choose the question and I was in no position, obviously, to give the answer, so conversations take their own pace and you've got to be very careful of the questions you ask, it is as simple as that.

Q. Just tell us, and loudly enough for the jury to hear please, you raise Copenhagen; it was a short conversation, was it not, you did not keep driving him mad about Copenhagen; it went on for some seconds, did it not?

A. I accept that from the clip there, yes I do.

Q. Thank you. Are you saying that it would have been dangerous for you to have said, after he described 20 people getting him off the floor, at least you were able to get back later? I want any words you choose.

A. I am saying that, you know, you cannot script an undercover conversation in the company of people like Jason and that is simply the way the conversation went.

Q. Tell me why, please, you erase the mini disc in Copenhagen?

A. I did not erase the mini disc in Copenhagen.

Q. Tell me why, please, you expressed an intention to erase the mini disc?

A. It was a difficult night, a very stressful night and my colleague Paul Atkinson had just been beaten up and, you know, kicked in the head and punched and assaulted and when I met him he was very, very stressed and agitated and he said he was afraid after even being beaten up that, because obviously he couldn't fight back, that Jason would think that he ran away. And he was distressed by running away and obviously not fighting back as a BBC journalist, that perhaps he would expose himself as a rather cowardly non-hard man. He said to me, you know, he wanted a black eye because he thought that if he had a black eye Mr Marriner would think that he had been involved in a scuffle and had stood his ground, so when he asked me to punch him in his distressed state I gave a very human reaction to a personal situation and I said hold on, whatever, I'll wipe the disc. In any event, the tape is there and that full conversation is recorded and with the defence.

Q. Mr Atkinson has been beaten up. Mr Atkinson on this story is scared that Jason Marriner will think he has run away?

A. Yes.

Q. Mr Atkinson asked you to give him some sign of injury?

A. Yes he does.

Q. The very human response to that is I will erase my mini disc?

A. It is a personal moment, he was distressed and there was nothing or nobody evidential on the tape and it was a human response to a human moment and I did not and I wouldn't but it was a human reaction to a human situation.

Q. Because you did not erase the disc we can now watch if you direct us to where we find it the bit where Paul Atkinson asked you to punch him in the eye. It is obviously on the tape, is it not?

A. I think the defence have the tape.

MR WOLKIND: Can we see extract 21 please. You listen carefully before describing his request for you to punch him.

MR VAUDIN: Your Honour, may I remind Mr MacIntyre to raise his voice. It is difficult for us to hear, it is difficult for me to hear and I think it is probably difficult for the jury to hear. I see they are nodding.

JUDGE BYERS: It is a difficulty that a lot of people have particularly people who are used to working with microphones because you have to tone down your voice when you are speaking with a microphone, so I am afraid you have got to get yourself back into cheering on the terraces mode. (extract 21 is played back)

MR WOLKIND: Was it on that?

A. When he asked me to punch him, yes it was.

MR WOLKIND: Can you stop it so we can actually hear it.

JUDGE BYERS: I may have identified the words and if I have it may be helpful. It was something like, "Take me around the back and smack me." I thought it was 25.38. I may be wrong with the footage. But I say that so that members of the jury and others can listen for that in case I am mistaken but that is what I thought I had picked up.

MR WOLKIND: Can we note 25.23 please. Was it one question too many when he spoke to you in the car to ask him what damage he had inflicted?

A. Not at all. When you are working undercover you cannot script your conversations.

Q. I am not asking you to script it but as you spoke to him were you scared in the car to ask him for any details of his revenge?

A. This is the journey back home from the airport?

Q. But where you claimed that he had told you that he had got some mates and they had gone for what I have described as revenge, were you scared to ask him?

A. I can't remember and recall my specific thought process at the time.

Q. Did you see Jason Marriner involved in any violence in Copenhagen?

A. No, I did not.

Q. Did you see Jason Marriner involved in any violence in Leicester?

A. No, I did not.

Q. You spoke to him after the Leicester match in the MacDonald's car park at Feltham, did you not?

A. Yes, I did.

Q. We know some of that from the radio clip and the roar that part we played this morning.

A. Yes, we did.

Q. That is when he described that it went off and it was going berserk?

A. Yes, he was.

Q. You do not, of course, take that to mean that he was involved but did you not tell Mr Vaudin for the prosecution yesterday that meant that he saw violence and there was violence?

A. That was my interpretation.

Q. So you did not see him in violence in Leicester and you interpreted that to mean that he saw violence, you did not take it to mean that he was involved?

A. I did take it to mean that he was involved in violence.

Q. He was involved, personally?

A. That is what I took it to mean.

Q. It may be something that is worth checking and I will not trouble the jury now but your Honour may recollect that yesterday you told Mr Vaudin you took it to mean that there had been violence at Leicester, you offered to us that he had been involved?

A. That's my interpretation.

Q. So it remains your interpretation or it is your interpretation today, that he had been involved in it but you never saw him involved, did you?

A. No, I did not.

Q. What you have seen, subsequently, is a number of videos from Leicester. Have you had a chance to see the police videos?

A. No.

Q. Never? You have not seen any of those at all?

A. No, I have not.

Q. You proceed throughout the making of the programme and throughout your evidence, do you not, on a presumption of guilt?

A. No. Mr Marriner demonstrated very clearly how one went about organising violence. It was clear to see and absolutely he told us of many occasions in the past and since of how he organised it, he did it in front of our very eyes and so it is not a big leap of faith to suggest or to interpret that when he said he went berserk, that perhaps he might have been involved.

Q. You have a general view of him. You apply it to each particular situation. So when he says that Leicester was going berserk for you it is an acceptable leap of faith to presume that he was involved in violence?

A. Mr Marriner has a long-term representation — am I allowed to say that?

Q. No. For you it is an acceptable leap of faith that he must have been involved in the Leicester violence?

A. Well, Mr Marriner spent some considerable time attempting to organise football violence prior to the Leicester game. There was an interpretation I made after he said it had gone berserk although he did not clearly explicitly say to me that he was involved but it was my interpretation.

Q. Of course one possibility which I suppose you would say would be a question much too far, was to ask him in the car park at MacDonald's whether he had managed to get any of the fucking Leicester mob or any of the Leicester cunts, you could have asked him that, could you not?

A. It didn't occur to me at the time. I could have asked him that, yes.

Q. It did not occur to you?

A. You cannot script an undercover conversation, it is as simple as that.

Q. No, of course not. But even without your script would you like to identify any occasion through the year or hundreds of hours of tape where you asked him if he did anything. Is there one occasion where it has occurred to you to ask him whether he did anything himself?

A. It was quite clear you did not have to ask him if he had organised football violence at Leicester, he had organised it. There were many occasions in which we did not have to ask him, he admitted being involved in violent football incidents which are not before this court.

Q. Shall we explain the technique to the jury? If you can interpret some behaviour of Marriner in a way that you say shows he is organising then you can present it to the jury, can you not, with your interpretation?

A. I am sorry, I do not understand the question.

Q. See if you can stay with this, because I am going to ask you if this is your technique. If you can offer an interpretation to the jury for Mr Marriner's behaviour then you do not have to ask him directly because you might lose all you have got. Do you follow?

A. That did not happen. Mr Marriner told us on many occasions about his past involvement in football incidents as late as — before — I mean just some months before we met him and it was quite clear that football violence and Mr Marriner were not a new thing. We did not turn Mr Marriner into a football hooligan,

Q. Tell me a single occasion, please, when you asked him if he was involved in violence, even one will do?

A. I think Mr Marriner — I did not need to ask him the specific question but there was no need to he was happy to tell us about his involvement all by himself.

MR WOLKIND: We need to pause to hear your answer. The explanation is that you are happy interpreting what is said. But just pausing to save your answer —

JUDGE BYERS: No. That is what he said. He said we did not have to ask him about — you asked the question: when did you ask him about violence? His answer was, I did not have to ask him.

MR WOLKIND: Absolutely, and you went on to explain that was because you were happy with what you had heard him saying and doing.

JUDGE BUYERS: No, Mr Wolkind, the reason I intervened is this. It is not this witness' interpretation of what was said. Your question was to tell me when you asked him, it was not an interpretation. He said I did not need to because he was quite happy to tell me. So it is nothing to do with interpretation, that is what I am trying to put an end to.

MR WOLKIND: Thank you. Do you remember I was asking you whether you asked him, on a single occasion, if he was involved in violence. Can I at least save the answer before we move on, you did not ask him on a single occasion?

A. I can't recall a specific occasion but as my view was that there were so many occasions when Mr Marriner himself comfortably told us about his involvement that there probably was no real need to ask.

Q. You give me an occasion, please, when he told you about him organising football violence, that he told you, where was the occasion and what did he say?

A. Well I recall him telling me in, I think it was in late '98, telling me how he was involved in a fight against Tottenham hooligans in I think Leicester or Trafalgar Square and how a number of his friends had been convicted but that how he had not been nicked because he wasn't tooled along with a couple of other associates.

Q. So first question please. Is it an occasion which was within the period that we are interested in this trial? I asked you about it, of course, but just to clarify it, is it an occasion within that period?

A. He told me about that admission during the time which we were under-cover.

Q. Absolutely. But was it an occasion that happened within this period?

A. No, I think after Leicester he went home to a party before a number of his associates went down, he went to a party, so the offences I think took place in January 1998 or before the time which we are talking about in the court.

Q. It is not an occasion when you saw him involved in violence, it is before you had ever met him?

A. That's right.

Q. What did he do?

A. In respect of what?

Q. That occasion, what did he do?

A. I am sorry, I do not understand the question.

Q. It is a description of an occasion involving violence?

A. Yes, it is.

Q. What did he do?

A. I can't recall the specific words but what he said was because he wasn't tooled up he wasn't nicked.

Q. Yes. But you are not tooled up, are you, there? What did he do not what he did not do?

A. From what he said to me it was clear that he was involved in a group fight against, erm — that was my interpretation.

Q. Did he punch someone?

A. I can't recall him say.

Q. Did he kick someone?

A. I have no idea.

Q. Did he touch someone?

A. That is for Mr Marriner to say.

Q. Well did he say it to you?

A. I can't recall. No, in fact I don't think he spoke in detail about it except for the fact that he was lucky he wasn't nicked because he wasn't tooled up.

Q. Forgive me, Mr MacIntyre, you worry at a number of occasions in your book about being arrested, do you not?

A. There were a number of occasions in which I worried about being arrested.

Q. Alongside your worry about being arrested is your declaration you had done nothing wrong.

A. I was worried I would be arrested because I was in the company of football hooligans who would obviously attract significant attention from the police.

Q. They are guilty, automatically, are they not, because they are followers of the Football Club? They are automatically guilty, are they not, which is why you were worried? In your mind they are automatically guilty, are they not?

A. No.

Q. What did Marriner do on the January '98 occasion, what did he do that makes him guilty of any offence, please?

A. Well, it's for Mr Marriner to say, not for me.

Q. What did he do on any occasion that is described to you ever that makes him guilty of any violence?

A. I am aware and was there when he attacked the march.

Q. The march we may be able to judge for ourselves but you are entitled to answer that. You were not clear not because you ever once asked him a question but you say from his own volunteered comments of his involvement in football violence, select please from anything Mr Marriner has ever said to you words that show he has touched anyone, tell us?

A. Well, he told me coming from Copenhagen, he told me many occasions of his interest and his previous involvement in football hooliganism.

Q. Copenhagen, we are going to look for the tape then we can better discuss it, perhaps. So we have Copenhagen and?

A. He told me — well I was there at the attack, I saw him attack the march.

Q. That we will judge for ourselves; and?

A. I can't recall other instances but you know.

Q. No, but I do not know. I want to know about those many occasions when it was so obvious to you of his involvement, what did he ever tell you that he did?

A. Well, I mean he told us many occasions of his involvement in football violence and we demonstrably saw him organise football violence and were it not for the police – –

Q. I want to know about those occasions when you claimed he told you?

A. Well, we saw him organise football —

MR WOLKIND: I am just going to pause because there is a question.

JUDGE BYERS: I have a question from jury. Mr Wolkind, I expect the witness will be able to help us: "What does tooled up mean?"

MR WOLKIND: As far as you were concerned, it meant armed with a weapon, did it not?

A. A weapon of some description.

A JUROR: Are you saying that Jason Marriner was carrying a weapon?

A. No, what Mr Marriner said to me was that if it wasn't for the fact that he was tooled up then he would have been nicked along with some of the associates. That's what he said to me. Those were his words, as I recall.

MR WOLKIND: Through your Honour there are questions from the jury from time to time. With a break coming up we have obviously got no problem if any questions are written down we will deal with them afterwards.

JUDGE BYERS: Yes, of course. This one was written down.

MR WOLKIND: I know it was.

JUDGE BYERS: But do not worry about it the jury know that if they have a question they can write it down on a piece of paper and it will be answered as soon as it can be.

MR WOLKIND: Yes, any question at all, of course. Have we reached this point? You cannot tell us of a single description from Jason Marriner of his being violent in the past before you had met him? Name that kick, that punch, that weapon?

A. There were many occasions, to answer your question, where he told us he had been violent in the past, many occasions.

Q. If he did not describe it did he turn to you and say, "Mac, I've been violent in the past"?

A. No, he told me specifically about how he took on Millwall. He told me – -

Q. Wait? Just check. This is not a reference to Millwall 1984, is it?

A. He did tell me about his involvement in that.

MR WOLKIND: The 16 year ago job?

JUDGE BYERS: Mr Wolkind, in great fairness to the witness you asked the question and the question was as follows: Tell me of an occasion when you referred to him being involved in violence before you met him? So the witness has answered your question.

MR WOLKIND: Absolutely. But before we hear the details it is nice to know it is 16 years before you met him. I am not going to stop you so carry on. What did he do on that occasion, 16 years ago?

A. Well, on that occasion and others Mr Marriner first told me he became involved in football violence I think at the age of certainly 15. He also mentioned the Millwall incident and he talked about as recent as the '98 incident and he talked when we were in Copenhagen about other incidents when he had been involved abroad with England.

Q. Pause on the Millwall, please. I did not hear you describe to us the violence in detail which no doubt Mr Marriner gave to you. What did he do?

A. If you could refresh my memory it would be useful with the tape.

Q. You tell me. What did he tell you he had done? Did he kill anyone?

A. No, I mean, I can't recall the words but, you know, I think if he had killed somebody we would probably have known about it.

Q. Maimed or stabbed someone, used a weapon?

A. I can't recall the conversation but I do recall the incident.

Q. Hit or kicked someone?

A. I can't recall the specifics.

Q. Say boo or down with Millwall. Can you find us a kick or a punch or any violence anywhere, please, from 84 onwards?

A. I think he talked in Copenhagen about his experience abroad. I think at one stage he told us that he had been, erm — although I am not too sure if I can say that. It may prejudice the defence.

JUDGE BYERS: You have been asked the question. If it is relevant to the answer you may answer it.

MR WOLKIND: That is not guaranteed to be relevant, which is why there may have been some hesitation. It may be something we will raise in a few moments if your Honour thinks that is a safer approach.

JUDGE BYERS: All right, well it is 12.55. Members of the jury, have a longer lunch hour. 2.05 please. (The jury withdrew from the court)

MR WOLKIND: The question was what Mr MacIntyre wanted to say and there is some hesitation it may be easier to hear it now.

JUDGE BYERS: I normally prefer to hear evidence in front of the jury if the question opens the door to it, but because of the sensitive nature of this particular aspect of the cross-examination then it is probably better that we do hear it.

A. I think he told me how he had previously, abroad as a hooligan, I think spent the night in jail abroad, and how he had been involved in violence in, erm — or and perhaps handcuffed on a previous visit to Leicester and I think he had talked about how he had beaten up a Catholic — I can't recall the specifics but involved in violence in some fish and chip shop.

MR VAUDIN: Your Honour may have the original transcript of course but it is — well I would submit in re-examination if it is not dealt with in this way I would apply to have the whole of it dealt with. Page 10 of the original transcript —

JUDGE BYERS: Are you looking at the transcript bundle or are you looking at the —

MR VAUDIN: I am looking at the original transcript rather than the jury's transcript bundle. But if your Honour looks at NWE100, it is all on tape, it is all on film, we have been invited to exclude all this. He is talking about extreme violence in Leicester Square, he talks about violence in a fish shop where he smacks someone, he talks about violence in a public house where they were tooled up and they have smashed the place up so that they may have tools. It is so extensive that I am afraid this line of cross-examination may well mislead the jury completely.

JUDGE BYERS: I was looking at page 13 of his witness statement actually.

MR VAUDIN: It is also, of course, in his witness statement but more extensively so on tape and in the original transcript.

JUDGE BYERS: No, I was merely looking at his witness statement. I would invite you and Mr Wolkind to do so as well. Page 13, paragraph middle, prefacing what he is no longer interested in. It starts, "I am never a bully...."

MR WOLKIND: I have a different page 13 for the moment.

JUDGE BYERS: Page 19 of the bundle.

MR WOLKIND: Thank you.

JUDGE BYERS: Page 13 of the statement.

MR WOLKIND: That paragraph gives me no concern.

JUDGE BYERS: But if there are other transcripts which are recorded which — and this witness has a lot of conversations to remember — then he must be entitled to refer to those tapes and he must be entitled to put that evidence before the jury if it answers your question.

MR VAUDIN: Your Honour, if I may suggest if it might assist, your Honour, I have underlined and crossed out but apart from that made no real notes of my own on any of these transcripts but because we have been asked to keep them out I have put lines right across it and underlined other parts. It may assist your Honour to go through the original transcript which is NEW101. Your Honour ought to have a copy of it. The violence described, in my submission —

JUDGE BYERS: I am not sure that I have. I have the jury bundle and I have an original bundle of transcripts which is different to the jury bundle.

MR WOLKIND: Can I just say that there are good reasons why the witness should withdraw really, as we are discussing the transcripts they must not be a memory refreshing now.

JUDGE BYERS: Mr MacIntyre, subject to looking for that tape obviously do not talk to anyone about the evidence that you are going to give and please wait outside so that you can assist with that if you would not mind. Thank you. (The witness withdrew from court)

MR VAUDIN: I am referring as an example, and only as an example, to the Leicester car journey. The transcript of that car journey and the film of that car journey in its original version is peppered with accounts of violence that we have been asked to exclude, violence at previous games, violence — I was referring a moment ago to page 10 of that transcript where he is talking about really the throwing away of the Marquis of Queensbury rules.

JUDGE BYERS: Is this the car journey?

MR VAUDIN: Yes, the car journey.

JUDGE BYERS: Is this GP59?

MR VAUDIN: Yes, GP59.

JUDGE BYERS: Just a moment. Let me find it. Page 10.

MR VAUDIN: Page 9 and 10. It starts at page 9 and goes on to page 10. It describes an incident where a man — and he mentioned it in a fish shop — was beaten up.

JUDGE BYERS: I have, "There was proper fist stick ups." Mr Frain joining in and the person has already to at 18.42 having started it. Then there is various other pieces and that is all during the course of the car journey. It seems to me that he must be allowed to refresh his memory from that.

MR WOLKIND: Oh yes. I have no trouble with that at all.

MR VAUDIN: Your Honour, page 12, if I may go on and page 13, page 14, page 15, page 18, 19, 20 and page 21, and that is only in the Leicester car journey let alone all the unused material which we have kept out. I am afraid if this goes on the whole of the unused material is going to have to be played because it contains —

JUDGE BYERS: It would not necessarily have to be played where there is a transcript of it.

MR VAUDIN: But we do not have transcripts of it because they were unused material.

JUDGE BYERS: No, no, where there is a transcript of it. But certainly he has been asked questions about that, that being material within the Leicester car journey, certainly he can refresh his memory from that and it may be that there are other things from which he can refresh his memory on other incidents.

MR VAUDIN: Your Honour, there are.

MR WOLKIND: The Leicester car journey is in a clear category, it is obvious that it can go in. I am not troubled and never have been about that. In re-examination if there is any other film that my learned friend wishes to play he will have to argue it first because otherwise the damage is done.

JUDGE BYERS: I suspect that he will have the weekend to think about it, yes.

MR WOLKIND: Yes.

MR VAUDIN: I am certainly going to apply for the whole of the Leicester car journey now to be played in its original version.

JUDGE BYERS: Let us hear the witness' answer. The way in which I suggest that the matter is dealt with, although strictly speaking it is a matter for counsel, is that Mr MacIntyre be given the transcript of the Leicester car journey, he can then look at it and if he wishes to he can answer questions from that transcript.

MR WOLKIND: We may have some submissions, although I have asked in the generality, I am surprised — I made one presumption about my learned friend — he means the whole journey. He surely does not mean a passage that includes a co-defendant, so it may be an ill-considered comment that he has made.

JUDGE BYERS: We will have to wait and see what cross-examination there is so far as the co-defendant is concerned because I have a balance to strike on fairness to both defendants and fairness to the Crown. But for the moment the transcript of the car journey seems to me to be a good starting point. The witness statements, he may wish to have another look at his witness statement which he is perfectly entitled to do. It is not for me to suggest what sources of material he may need to refresh his memory from but a general question of: can you tell me of one occasion when he mentioned himself being involved in violence? opens the door to him being able to go back to the year dot.

MR WOLKIND: Yes, subject to me raising other arguments that is the starting point, certainly. (general discussion re timetable)

MR VAUDIN: Your Honour, I was not quite clear whether your Honour meant that we should ensure that Mr MacIntyre has a transcript of the car journey now?

JUDGE BYERS: Yes, I think that he should. I think it is a document which he has been given leave to refresh his memory from. It is a category of evidence which is important to this trial. He has been asked a specific question about whether other incidents of violence were ever mentioned to Mr MacIntyre. Mr MacIntyre is therefore entitled to refresh his memory from the documents that he has and that are appropriate.

MR VAUDIN: Your Honour, then I propose to ask that he be given all his statements and that he is given the transcript of the car journey during the course of the luncheon adjournment and without any directions to any pub that he be allowed and told that he should read through it.

JUDGE BYERS: Nobody should tell him anything other than here are your documents and no doubt if a little more time is needed, because he is going to assist in finding that audio tape in order to assist Mr Wolkind, I shall be sympathetic to any application. But I am not anxious to lose time if we can help it.

MR VAUDIN: I do not know if that can be done during the luncheon adjournment plus his looking at these documents. They are extensive documents.

JUDGE BYERS: Let us see where we go. It may be that the tape cannot be found at this stage but if Mr MacIntyre is going to be in the witness box as I suspect on Monday and the matter can be dealt with then.

MR VAUDIN: Yes, so be it.

MR OLIVER: Your Honour, I was very guarded a moment ago. I think now I have to be a little less guarded. We currently plan to be very short with this witness. If he is now to see the transcript, but clearly he will have to be warned as to which is relevant in his answers and that which is not relevant.

JUDGE BYERS: I am afraid that is one of the difficulties that one has in a joint trial. If evidence is cross-examined in then it goes in and I will obviously have to give the jury careful directions as to how they approach that.

MR OLIVER: Your Honour, yes, of course, could lead to an application on behalf of Mr Frain about (inaudible) his trial.

JUDGE BYERS: I understand that. Quite how I view the application would be a different matter. 2.05 please. (luncheon adjournment)

MR WOLKIND: May it please, your Honour. We have found that part of the tape that provides the material for the section of the book dealing with Jason and Copenhagen and so I need to ask you this. Did any cunt get up from Jason after he had been beaten up?

A. I mean, I do not know I just know Mr Marriner said to me which I think it is on the tape.

Q. So you being sensible and knowing Jason, you will tell us that you do not know if he was just boasting, to keep up his image?

A. No. Mr Marriner said that he went to — off and I think it will be on the tape and I took it from his words that he did indeed go off and beat people up.

Q. I want to move on from the fact he said it. I was asking you for your help knowing Jason, it must have crossed your mind that he may be boasting, in other words, they had got the better of him and he was boasting to the flash drug dealers who had recently come into his life that he had got revenge. It is a possibility, is it not?

A. I didn't — I do not accept that. It is my belief that he did at that incidence do in fact what he said he did.

Q. Do tell me what it is that drives you to prefer the version that he was telling the truth from the possibility that he was lying?

A. I think if Mr Marriner had been a greengrocer, had never attended a football match in his life and did not admit to several incidents of football violence and did not organise or attempt to organise football violence in the back of my car, I think I might have given some consideration, but I was left with no doubt. That was my feeling, that's my view.

Q. I mean sometimes feelings are backed up by evidence of seeing it with your own eyes. You have told us already Jason may have said it, you never saw him do it?

A. No, I didn't see him attack anyone in Copenhagen, that is true.

Q. Sometimes feelings may be backed up by an occasion when you look back, such as March 3rd in your flat, and it is said again. Do you remember we saw that excerot this morning, you introduced Copenhagen, he does not mention any revenge, do you remember that?

A. Yes, I do.

Q. As we leave this subject, I wonder if you agree with this, one more question from you and you may have found out whether anyone got it from Jason?

A. Well, previously Mr Marriner had said that he had gone out to beat.

Q. Absolutely.

A. — and I felt that we had already had that but I was keen to discuss it again, As I said it is very difficult to organise a script of conversation. Before you go into the field you try and prepare yourself for areas of discussion but not — you obviously can't push it too hard, because otherwise they might get very suspicious.

MR WOLKIND: It is not as if you are an investigative journalist or anything like that trying to find out the truth, is it?

JUDGE BYERS: Is that a question?

MR WOLKIND: Yes, it is a question   waiting for a response. As an under-cover reporter you are still an investigative journalist trying to find out the truth, looking for confirmation, looking for real evidence, is that your role?

A. Well, I think in relation to that specific matter Mr Marriner gave his own confirmation. You may have a different view.

Q. Yesterday you told us, because I said I would check the note, that when Jason was telling you it had gone berserk at Leicester, you took that to mean that there had been violence in the ground. Today you yell us you took it to mean not just that, but that he had been involved?

A. Yes.

Q. You also told Mr Vaudin yesterday that to you naughty in anticipation of Leicester could only mean trouble?

A. Specifically in relation to that specific comment Mr Marriner had said in relation to the organisation of buses and he said he was going to be naughty, Leicester would be naughty, then I said qualifying it, you know, in the terms which I thought that he had meant, i.e. violence, I said, "Stand up for yourself" defensive proposition, and he said, "We will be all right. We will be all right," that seemed to indicate that the conversation was related to violent organisa-tion, some kind of confrontation.

Q. You, of course, would reject the possibility that if you said stand up for yourself he may think you are a complete idiot but nonetheless keeping in with his new flash drug dealer friends, he would reassure you that he would be all right?

A. Could you repeat the question?

Q. Of course. Do you rule out the possibility that in order to keep his new friends, the flash drug dealers happy, he would of course agree with you. He may have been thinking to himself you are a complete idiot but he would agree with you to keep in with you?

A. It was Mr Marriner who mentioned the word naughty.

Q. Forgive me. It is the actions to your comment that we are discussing, stand up for yourself. He may have heard you say it he may have thought you an idiot but nonetheless reassured you that he would be all right.

A. Mr Marriner clearly was organising football violence in the back of the car. I was quite confident that — and remain so — what he meant at the time pre-Leicester by the word "naughty" was in fact that there would be trouble. I stand by that.

Q. You know that after Leicester he went with other Chelsea friends for a good drink?

A. I know that after the Leicester incidents he went back down to London and had a drink with some colleagues.

Q. Yes, that is right. Mr Vaudin asked you yesterday about drinking habits after funerals. Do you remember he asked you that?

A. Yes, I do.

Q. That you expected trouble at Leicester to include people being tooled up, did you not?

A. People may very well have been tooled up at Leicester.

Q. Sorry, you thought they may well be going tooled up or are you actually saying they may in fact have been tooled up?

A. Tooled up, is that the phrase you are using?

Q. Well what phrase are you using?

A. Tooled up.

Q. The one the gentleman in the jury asked us about?

A. Tool up, yes. Hooligans often go tooled up.

Q. When you said or when you used the word "may" before, was that a reference to you anticipating they may go tooled up? Are you telling us even now that they may have been tooled up in the event?

A. No...I don't know whether Mr Marriner or Mr Frain were tooled up but hooligans often go tooled up.

Q. Why were you driving him to trouble, please?

A. We were attempting to see how organised football violence was organised. Mr Marriner was going to the game in any case and in order to witness how it was organised we thought we would go up and we would phone him and we would try and find out how he interacts with people. It was to our surprise that he had guests in the car with him.

Q. Never mind the others, and concentrate on Mr Marriner, to whom you had offered a lift. But why were you aiding his crime, please, if you thought he was going to cause trouble and may even be tooled up at Leicester, why were you aiding his crime?

A. We were — Mr Marriner was going to the game in any case so he was going to make his travel arrangements and would have got there any other way. We wanted to give him a lift so we could witness him organising it, so we could have evidence of people organising it in actually the act of it and that is a field which we did (inaudible) and that is why we are here now.

Q. Mr MacIntyre, are we back to Mr X that if you wanted for your TV programme that remains the most important point, more important than the law, more important than the guidelines under which you are meant to operate. We want, we want, we want. Why did you drive him to the crime, please?

A. Well, Mr Marriner was — when we were in the car indeed did commit a crime, he was organising criminal football violence and we wanted to witness that and we wanted to — we wasn't sure what he was going to do. We were quite clear that if the police had not been aware of the anticipated violence between Chelsea and Leicester, and it is a rare police officer who isn't aware that there often is trouble between these firms, and as indicated by their substantive police presence at Narborough where we left — where we arrived. But if there was going to be a substantive altercation and we would certainly have taken every opportunity to have dialled 999 and advised the police of the plan. In any case the police obviously became aware of the plans and were there, there was therefore no need to do so.

Q. Where was the crime going to happen?

A. We wasn't quite too sure. It was difficult to know.

Q. I am not that interested, actually, in the real details but it was going to happen towards Leicester, if not at Leicester, somewhere on the way to Leicester.

A. It was difficult to know because the meets were being changed and as Mr Marriner said he himself wanted to have changed the meet, so if he was confused we who were not party to it except in the company of the car we ourselves could not be certain exactly where the altercation that was being planned was going to take place.

Q. Mr MacIntyre, I am not actually really interested in where it was going to happen. The point may be this, it was going to happen en route, somewhere you were going to take him on the way to Leicester problems were going to happen?

A. It would have happened at a designated place. It is difficult to know where it would have been but clearly the first stop on the way to that would have been Narborough but initially it was going to be Loughborough but we – -

Q. I am still not interested, I can tell you how we can deal with this. Either Leicester itself or a point on its way. We can probably agree with that?

A. I think that is fair.

Q. Thank you. How did he get to the point on the way to Leicester? Was it by car, did he walk or did he go by train?

A. I think Mr Marriner was as indicated by the tapes, given a lift.

Q. Sorry, I can hardly hear you.

A. Sorry. Mr Marriner was given a lift to Leicester by myself and Mr Atkinson.

Q. You and Mr Atkinson, knowing on your version, that a crime was going to be committed, did you help him by giving him a lift to Narborough or could he just have materialised at Narborough without a lift? What do you think, did you help him to get there?

A. We wasn't too sure exactly what was going to happen. We thought we were just going up to give Mr Marriner a lift by himself. It did come as a shock to us that he was in the company of two other men and that did change the dynamic and certainly it did make the situation much more stressful and we did not expect to see the witness — the organisation explicitly as it transpired in front of us. But Mr Marriner was going to the match, anyway, he would have found his own means. I think he indicated as much as he was going to, you know, if we did not bring him there he would have gone there.

JUDGE BYERS: Can I just get one thing plain? When you started the journey where were you expecting to drive him to?

A. We were expecting to drive him to — I think there was some mention of Loughborough, initially.

Q. When you started the journey, did you know that there was likely to be trouble at Loughborough or anywhere else en route?

A. We had information that there may be trouble en route

JUDGE BYERS: Thank you.

MR WOLKIND: Well for you naughty left no doubt. It has no other possible meaning, Mr MacIntyre, naughty could leave you in no doubt you were taking him and aiding him to get to the scene of a crime? There is no doubt, is there, what else could naughty mean?

A. Well, as far as I read it at the time and in the context of the journey, I felt comfortable that Mr Marriner was intent. Of course, my version of events is now made much more secure by the fact that we did see him organise it, attempt to organise it in the back of the car. But there are many times in which, you know, you think something may happen and it does not happen. There are surprising events like the two gentlemen turning up. But if —

MR WOLKIND: Which you have mentioned probably six times so far. But you were driving him —

JUDGE BYERS: Can he finish his answer please, Mr Wolkind?

MR WOLKIND: Yes, certainly.

A. We were surprised that two other people turned up and we did not expect that to happen and that obviously had changed the situation quite dramatically. But we had BBC cars following us and keeping tabs on us and where we were going and if, for example, we had arrived in Narborough and there was no police presence and there was no expectation that, you know, that there was obviously going to be riotous assembly, then we clearly would have informed the authorities.

Q. See if you can leave out of your next answer your surprise that two extra people turned up. See if you can leave out your escape route and your decision that you were going to phone the police and see instead if you can straight answer this question, please. When you set out, because there is no other meaning of the word "naughty" you were helping him to the scene of a crime? See if you can do it without mentioning your surprise and your escape.

A. Well, we could have no confidence that a crime was going to be committed. We could have an expectation from his language and of course and the word he used. But there are times when Mr Marriner went to the game and violence did not happen or was not organised.

Q. Well, for example, you went to West Ham or he picked up a West Ham supporter and no violence?

A. There was no violence in that game.

Q. For example, went to Derby, no violence?

A. Mr Marriner did not go to Derby.

Q. See if you recognise one of the guidelines from the producers guidelines BBC and the reference. It is page 153 of the latest edition. The principles we should follow are — and I shall just pick out one: programme makes must not be involved in commissioning aiding or encouraging a crime. Aiding obviously includes, does it not, driving someone there? There is no escape clause just because he could have got there some other way?

A. We thought that indeed violence may take place at the end of the route. We thought that it may be organised. So we had an expectation we could not know for sure. The only reasons we are standing here right now is because we gave Mr Marriner a lift and because we thought that would give us an opportunity to witness the organisation of it. You can never tell what is going to happen on the journey.

MR WOLKIND: Once again, just like the drugs in the pub, what Donal MacIntyre wants is more important than the rules and the law, otherwise you might get in the way of your TV programme.

JUDGE BYERS: Mr Wolkind, thast is a statement not a question.

MR WOLKIND: It was becoming a question for sure.

JUDGE BYERS: Just a moment, Mr Vaudin has an objection.

MR VAUDIN: It is a statement, in my submission, but more than that, your Honour, with respect, I think my learned friend is losing sight of the offence. The offence this jury is trying is conspiracy. That conspiracy has been organised before Mr MacIntyre gave a lift.

JUDGE BYERS: Yes, but these were acts done, say the Crown, in the furtherance —

MR VAUDIN: It was the act in furtherance of the conspiracy that was taking place in the car, so the offence had already been committed.

JUDGE BYERS: No, these are acts done in the furtherance of the conspiracy and if they are acts done in furtherance of the conspiracy, strictly speaking they are part of the crime that is committed. Mr MacIntyre has already acknowledged that a crime was committed in his car.

MR VAUDIN: Exactly. He was witnessing it going on.

MR WOLKIND: So what I was going to ask you to do is to add together, please, your behaviour in the pub and your behaviour in giving a lift to Leicester, and do you agree that the true position is that what Donal MacIntyre wants is more important to Donal MacIntyre than the rules or the law?

A. No.

Q. Away fans stick together mostly because they are in a minority? It is a question, you can answer yes or no.

A. Yes, that would be fair.

Q. I suppose because they are in a minority they may feel more comfortable sticking together?

A. I think that would be fair too, yes.

Q. Are they allowed to meet in a public house on the way to a match?

A. Yes, I am sure they are.

Q. That is all right with you? I mean that is not a presumption you would say that that would be a conspiracy if they met in a pub?

A. No.

Q. Now are they allowed to meet in a second pub if the first one is closed or is that in itself sinister to you?

A. No.

Q. Do you know about pub talk, when people exaggerate or boast or fake what they are going to do and about their achievements when they have been having a little bit too much to drink?

A. Yes, I am aware that that happens.

Q. People can exaggerate when they are drunk, can they not?

A. Yes, they can.

Q. Sometimes they want to keep up with their peers, their group?

A. That may be the case.

Q. Sometimes people are just so drunk they do not really know what they are talking about?

A. That too may be true, yes.

Q. If, for example, they are in an exciting situation, they might show off?

A. That they may do, yes.

Q. If the situation is naughty lots of drink and fun and excitement like a BBC award ceremony people might say things that are a gross exaggeration; what do you think?

A. They may do, yes.

Q. Have you been to any awards ceremonies recently?

A. Yes, I have.

MR WOLKIND: What is the real name of the Daily Mirror reporter, Lucy Rock, which I presume is not her real name?

JUDGE BYERS: Is it essential that you know that for the purposes of you cross-examination?

MR WOKIND: Vital

JUDGE BYERS: If it is not —

MR WOLKIND: If your Honour meant if that is a serious indication —

JUDGE BYERS: It is a serious indication.

MR WOLKIND: Forgive me, she is a show business reporter, but if your Honour thinks there is any question of confidentiality —

JUDGE BYERS: I am not anxious, if she writes under a pseudonym, I am not anxious that that should be revealed unless it is essential.

MR WOLKIND: I am sorry, I did not immediately spot purpose behind your Honour's question. So the journalist, Lucy Rock, who writes for the

Mirror, just tell me please after the award ceremony you attended, it is not accurate for her to write, is it, that you, Donal MacIntyre, had moved 16 times in the past two months, going backwards from this month November 2000, is it?

A. Yes, it is.

Q. 16 times in the last two months?

A. I have moved from various people's floors, beds, and I've just recently moved into a new secure safe house.

Q. 16 times in the last two months, have you counted them?

A. I have moved backwards and forwards. I have not counted them explicitly but around that time, yes.

MR WOLKIND: Have you been in 16 addresses in the last two months for security reasons, come on?

JUDGE BYERS: No, no, not come on, let him answer the question.

MR WOLKIND: Yes, certainly.

A. I have moved housing locations, sometimes back to the same location for safety reasons on police and security advice. I am sorry I have to say that.

Q. Is it 16 times, Mr MacIntyre?

A. Yes, it is around 16 times.

Q. How many times do you think it is?

A. Yes, it is 16 times.

Q All right. Take a moment, please, do you have a pen there, I do not want to see the addresses, just take a moment and tell me if it is truthful? Keep it on a piece of paper and you can throw it away afterwards so that it is not left with us, just jot it out for yourself.

A. I mean, I do not obviously have a diary here but I can tell you that I have moved backwards and forwards to friends houses, to hotels, to a lot of people's homes, backwards and forwards around that number of times. It wasn't 16 different addresses but I have moved backwards and forwards. I have been sleeping on people's floors, on their sofas, and it was under security advice given to me by the BBC.

MR WOLKID: Tell me if this is accurate, that you spoke to a reporter when drunk, realised —

JUDGE BYERS: No, Mr Vaudin. He is putting a situation which he is perfectly entitled to do.

MR WOLKIND: You spoke to a reporter when you were drunk. When you sobered up later you realised your loose talk, your pub talk, drink talk, may lead to an article in a newspaper weeks or even a week before a trial was about to start and you did your best to try and stop any publication. Is that overall situation accurate as I have described it?

A. I had a very difficult evening that night which I won't go into.

MR WOLKIND: You did not win, did you, the award?

JUDGE BYERS: No, Mr Wolkind, if that sort of remark is put it may provoke an answer which you do not want. He said he has had a difficult evening and he did not want to go into it, now he may be being fair, I do not know.

MR WOKLIND: All right. So I get the background and, of course, you can fully answer, you gave an award?

A. I was presenting an award for a documentary prize giving which I had been asked to by the BBC. I did not really want to do it because I tend to avoid those but I had given a commitment. Then I came after the event and was brought around and hadn't really expected to be asked any questions but in any event I was and I was courteous and I explained the security situation and then I realised afterwards, because I did not stay very long, I left the premises around 11.30 because I had arrived around 9.30, quite late in fact with Fergo Keen, another BBC reporter, and we took a taxi home together and I realised there I said, Mmm, I said perhaps discussion, the mere discussion of my security situation may be prejudicial to the defendants and that we have been very, very careful to be very careful about that and I phoned up the organiser there, a Joanna Hanley and said I may have discussed my security arrangements. I would like I am afraid if that was printed in advance of the trial that may be prejudicial. And she said she would mention that to the BBC press officer and that's what happened that night.

Q. The article duly came out, did it not, in November 16th including your words that you had moved 16 times in two months?

A. Yes, it did.

MR WOLKIND: Please understand, I hope it was clear that until you give me any list or details I do not accept it.

JUDGE BYERS: Are you in a position, in fact, to challenge it?

MR WOLKIND: We do not accept it is anywhere near that number. If you say what information do I have it is not for me to call evidence at this stage. We do not accept it.

JUDGE BYERS: I know, but I merely put down the marker that as it is challenged that that is untrue then obviously the rules apply.

MR WOLKIND: Yes, inaccurate and exaggerated. Just to check please when we are talking about publicity, is this the Radio Times cover, November 1999?

A. Yes, it is.

Q. Just let me into a secret, does the photographer sort of touch up to make the eyes blue and things like that? That is you, is it not?

A. That's me.

JUDGE BYERS: Why, were you thinking of having some photographs taken, Mr Wolkind?

MR WOLKIND: They cannot make my eyes blue. But yours are blue to begin with, are they not? You do not know, you have not looked. All right. Pub talk, "Fulham Dray" that was the occasion when the Chelsea/Aston Villa match had been postponed?

A. Yes, that's right.

Q. People in the pub were disappointed about that and were talking about the match being off?

A. Yes, they were.

Q. If the jury please look for the first transcript in their bundle, the very first one, it deals with some of the conversation there. And you must be given a copy as well, of course.

JUDGE BYERS: Do we have a copy of the transcript for the witness please? There must be a jury bundle available for the witness. Which divider do we find this in?

MR WOLKIND: I say it is the very first transcript. For me it is in front of number one, either side of number one divider.

JUDGE BYERS: Just so that we have the reference. I have at the top of that in the right hand corner GP65, GRF14.

MR WOLKIND: Your Honour, yes.

JUDGE BYERS: It starts with 00.17 and goes on down the clock.

MR WOLKIND: Precisely. (to the witness) Looking that you no doubt satisfy yourself that is the occasion Fulham Dray after the postponement. You will see, for example, at the second page, 0.16.10 MacIntyre and Marriner discussing the rain and why the game was called off. So the subject for discussion there is still Villa/Chelsea?

A. Yes it is.

Q. Is this the occasion when you say Marriner left the pub as far as you believed to find people at Victoria, perhaps five of them?

A. I think on this transcript it says here, I think it is four minutes earlier when he says —

Q. Forgive me, I meant the overall occasion not that precise second. This is the occasion when you say he was going off to Victoria to look for opposing fans?

A. This is, he says, I am going to have a walk about and see if they are about.

Q. Right. Despite saying that he is there still, is he, at 16.10 when you are discussing it?

A. I think, yes, he is. I think at some stage he does leave the pub.

Q. We shall come to it, do not worry. Pub talk, boasting or real intention?

A. Well, I felt there was real intention there, others may have a different view.

Q. You have to talk up the whole time. Trying to impress other people, is that a possibility for you?

A. I don't think there he was trying to impress me at all. In fact I felt slightly cold-shouldered, because in many cases he wasn't actually talking to me directly, and sometimes he was talking with his back directly, erm.

Q. Trying to impress those to whom he was talking directly, to show that he was on that day interested in violence, possible?

A. That wasn't my view.

MR WOLKIND: No, possible?

JUDGE BYERS: He can only tell you what his view was, Mr Wolkind.

MR WOLKIND: I can ask him to think back in the circumstances and see, in fairness, whether that is possible.

A. Well, it wasn't my view, others may have a different opinion.

Q. Do you see again, as I suggest, with the Copenhagen words as well, it is one thing for a person to say they are going to have a walk to see if they are about and it is one thing for you to record him in Copenhagen to say any cunt was going to get it. Do you see, that is different from the other thing that he actually did find?

A. Sorry, could you repeat the question?

Q. Of course, far too complicated. Can you see the difference from someone saying they are going to look and someone who has told you they found? You cannot follow still. Is there a difference between someone saying they are going to look for trouble and someone who tells you they have found trouble?

A. They are two different statements.

Q. Two different statements you said and I have just about heard. Did you hear during the tape of the Fulham Dray sequence the name "Girty (?)" called out?

A. I can't recall.

Q. Did you know where Jason Marriner went from the Fulham Dray?

A. No, I do not know where he went to afterwards.

Q. Because I suspect you can see the difference between you telling us that he may go and look for them and you knowing he did go and look for them. Can you help us whether he did go and look for them?

A. Well, I am just taking the word from Mr Marriner. He says, "I am just going to fucking have a walk about and see if they are about, the cunts."

Q. All right. But he is still there at 16.10, so moving on from 16.10, what can you tell us moving on from that?

A. I think he left and I think previously there was a conversation about meeting the twins and people at this stage door in Victoria at 3 o'clock. That's my recollection.

Q. No, I am moving on from 16.10, please. The third one up, you are still talking about the game — bottom of the second page. Move on from 16.10 because he is still there talking about the game. Any hint after 16.10 of an interest in going over to Victoria?

A. That's erm....

Q. You have 16.10, have you not?

A. Yes I have.

Q. So move on from 16.10.

A. Mr Marriner left at 17.08, is that the point you are referring to?

Q. No. Start at 16.10 and why do you not go through the entries from 16.10 onwards?

A. Erm, there is a discussion about Copenhagen which I recall. "Are you going over?"

MR WOLKIND: I'm sorry, it is a discussion about what?

JUDGE BYERS: Are you going over?

MR WOLKIND: It is a discussion about what, not are you going over, it is a discussion about what did you say?

A. Copenhagen.

Q. I can see the transcript that at 16.25 it says, "Atkinson, are you going over?" Marriner, "Yeah, yeah." 16.35, "Yeah, I'm going over there." How do we know that is Copenhagen?

A. Well, I think there was another conversation, word, when Mr Marriner left at one stage and he had a conversation with somebody else in that pub and he said, "Am I going to see you," or something like that and Mr Marriner said, "I'll see you in Copenhagen."

Q. Looking at 16.25, is it your colleague, Paul Atkinson, saying "Are you going over? Answer "Yeah, yeah." 16.35, over the page, "I am going over there". How would he have known from looking at the transcript that that is Copenhagen?

A. Well, that's my recollection. Perhaps if I could see the primary material I could give the Court a bit of help on that.

Q. I do not know if you can answer this question. How would we know from the transcript, you see, I am asking about the transcript, that that is a reference to Copenhagen?

A. I think it is not altogether clear but maybe for the Court — maybe the tapes are clear.

Q. No, I am asking you about the transcript, and you say it is not altogether clear, where is a hint or a sign that that is Copenhagen, please?

A. Because Copenhagen isn't mentioned specifically.

MR WOLKIND: Exactly. So where do we find a sign or a hint that it is a reference to Copenhagen on the face of the transcript, please?

JUDGE BYERS: No, he cannot answer that, Mr Wolkind. He has told you he cannot.

MR WOLKIND: He has not yet. He has said about the film, he has not answered me.

JUDGE BYERS: no, he has said the only way he can answer you is by looking at the primary material.

MR WOLKIND: With the greatest respect the question is not about the primary material, the question relates to the transcript. If the answer is there is no hint that it refers to Copenhagen on the transcript, then all Mr MacIntyre has to do is say there is no hint on the transcript.

JUDGE BYERS: I think we can see that for ourselves. No, Mr Vaudin, it is all right.

MR VAUDIN: The difficulty is it is not in his transcript.

MR WOLKIND: Yes, but that is not the difficulty.

MR VAUDIN: He has not prepared it and he has been asked about somebody else's transcript, with respect.

JUDGE BYERS: This is a question that has now been answered. He cannot assist with the transcript. He has asked about that remark he has given you an answer that it refers to Copenhagen as does the one at 16.35, and as far as he is concerned a greater clue would be given if one was to look at the primary material. Now if you want him to see the primary material —

MR WOLKIND: I will soon but there is more yet. You, of course, are not responsible for how the transcript is put together, are you?

A. No.

Q. You will be pleased to know that this is the rare occasion when I absolutely agree with you that that part refers to not going to Victoria to look for other fans but refers to Copenhagen. It is not your fault how the transcript is put together, is it?

A. Pardon?

Q. It is not your fault how the transcript is put together, is it?

A. I did not put these transcripts together.

Q. The statement dated 2nd June 2000 with the name Donal MacIntyre and signed by Donal MacIntyre on each page, would that be your responsibility or is anyone else to blame for the contents of that?

A. No, that would be my responsibility.

Q. Then let us find that before we check the film.

A. Sorry, what date is that?

MR WOLKIND: 2nd June, please, 21(a) it begins at if you have a typed bundle. 21(b) is the relevant part.

JUDGE BYERS: It may be that you do not have the same pagination as us. It is the statement apparently of 2nd June and it is page 2 as I understand it.

MR WOLKIND: This relates to the Fulham Dray because you begin on 21(a): Firstly, I would like to detail meeting that occurred in the Fulham Dray, do you see that? The rest of the page continuers with Fulham Dray, does it not?

A. Yes, it does.

Q. Second page details with Villa perhaps being at Victoria, "I am going to have a fucking walk about to see if they are about." You took that as a serious intent. You rejected my suggestion that it might be a boast to impress. Then you do come to a paragraph at the bottom of 21(b) that says, "Marriner and a man in a green coat then left the bar. A couple of minutes I saw Marriner return. Paul then spoke to Marriner and I heard him say words to the effect of "Are you going over?" Do you see that?

A. Yes, I do.

Q. Copenhagen, can I ask you, has that had a mention so far?

A. Erm....

Q. — in this statement?

A. No, it hasn't.

Q. Marriner replied, "Yeah, yeah, yeah, I am going over there." Paul continued to speak with Marriner, "I bet Villa scarpered." See if we are in this position. Lots of conversation about Villa and threats or boasts. There comes a time when you say to Marriner, "I bet Villa scarpered," and in between those two parts dealing with Villa you have recorded Paul asking, "Are you going over?" Marriner, "Yeah, yeah, yeah, I am going over there." Why did you not, please, in a statement which you swore would be true to the best of your knowledge and belief make it clear that the passage was to do with Copenhagen as you knew when you made that statement?

A. If that's an omission I am happy to say it is an omission.

Q. You took part in that conversation. It is not as if you want the jury to believe that it was only Paul asking, are you going over, and Marriner saying yeah, yeah, yeah, I am going over there; you took a part, did you not?

A. I took a part in that conversation and hundreds of other conversations in the course of this investigation and there were others, so sometimes it is difficult to actually recollect the specifics all the time. That is the nature of the work which we do.

Q. Do help me, when you made the statement on 2nd June, were you not making these words — the ones you had put down — from listening to the tape?

A. Yes, I can't recall the exact.

Q. No, I asked you as whether you were listening to the tape when you made this statement?

A. I can't recall. I can't recall the specifics of that while I was giving the statement.

Q. No, what you said to me, Mr MacIntyre, what you offered as an explanation for you not including Copenhagen in your part, was that you do hundreds and hundreds of conversations and tapes. Why do you not tell us whether on 2nd June you made this statement with the benefit of listening to the tape because then we could get rid of the excuse of hundreds of conversations, do you see?

A. I just can't recall.

Q. But where did you make the statement?

A. I am not too sure whether I made it at the BBC or I did it at the police station.

Q. It may come back to you if you look at the signature of the person who witnesses it. I cannot interpret it. It may be Smith, is it a Detective Constable Smith? Yes, it is much clearer on another page. I see his signature as a Mr Smith, Detective Constable. Does that help you remember whether you were sitting with the benefit of a tape or what the circumstances were when you made this statement?

A. I can't recall. I certainly have viewed that tape many times, I just can't recall specifically.

Q. What you said on the tape was that he should go to Copenhagen by Easy Jet. It was your recommendation, you were involved in that conversation?

A. Sorry, this is another conversation.

Q. No, this conversation. Part of the same conversation in the Fulham Dray Paul says, "Are you going over?" he says, "Yeah, yeah, yeah, I am going over there." And you Mr Donal MacIntyre say these words, "You want to go Easy Jet." Were you suggesting he should go Easy Jet to Victoria to beat up Villa fans?

A. No.

Q. What were you suggesting he should take Easy Jet for?

A. Well, I think I was talking about cheap flights that were going to Copenhagen.

Q. Why is it not in your statement, please?

A. There are a lot of things related to what Mr Marriner said to me, related to his past experience of football violence which isn't in the statement and it may be it is not detailed as it should be but I certainly tried my best to help the police and the Court.

Q. Of course. If you had the tape running in front of you it would be odd indeed, would it not, for you to exclude the part that tells us it refers to

Copenhagen? It would be a conscious decision to exclude it. Did you make such a decision?

A. Absolutely not.

Q. So we are left in this really unlucky position that the statement deals with violence at Villa, he is still there although you will not accept it may have been just a boast, he is still there, you bring the conversation back to Villa and in between we read, "Are you going over?" "Yeah, yeah, yeah, I am going over there." And not a clue that it is anything other than Mr Marriner saying I am off to beat them up at Victoria. There is not a clue, is there, from your sworn statement?

A. I think Mr Marriner —

JUDGE BYERS: Just pause a moment. It may be helpful if one goes to the bottom of the page, because although Copenhagen is not mentioned – -

MR WOLKIND: Once you had reintroduced the subject of Villa Marriner again talks about that, does he not?

JUDGE BYERS: I think one has to set it in context, Mr Wolkind, for this reason, that they will go over is used again in the context of Victoria and it is on the transcript that the jury have.

MR WOLKIND: Yes. But as to the question: are you going over there, which the jury see at the bottom of page2 of the transcript, answer, yeah, yeah, yeah I am going over there, at the top of page 3, we can all write in now, can we not — it is not going to be a comment but a bit of evidence — that refers to Copenhagen?

A. This is the Easy Jet line.

Q. It is actually Mr Atkinson on the transcript saying "Are you going over?" Marriner saying "Yeah, yeah," and on the next page Marriner saying "yeah I am going over there." One can bracket those three together and mark it Copenhagen and one can also mark it, could one not, Mr MacIntyre says, "You want to go Easy Jet?" That is what we could do because that is the state of the safe evidence, is it not?

A. I am slightly confused because this is one statement involving several different events, including the Malrborough Public House, including the, erm....

Q. Do not worry at all, see if I can help. At 16.10 if you go back to the transcript, please. That is the part I am referring to in case you got confused with the statements. At 16.10 on the transcript you are still discussing the game, all right. Now I am going to suggest we can all safely bracket the next three entries. (16.25 Atkinson, Are you going over?) (16.27 Marriner, Yeah, yeah) (16.35

Marriner, Yeah, I am going over there). We can also safely bracket that and mark it Copenhagen. If the jury choose to they can add MacIntyre, You want to go Easy Jet? Do you follow?

A. I think, you know, it would probably be more helpful to me if I can see the primary material.

MR WOLKIND: Certainly, you are absolutely entitled to.

JUDGE BYERS: Yes, of course you can. Then, Mr Wolkind, when this piece of evidence is complete, this particular part of your cross-examination we will have a ten minute break because it is getting hot in here.

MR WOLKIND: Yes, certainly. (extract of video is played back in court) Just to explain what is happening, I think you all turned to a television where the explanation was given for why the match was being abandoned. Something about responsibility for safety to which you said fuck off and you continued to say fuck this and fuck that to the next passage. And then when the question from Mr Atkinson about whether he is going over to Copenhagen comes in did you hear yourself saying you want to go Easy Jet?

A. Yes, I did. Could I just put my bad language into context. No, I wouldn't want my mother to hear it but when you are working undercover you steal the clothes and language of the people that you are with and that they would feel comfortable with, that's all.

Q. Of course that means, I suppose, that when you are alone with Mr Atkinson there is no real need to swear, is there?

A. May I answer that, your Honour?

JUDGE BYERS: Yes, you can.

A. It is a difficult job which we do and sometimes we role play and some-times in this bad language does seep out and sometimes when you leave the world you have retained some of that language and there is no doubt that before I went into the world, I certainly in my own personal life had used bad language. When I went into the world of football hooliganism I used a lot more and now that I have come out I use an awful lot less.

JUDGE BYERS: Have you concluded?

MR WOLKIND: No.

JUDGE BYERS: But you have concluded this particularly piece?

MR WOLKIND: Yes, certainly.

JUDGE BYERS: We will have a ten minute break. (the court adjourned)

Cross examination by MR WOLKIND con't

Q. May it please, your Honour.

A. Your Honour, could I clarify something earlier related to the suggestion that I was drunk and in relation to the fact that I was obviously trying to retract a statement made in some exotic state? Before that award ceremony I contacted the legal department to ensure that none of the rushes or video clips from our show would have been broadcast by accident. I ensured that a duty lawyer was informed that they would be aware that because of the upcoming trial and the mere mention of our programme may be prejudicial to the clients.

I was not drunk, indeed I had perhaps one or two drinks there and I left for home very early, two and a half hours before the event was over, in a taxi, with Fergo Keen and I am sure that he would testify that I was of full and fair mind and it was on that journey home when I thought I should phone the press office.

The next day I also phoned the editor of our programme to ensure that once again the legal office in the BBC were aware that none of the pictures related to that event would be broadcast and would be prejudicial.

What I also should have done then again is phone back the press office again to ensure (which I had requested) that the two journalists, agency journalists, who took and wrote their pieces they were made aware that any mention of security and me would have been possibly prejudicial to the clients. So I thought I had done my best and I was sober. I am sorry if — I had to clarify that.

JUDGE BYERS: No, no, thank you. You had clarified most of that already. What you have not told us was that you had been in touch with them prior to the ceremony, but I do not think it is persisted with.

MR WOLKIND: Did you realise that at times Jason Marriner was keen to impress you or keep up with you?

A. Mr Marriner had got increasingly comfortable with us. Initially he was very diffident and separate to us and I do not suppose it took him a long while for him personally to get comfortable with me.

Q. You in turn were like a little groupie to him, for laughing at his jokes and encouraging and apparently welcoming any old stories?

A. Mr Marriner often told us about — he told us some occasions about his past related to football or football violence.

Q. It does not quite acknowledge the question. You in turn were like a groupie, do you understand, I mean sycophantic towards him. Laughing at his jokes and very readily encouraging him and apparently always keen to listen to him, made him feel important.

A. We were keen to obviously build a connection with Jason but sometimes he was genuinely funny and sometimes he wasn't, but we slowly built a relationship over time and I think if we had been too full-on with and Jason would have immediately suspected that we would have been — we were not who we claimed to be or pretended to be, so we couldn't be too sycophantic otherwise Jason would have been alerted to our journalistic intent.

Q. I am not sure if you agreed or not. You laughed very readily at his jokes and he could see all the signs from you that you enjoyed him, you enjoyed his company?

A. Yes, I accept that.

Q. He is a joker, is he not, a story-teller?

A. Jason is, you know, an affable chap sometimes.

Q. And a story teller?

A. He can tell stories/

Q. Affable and a story teller is a decent enough and accurate description of at least part of him, is it not?

A. Yes.

Q. It has to be, you know, because I took it from your own book. Page 50, "Jason Marriner, affable and a story teller." One approach you used to him in your relationship was flattery.

A. Yes, flattery is a useful tool, it least of all makes him feel comfortable in your presence and considering perhaps the danger involved we felt that was appropriate. Of course there was also another danger — and I think I had slipped into this — in relation to his football and in relation to the first football match I attended with him I was offering him too much praise which made him feel uncomfortable, so you have to be very, very careful about — you have to take a careful line.

Q. Have you to find something you could flatter him about and it was his football skills. He is not bad and you told him he is pretty good?

A. Well, indeed, Jason himself is quite a nifty footballer and I am sure I think he had a trial at one stage for Brentford Football Club. So at one stage before he went into the violence he was a talented footballer.

Q. He has got a trial now as well and during it we are going to see extract 3 please (extract 3 is played back in court) Did you say, "No-one has got your vision. On your (?) part, four stops ahead. The only one with vision is you."?

A. I did. I think it is fair to say that Jason is also quite a nifty footballer and although he may be here but it doesn't take away from his genuine football skill.

However, there could have been a moment and there certainly were when I might have heaped more praise upon him than he deserved.

Q. Let us see, please, how important to you Jason taking praises from extract 5 (extract 5 being played back) There we have confirmation that it was important that he was taking praise that you flatter and he is a deceit by it?

A. I think it is in the context of a previous game when I had praised him extensively and he pretty much blanked me and was making him feel uncomfortable and therefore I was keen to get him to feel comfortable with us and we talked about his football.

Q. So now you are happy because he is falling for the deceit?

A. No, I was pleased and comfortable that at last we had a common bond that he could feel comfortable talking to me which would offer me some protection. Because if he felt uncomfortable with me then, of course, he would feel nervous in my company and he wouldn't feel comfortable enough and engaged enough to discuss his behaviour.

Q. Sorry, was there anything wrong in the proposition I put to you, now you are happy that he is falling for your deceit?

A. Well, I think that he was comforting with the football thing. There was a measure of truth in the fact that actually genuinely, you know, he is quite a nifty little footballer.

Q. You had to decide or at least provide for the producer some material for how Jason could be effectively introduced to the viewing public on the documentary. There is going to come a time when they are going to see him talking and walking for the first time, is that right?

A. That is right.

Q. There has to come a time when Jason makes his debut walking and talking for the viewing public?

A. Yes.

Q. You want to get something appropriate. You would not want him walking into church, for example, something that fits in with the theme of football violence?

A. Well, I think the programme as broadcast demonstrated to us and my year or so demonstrated to me that he was a football hooligan and I felt that our programme fairly represented him as that.

Q. No, I am asking you about the opening shots? Sorry, was it not clear?

A. No, no, not at all.

Q. I must have introduced that, that could of course mean the whole programme so I am sorry. The first time within the programme that is shown, that is as an introduction walking and talking, now I am saying you would not want the opening shot to be something that was against the theme of the film like coming out of church or something, you wanted a nice opening introduction within the programme of Jason Marriner, did you not?

A. The editing of the programme was the responsibility of Mr Clothier.

Q. Forgive me. Is there anything wrong with the idea I am putting forward, that anyone associated with that programme would want a decent introduction of Jason Marriner? You would be shocked and pretty upset if it was a picture of Jason Marriner coming out of church, would you not, it would ruin your work?

A. No. All I am saying is that the specific editing of the programme was the responsibility of Mr Clothier. But, you know, I can understand what you are saying, yes.

Q. I mean you would not want, for example, a film of the occasion he took you to a charity do, that would really not fit in with the story, would it?

A. Not at all. We had limited footage, we went to one charity do and there wasn't much footage there because when we arrived there, myself and Atkinson, we suddenly and to our shock and horror recognised somebody who we see on a daily basis with our work for the BBC and for both his security and our own security we quickly left.

Q. Mr MacIntyre, that may have happened, I am sure it did, but do you want to tell me what that has got to do with the point that a charity shot regardless of whether you meet someone or not would not fit in with the theme, do you see? You do not have to tell me the fact about the charity it would not fit in with the theme of the story, would it?

A. Well, it may have been done but you are making a film about the organisation of football hooligans or football violence.

Q. Was it a charity do to raise funds for Combat 18, the National Front or the British National Party?

A. No, I understand it was a charity for a friend or a colleague who had cancer.

Q. Can we look at extract 20 please?

JUDGE BYERS: When was this taken?

MR WOLKINID: Yes, certainly. This is from the television documentary and it is the first day of the football season.

JUDGE BYERS: Do we have a transcript of it?

MR WOLKIND: No, there is no transcript of it.

JUDGE BYERS: I think it is a shot we have already seen, is it not?

MR WOLKIND: Yes, it is with a different witness. 22nd August 1998 (extract 20 being played back in the court) Just stop there please. The voice over is yours, is it not?

A. Yes, it is.

Q. It tells the millions watching that your first glimpse of Jason Marriner is as he is harassing a man in a phone box?

A. Yes, it does.

Q. Why did you say that?

A. As a journalist and as a presenter, a narrator of a programme, I take on in the first person the work of other people representing me. So it is traditional in television grammar – –

Q. Forgive me, there is a misunderstanding. I did not mean why are you doing that, we know what a voice over is. I am sorry you misunderstood. I understood it was your job to say something, but why did you say those words?

A. Erm.

Q. That he was harassing a man in a phone box, why did you say that?

A. That was the view of Mr Clothier and Mr Holmes who had witnessed the incident, as I understand.

Q. Oh, it is Mr Clothier's view, is it? So just so I understand it had you in fact had your first glimpse of Jason Marriner at the phonebox regardless whether he was harassing or not, did you see it as well with your own eyes?

A. No, I did not. I can't recall whether I did exactly or not but in traditional television terms the presenter or reporter takes on the voice of his colleague and workers.

Q. So are you not sure whether you saw it or not. Do you want a moment to think?

A. I can't recall that I actually saw that incident.

Q. Did you see the original material before it was cut down over which you did your voice?

A. I mean that particular shot.

Q. Yes.

A. Yes, I did.

JUDGE BYERS: No, wait a minute, there may be a misconception here. Did you see the base material from which that shot was taken before you did your voice over or did you just see the voice over or the programme?

A. I saw the voice over and the programme on that particular shot. That is my recollection.

JUDGE BYERS: Can you help the jury with this because it may be important. The voice over on a documentary of this sort, is it put on after all the pictures have been put together?

A. Yes, it is.

MR WOLKIND: So it may be in some circumstances the man who does the voice over cannot be responsible for the pictures. He may not know what really happened he is given the edited version?

A. That may be reasonable.

Q. But on this occasion we are not quite in that position, we are in the position that a witness, yourself, sir, cannot remember whether you saw it or not with your own eyes, so therefore I'm going to show you the full version. 19 please perhaps. Mr MacIntyre can we just remind everyone what the quote from your book at page 13. "For the first time ever it would be an honest and detailed TV portrait." So just watch 19, bearing that in mind please. (extract 19 being played back in court) Thank you. Can you tell us if you have ever seen that full material before?

A. Erm, I can't recall seeing the full material.

Q. Now you see it and you know you broadcast to the watching millions that this was the glimpse of Jason Marriner harassing a man in a phone box, you must I suppose feel embarrassed and wish to apologise, do you not?

JUDGE BYERS: Let us ask the questions in stages, shall we?

MR WOLKIND: Happily. Do you remember feeling embarrassed?

A. No, I mean that was the view of the....

Q. I can hardly hear you.

A. Sorry. It looks like he was certainly interacting less than politely. I can't recollect being there or seeing the extent of the footage. I think that is probably best answered by the producer. I really......

Q. The less than polite words were what?

A. I said it appears to me that — but I have no doubt, I really can't speak for that occasion because I can't recall being there or seeing the full material. I am sorry.

Q. What, have we reached the stage now when you are sure you were not there or you still just cannot remember?

A. I did a lot of work in 18 months and it is difficult to catch up.

Q. But you see it would have been your first visit to Chelsea, would it not?

A. On the 22nd?

Q. Yes.

A. That was the first game of the season.

Q. Yes, because unless you are a secret Chelsea supporter yourself, first game of the season, your first visit to their ground, so that may help you to bring back what happened. People were excited, were they not, first home game of the season, there was a buzz?

A. I am sure there would have been a buzz. I just can't recall seeing that incident or I can't recall that specific incident because I did a lot of work in the course of 18 months and it is difficult to attach, you know, a memory and I really do not want to speculate, it wouldn't serve the court.

Q. Were Jason and the man talking about football?

A. I have no idea

Q. Did Jason touch him?

A. I can't see

Q. Did he throw him out?

A. I don't think he did.

Q. Did the phone call continue after Jason first spoke to him?

A. It seems to have done, yes.

Q. Did Jason wait outside?

A. Yes, it seems that he did, yes.

Q. Did he knock on the door whilst he was waiting or did he just wait outside?

A. I can't recall.

Q. Did the man run away?

A. He did not seem to run, no.

Q. But you have seen that material, based on that material, please, was Jason harassing the man in the phone box?

A. Well, it is difficult to see but it seems to me that the first interaction was not altogether polite.

Q. It does not really matter whether he was harassing him or not, does it, you were involved in an operation which as long as it could fake the story was happy, as long as you could cut and edit in a way that allowed the voice over of Donal MacIntyre to say here is the man the programme is about harassing a man in a phone box, that is all that mattered to you and your team, is that right?

A. Absolutely and utterly not. This was a programme about the organisation of football violence.

Q. It is not an honest programme though, is it?

A. This is a thoroughly honest programme and part of our evidence, this programme, this man, is an organiser of football violence and I think he demonstrated that to us and we broadcast to the nation.

Q. Do you remember I have asked you a number of times about whether you understand the difference between Jason talking and Jason doing, things might just be boast, for example. Do you remember, we discussed that?

A. Earlier this afternoon?

Q. Yes, a number of times. Do you remember, for example, how he told you that 0961 mobiles were special because they gave you a protection, you could not be traced in a certain way. Do you remember all that?

A. Yes, I do.

Q. Would you be kind enough, please, to tell the jury the rest of Jason Marriner's 0961 mobile number?

A. I have no idea.

Q. Tell us what his number was, please just the beginning of it? You must have rung it many times?

A. I genuinely can't recall. He did change his mobile a number of times but I am sorry I can't recollect.

Q. That is perfectly understandable, I will give you the beginning and you will tell me that you recognise it. 0777, that must come back to you now, I suppose?

A. I think that was one of the number of mobiles which I think we phoned.

MR WOLKIND: The other number you may have phoned — if the jury look behind their tab 8, exhibit JP1, his business card — was beginning 0802 for his tyre business.

JUDGE BYERS: Mr Wolkind, we will deal with this point and then we will conclude for the day. Are you asking us to look at JP1?

MR WOLKIND: Yes, it is the business card.

JUDGE BYERS: It does not have a name on it except on the back.

MR WOLKIND: It does in the one I was shown, so I had better check I am looking at the same. You see the address, do you not, and you know from having visited that is his business?

A. I am sorry, I have not seen the card.

Q. I am sorry (handed)

JUDGE BUYERS: Mr Vaudin, can we make sure that by Monday we have a proper bundle for the witness.

MR VAUDIN: We do.

JUDGE BYERS: I do not know if it is tabulated in the same way, is it?

MR VAUDIN: It should be.

MR WOLKIND: Hanworth tyres with an address in Hanworth and I expect you now recognise that as the business of Jason Marriner?

A. That's the business address of Jason Marriner.

Q. There is a mobile number on that beginning 0802. The only phone numbers that you ever used to contact Jason were the 0777 one I mentioned plus one on this card?

A. I recall Mr Marriner changing his mobile a number of times and being directed to other mobiles he was on, I can't recall the details but that was my recollection.

Q. I can barely hear you. But I think you said change a number of times, cannot recollect details. Perhaps you would be kind enough to end the evidence for today by confirming you never ever contacted him on an 0961 number, did you?

A. I really can't recall.

Q. What do you think, does it ring any bells? Here he was telling you about the benefits of 0961 numbers, a prime example of Jason Marriner talking but not doing, you never phoned him on such a number ever, ever, did you?

A. I mean, I genuinely can't recall the specific details about his phone number, I am sorry.

Q. Because you would help us if you could, would you not?

JUDGE BYERS: Yes, very well, we will adjourn until Monday at ten o'clock.

Members of the jury, before we depart can I say to you it is doubly important now that you are involved in this trial fully and receiving evidence that you do not discuss the case with anyone else, particularly as it has attracted a certain amount of publicity. If a friend or relative gets to know you are on the jury that is involved in that trial, please if there is a discussion about it, walk away from it, because it is very important that these defendants are tried on your view of the evidence and not on somebody else's opinions gleaned through a snapshot of the trial. I am sure you understand the sense of that. So with that please try and put the matter out of your mind until Monday and come back fresh to it on Monday morning. Thank you for your attendance this week.

Mr MacIntyre, obviously you are free to go. Please do not discuss your evidence with anyone and be ready to start again at ten o'clock on Monday.

(The court adjourned until Monday morning at ten o'clock)

****

We hereby certify that the above is an accurate and complete record of the proceedings, or part thereof.

Signed SMITH BERNAL REPORTING LIMITED
File: 300101/JB

20

WHAT'S THE SCORE?

Document 2: The cross-examination of Donal MacIntyre (continued from Friday 24ᵗʰ November) 27ᵗʰ November 2000.

BLACKFRIARS CROWN COURT   No. T20000418

Pocock Street
London SE1 0BJ

Monday, 27ᵗʰ November 2000
Before:

HIS HONOUR JUDGE BYERS

R E G I N A

-v-

JASON MARRINER
ANDREW FRAIN

MR C VAUDIN and MR O GIBBONS appeared on behalf of the prosecution

MR M WOLKIND and MR A BUDWORTH appeared on behalf of the defendant MARRINER

MR M OLIVER and MR J WHITFIELD appeared on behalf of the defendant FRAIN

CROSS-EXAMINATION OF DONAL MACINTYRE con't

Computerised transcript of Smith Bernal Reporting Ltd (Official Shorthand Writers to the Court)

Monday, 27th November 2000

JUDGE BYERS: Mr MacIntyre, as normal I remind you that you are still bound by the oath that you took on Thursday.

Cross-examination by Mr Wolkind con't

MR WOLKIND: On what date did you acquire your tattoo?

A. I am not too sure of the exact date but I, erm, can't recall the exact date, I think it was some time in November or maybe — yes, early November.

Q. What date did Jason Marriner acquire his?

A. I am not too sure.

Q. Yours was part of your disguise as a keen Chelsea supporter?

A. Yes, it was

Q. You had learnt your history of the Chelsea Football Club so that you would be able to discuss it with people on equal terms?

A. Yes, I did.

Q. Tell us, please, about the occasions when your knowledge was laughed at by London Cabbies?

A. Well, there is some occasions when I would be using taxis, black cabs, and I would discuss football with them and they would ask me about a notable Chelsea player from the past and I would have known nothing about them, so it was sometimes useful because at that stage I was not knowing and at that stage I actually had not met Jason, it would be useful to be able to have a discussion about football with people who did not know why I should have an interest in Chelsea Football Club.

Q. You were testing how your knowledge was progressing?

A. Yes, I was.

Q. All I wanted was one example, because I have read within your book about how you were laughed at by London Cabbies and presuming it was not just a little flourish by you, I was just curious about an example of that please. What blunder did you make?

A. I can't recall this specific blunder but there were a couple of them.

Q. How many cabbies laughed at your blunders?

A. I mean, I can't recall, sorry.

Q. It would not be the worst thing in the world, would it, to just look at this jury and tell us that is an example, the rhetorical flourish, the little story you made up for the book because it sounded such fun you were laughed at by London Cabbies. But it is not really true, is it?

A. Erm, it is true.

Q. Tell us, please, just think back to the occasion when someone laughed at your blunder, what had you got wrong?

A. I can't recall but I think it was about the — it happened a couple of times, you know, about key incidents regarding famous Chelsea players of the past that somebody who was a Chelsea supporter really should know a little better about.

Q. What do you mean by key incident, the sending off, a missed penalty, tell us what sort of incident it was?

A. I actually can't recall it.

Q. Was it something on the pitch or some disgraceful conduct by a football player off the pitch, scandal, what sort of thing?

A. I am sorry, I just can't recall.

Q. Give us a little backup so that we understand you are telling us the truth rather than mucking something up in dock? On the field or off the field, that would narrow it down a bit?

A. Your Honour, I can't recall.

Q. A glorious hat-trick or a disgraceful sending off, what sort of thing was it that they laughed at when you flunked it?

A. I can't recall.

Q. Tell me this, as you were going to join the company of the keen Chelsea supporters, how did you assess the dangers, how serious did you think were the dangers facing you?

A. Well, the headhunters as a group of hooligans have very close associations with groups like Combat 18 and the National Front and I think Jason counts as a friend the head of the Combat 18, so obviously the headhunters have been responsible for some acts of violence as have Combat 18, so clearly we thought that was a very dangerous situation.

Q. You must not work backwards, but you did not have any knowledge of Jason apparently knowing someone connected with Combat 18 before you set out, did you? I mean you do not want to work backwards and mislead us for anything that happened later. So I will remind you of the question: as you set out to learn about Chelsea and as you were about to join the keen Chelsea supporters, how did you then assess the dangers, do not work backwards, please?

A. The research — before we do a programme like this we need to do a significant amount of research. That research was done by a Mr Clothier and that research and intelligence led us to believe that Mr Marriner had been involved in the attacks on that — or had been associated with groups like Combat 18 and the National Front before.

Q. In any event you probably noticed the question was the degree of danger, not how you came to the conclusion that there was danger, what was the degree of danger that you thought you faced?

A. The degree of danger obviously was related to the threat of exposure and the threat of exposure was related to either mistakes I would make in conversation or too many questions or perhaps even wearing equipment or even if a wire had dropped out, for instance. So at every stage when we wore equipment, in the company of these hooligans then that would represent a danger.

Q. I suppose that might just be a misunderstanding between us, Mr MacIntyre, but allow me to try again. You described the frequency of danger, would you be kind enough please to tell me the degree of danger you thought you faced; if things went wrong what do you think could have happened to you at worst?

A. We obviously had discussed this but I often did not really want to think too hard about it, but quite clearly if I had been in the company of Mr Marriner or Mr Frain and they had become aware that I was who I was , a BBC journalist, then I thought it could have been the most dangerous of circumstances. Including the — and quite explicitly I had thought on the Leicester journey that when I was turning on and off the key fob to turn on the camera, I was scared, I was terrified with some of the stories I had heard and I was very, very nervous.

Q. What could happen to you, you may want to tell me now I have been asking you for a little while. What could happen to you at worst?

A. Well, at worst I could have been stabbed or slashed, whatever the medical consequence of that could have been.

Q. You are not a person who easily exaggerates, are you?

A. I don't think so.

Q. So when I read at page 109 of your book: "We have to be so careful, a misplaced word could have us killed." Do you think that is an exaggeration?

A. I think stabbed and slashed represented to me a risk of being killed and absolutely was the case and specifically on that journey on the way to Leicester that had crossed my mind.

Q. But you see the context — do you still have a copy of the book available for you?

A. I do not have it but I am quite happy to answer without it.

Q. There is one here. (handed) Here is your commentary for the readers: "We have to be so careful a misplaced word could have us killed." That is no exaggeration?

A. I utterly stand by those remarks.

Q. Of course. There is no question, for example, you dramatising your descriptions of events for your own purposes?

A. Absolutely not.

Q. Better TV, better book, better evidence, is that the technique?

A. I stand by the threat that was posed by working undercover. Some moments were obviously more dangerous than others, some moments, some events were controlled or you had more colleagues around you or you were in the company of Mr Atkinson, or you felt your cover was very strong and secure, but clearly on the road to Leicester when we had two new occupants in the car, certainly I stand by those words 100 per cent.

Q. Leicester is an occasion when there is covert recording in the cars as we all know.

A. Yes, sir.

Q. But there are also other camera crews accompanying you or nearby?

A. Yes, there is.

Q. Not of course that you would be interested in filming violence, that was not the purpose of your TV programme, was it, but you had extra camera crews available?

A. We had extra camera crews available to film the car and other crowd shots and the events as they unfolded. But the primary purpose of the programme I think was demonstrated by the car journey was to show how football violence is organised between rival groups of football fans.

Q. One of your ploys to make Jason interested in you was to offer him legitimate work, was it not?

A. Yes.

Q. So that he being in the tyre business there came a time when you and Paul Atkinson told him about a possibility of 40 vans in one of your businesses needing tyres and could he help you.

A. I thought the figure was 20 vans but in any case we suggested that there was a possible tyre deal in the offering. That is absolutely the case.

Q. Substantial legitimate work?

A. Yes, that's the case.

Q. Tell us, please, about the details of the substantial illegitimate work you offered him. How much per drive for carrying your drugs was he going to get?

A. Well, sometime in March we had, erm —

Q. Can you give me a figure before the story please, how much per drive?

A. Sure, if I can just explain the context?

Q. No, can I have the figure then explain it, otherwise I would forget my questions the way you answer them.

A. Fine. We said to Jason that there was a possible £50,000 available for him to do a drive for drugs. This offer came when he was quite keen — Jason was keen to work with us. He was not keen to involve himself in class 'A's', drugs like cocaine, but said he would be prepared to drive on a cannabis run, a run that would obviously not take place. The first suggestion of this came some time after the January march and the Leicester journey, that came up in March 1999.

Q. Mr MacIntyre, I am keen that you do your best to give a straight answer to this, please, as I know you will. You posed as drug dealers, tell the jury, please, was it you who first raised the possibility with Jason of his working with you or was it him that approached you with the idea? A straight answer please.

A. I think it was, we had — I am not quite too sure whether it was involving a situation where Jason was keen to involve himself closely to us and we were keen to facilitate that, and to maintain contact with him in the New Year period beyond our main evidential gathering moments, and so we suggested that he would be a driver and he was prepared to do that.

Q. We suggested he would be a driver. Had he asked to work for you before your suggestion?

A. He had not explicitly asked to work for us.

Q. You attended the Bloody Sunday march in your role as the undercover reporter?

A. Yes, that's right.

Q. With your background you are trained to be an investigative journalist, is that right?

A. Yes.

Q. When did you discover that Red Action were a far right political extremist group?

A. I had not heard and do not know very much about Red Action to be frank. I presumed that in relation to Jason there was a far right group but we were aware in any case that Combat 18 and the National Front were going to be there as they always were.

Q. Are you a good and clever investigative journalist? I was just wondering if there was anything in the name Red Action that gave you a hint of what sort of politics they might follow? It is not the word Action, try Red?

A. I fully accept that I am not aware significantly of details and have not discussed or found out much about Red Action.

Q. Did you discover anything at all or are you willing to say the first thing that comes into your head?

A. I mean the research regarding those specific details were left to Philip Clothier.

Q. Did he tell you, Philip Clothier, a witness in this case, that Red Action were a far right group?

A. I can't recall that conversation. I don't think he did.

Q. On which tape can we hear the discussion or the information from Jason that he was going to attack the march?

A. The tape where it seemed to me where he is specifically — his intent to me was clear, is when I said to him: is this Fenian bottle you have in your hand is it a bottle of Balllygowan water?" And he says, "I do not give a fuck, that is ammunition mate," or words to that effect. That to me gave me a clear indication of that. And that recorded in the Penton Street pub before the attack was launched from that pub.

Q. Is that it? Is it the bottle conversation that is your understanding he was going to attack the march?

A. No, we had other information. It was quite clear at his attempts to evade the police. It was quite clear that the conversations in the pub, and it was quite clear that an attack was imminent, and of course the attack took place.

Q. We will discuss whether it was an attack in a moment please, but have a look at a statement dated 5th May 2000 and for me it is page 15 at the bottom, continuation sheet 9. It is when you are in the Tom Crib. We have the same numbering, Mr MacIntyre, 9 at the top, 15 at the bottom. Can you find a conversation about the bottle? It is the second complete paragraph on that page. Can you just se it? Then move on to the next paragraph. "We remained in the Tom Crib for about an hour. During conversation Paul asked Jason Marriner about what the plan of action was. "You have told us about a plan to attack, have you not?

A. Yes.

JUDGE BYERS: It may be as Mr MacIntrye has identified that as the tape from which he assumed there was going to be an attack, that the whole of that quote should be read out.

MR WOLKIND: I have not finished at all.

JUDGE BYERS: No, I understand. The jury should have the whole quote.

MR WOLKIND: They will because I have not finished. "He said that there was a Combat 18 spotter near to the official National Front demonstration." The he there being Jason, I presume?

A. Yes.

Q. — just trying to get it into context. "When the Republican march passed by he was going to call — that being the spotter — and then he would leave the pub and attack the march." Now that is the part of the statement that claims Jason told you of plans to attack the march, is it not?

A. Yes. I mean I took it, it was quite clear that there was an attempt to disrupt the march and attack the march. For me the line which Jason gave to me about that ammunition, "I do not give a fuck as long as it hits one of those cunts" that defines to me an aggressive stance and an attempt that an attack was imminent. So I was quite satisfied that that was his intent.

Q. See if we can separate the bottle from the plans for the attack and then I will ask you again on which tape we can see and hear that part of your witness statement on the plans for the attack, so the bottle first please. You made a witty comment about, "What is this Fenian water mate." Did you realise that you had caught him and embarrassed him drinking Irish water and that he gave in turn a witty response. Did you realise that?

A. That wasn't my view.

Q. Tell the jury, please, did you see him leave the pub with a bottle?

A. I can't recall Mr Marriner specifically leaving with a bottle. He may have done, I can't testify to that.

Q. Of course he may have done but you do not want to suggest that, do you?
You want to say in answer to the question: did you see, you want to say: Mr
Wolkind, no I did not. I know that is what you want to say. Have you seen on
any of the films of the Bloody Sunday march taken by the police or whoever Mr
Marriner with a bottle?

A. I have not.

Q. Thank you. Did you spot the difference or do you realise it now, the
difference between doing and talking?

A. Well, my view is that the attack took place and that was the intent on
behalf of Mr Marriner with that specific line, and that's my view that the attack
happened, so saying and doing in that case were an equal measure demonstrated.

Q. Equal measure. Well let us test that please. Saying a bottle was ammunition is one thing, using a bottle as ammunition is another, were they present in
equal measure on that day? Did he both say it and use it?

A. My view is that it was quite clear from his line that an attack was going to
take place, premeditated, and I was there and witnessed the attack take place.

Q. No, no, the bottle. Did he say it and use it equally?

A. I can't say whether Mr Marriner used the bottle or not.

Q. You probably can tell us, as he did not volunteer to you the bottle was
some ammunition until you had made your comment, "What's this Fenian
water mate"?

A. That's true. I asked him what he was doing with a bottle of Ballygowan
water.

Q. Just to test your fairness, Mr MacIntyre, can you even conceive of the
possibility that you caught him and embarrassed him and he came back with a
quick witted response. Can you conceive it?

A. That is for Mr Marriner to say.

Q. No, no can you conceive? Only you can say whether it ranges a possibility in your fairness?

A. It is certainly a range of possibility. It wasn't my view, that is all I can say.

Q. Were you remained in the Tom Crib for over an hour, so an hour passes
after the bottle, does it not, it seems?

A. I think he made the conversation some five or ten minutes in, but it was
approximately an hour.

Q. "During conversation Paul asked Jason Marriner what the plan of action was. He said there was a Combat 18 spotter near to the official National Front demonstration. When the Republican march passes by he was going to call them we would leave the pub and attack the march." On which tape please can we now hear and see that conversation?

A. That conversation took place after I had gone into the toilet in the Penton Street pub to flush away my microphone because to be stopped or caught while we were running with a microphone dangling or actually falling off would have revealed the nature of our investigation, so I had to flush the toilet. When we came back out and Mr Atkinson had that conversation and sometime shortly afterwards we all left the pub.

Q. Now I am completely lost. I asked you about tapes and you have told me about microphones and then you appeared to say when you came back out you understand he had that conversation. What do you mean?

A. Mr Atkinson told me of the conversation.

Q. You mean you did not hear it?

A. No.

MR WOLKIND: It is in a witness statement saying you saw it and heard it. What are you doing?

JUDGE BYERS: No, that is not what the witness statement says, Mr Wolkind. It says "During the conversation Paul asked Jason Marriner what the plan of action was." It may be taken either way, but it does not say anywhere: I heard him say it.

MR WOLKIND: Forgive me if I make the presumption, Mr MacIntyre, but when a person makes a statement of events that have happened they have actually witnessed it rather than been told about it. It is in a witness statement, is it not?

A. That Paul had the conversation?

Q. Mr MacIntyre, when you made a witness statement were you asked for what you had witnessed or were you asked to pass on prejudicial hearsay from what other people have told you?

JUDGE BYERS: No, that is a comment and when a witness makes a witness statement he cannot be expected to know the rules of evidence.

MR WOLKIND: No but the police officer who takes it may.

JUDGE BYERS: That may be the case, but you are putting to him his words. Now have a care, Mr Wolkind, because it is not fair to the witness.

MR WOLKIND: Your Honour, I do not accept that I have been unfair, but I will have a care, I promise. Mr MacIntyre, as I read the words: "he said there was a Combat 18 spotter," as I read those words in a signed statement by Donal MacIntyre as being true, does it give the impression that you know he said it because you were there to hear it?

A. I think the previous line might help the Court further.

Q. I am sorry?

A. It says, "during conversation Paul asked Jason Marriner what the plan of action was." After that conversation Mr Atkinson told me what took place in the conversation.

Q. Forgive me, Mr MacIntyre, how does anyone get a clue that you were not there to witness the conversation between two people? How do we get a clue as we read the statement?

A. I mean I am telling you now.

Q. No. You are keen to be fair, are you not?

A. Yes, I am.

Q. And so witness statements which are given in advance to the other side include a statement that during conversation he said certain things. How would we know that you were not there to witness it from reading the statement, how would we know?

A. But in the making of the statements I have only tried to be as helpful as I can, that's all.

Q. Helpful to who.

A. I am just trying to tell the truth as best I know and helpful to the Court.

Q. It is not very helpful. What stopped you saying, for example, "I was told when I came out of the toilet that there had been a conversation." Where is the clue that you did not witness that?

A. Well, I am just trying to be as helpful as I can.

Q. You see, suggestions have been made that I may not have been fair and you are keen to be fair as you have said, so we will test it together as to who is being fair. Let us read it together. "We remained in the Tom Crib pub for over an hour." That obviously means you. It is not something you were told after- wards, "Oh by the way Donal, do you know you remained in the Tom Crib." That obviously includes you, does it not?

A. Yes, it does.

Q. "During conversation Paul asked Jason...." How would anyone know who received this statement that it really means, "I was later told that during conversation," how would we know that?

A. Well, if anyone had asked me.

Q. I cannot hear you.

A. If I had been asked like I have been asked now, now you know and I am happy to help which way I can.

Q. So we have to wait until the opportunity arises. The defendant has to wait until Donal MacIntyre is ready to explain what the case against him is, is that the position?

A. I think, Mr Marriner, if he recalls the conversation that we had he would tell the Court.

Q. But it would appear, would it not, on the face of it, that you are a witness who is able to give evidence of what happened in that conversation. You are not, are you, because you were not there?

A. I am just trying to be as helpful as possible.

Q. Be helpful now and tell me if I am right. Are you a witness to that conversation?

A. I have already said that —

Q. Yes or no, please, are you a witness to that conversation?

A. No, I wasn't a witness to that conversation.

Q. Yes or no, if you can continue in that vein for the moment, is there any clue, on the face of the statement, that you are not a true witness to the conversation?

A. Well, if I had said in the statement I heard Jason say to me that would have been a clue. In fact, what I said during conversation Paul asked Jason Marriner what the plan of action was. He said — and I was reporting the conversation as Paul had told me. I am just trying to be as helpful as I can.

Q. Can I ask you please, what is this extra ploy today of adding on to every answer: I am just trying to be as helpful as I can. You are wholly bias against Marriner, are you not? What is this: I want to be as helpful as I can.

A. Well, I am trying to help the Court as I did I think last week.

Q. Have you ever spotted that your personal interests are in Mr Marriner being convicted?

A. I think that my view, if you want my view – -

Q. No, I do not want your view, I want you to answer the question. Have you ever spotted that your personal interests are in Jason Marriner being convicted?

A. It would be my view that it is in society's interest.

Q. No, I did not ask you anything of the sort. But why do you answer that when I have asked you about your interests? If you cannot agree with me or do not agree with me feel free to say so, why the commentary? Can you give an unbiased answer, please, concentrating on the question: have you spotted that your personal interests are in Jason Marriner being convicted?

A. It is irrelevant to me, personally, because my view, whether the view of this court, will be of Mr Marriner's organised football hooliganism. However, that is not my decision, that is the Court and the jury's.

Q. Because a conviction means that this jury are satisfied without doubt that he is involved in violence which is the whole theme of your TV programme, your interests run in parallel, do they not? Conviction vindicates your programme, had you not spotted that?

A. That very well may be the case.

Q. Thank you.

A. — however, it is for the Court to decide, not for me.

Q. That leads you to being wholly biased, does it not, in your evidence?

A. No, it does not.

Q. Tell us about views that Jason Marriner has expressed on violence to you rather than the ones you have been told about in hearsay? What views has he expressed to you of violence? Find some in his favour. Can you think of any?

A. There's some occasions where Mr Marriner suggested that he was getting too old for this game, football hooliganism, but he always seemed to caveat that with the break line, "my problem is that I am so passionate about it," or "there is no use trying it and valuing it unless you are with your mates," so hard Jason I think tried to escape from the world of football hooliganism it was just like a drug to him. That was my view. But there were a number of occasions where Jason did mention retreating from the world of football violence and hooliganism.

Q. Mr Fisher, please, can we have extract 16. Your Honour, this is 8th June 1999. We do not have a transcript.

JUDGE BYERS: Thank you. (video tape is played back)

MR WOLKIND: I can if you want to see if we can find the caveat. A caveat means a qualification, does it not, or an exception in this context. Because it appeared, did it not, as you listened carefully to that that Jason Marriner said, "Marching and football, it's all at an end for me. It's all over"?

A. That's the case. He said that on June 6th — your date — 1999 and at that

that was the moment where we were discussing his, you know, working with us as drug dealers and it was our view specifically on that — related to that, that part of his thinking along that was, part of it was that he would want to keep out of trouble with the law and but at the same time I do think that Jason sometimes struggled with the fact that he was getting old and he wanted to leave this game, absolutely, but he did not. I mean, after he had organised 150 hooligans to Leicester, he offered a little caveat and suggested that he was slightly getting too old for the game and then he said there was no value in it without your mates. So I can accept that Jason at sometimes struggled but he certainly did not leave that world behind, least of all not while we were with him and even if you accept the fact that he had left us at that time that was some time after we had gathered our evidence. My view was that he struggled and cannot leave that world behind because it is like a drug to him.

Q. You alone or you and Mr Atkinson perhaps have tried to think of an explanation before you have given evidence in this trial to write off things that Jason Marriner has said for which you have recorded on tape, have you not?

A. Absolutely not.

Q. You have come up with two particular theories. One we have heard for the first time today, struggle, Jason struggled, drug for Jason, another one which you premiered on Friday. Can I remind you what it was, Mr MacIntyre, in relation to the 3rd March meeting in the flat, you explained that Jason wanted to get out of football hooliganism so he would be available to work in drugs with you. Do you remember you said that in relation to 3rd March when we discussed it Friday and you repeated it here in relation to the car journey extract. It is a fabricated, fake, false fancy reason that you have thought up because you are embarrassed by what is recorded on tape. It exposes your whole theory and so you have fabricated an answer, have you not?

A. Absolutely not.

Q. The context I am going to remind you of when you first gave a debut to that explanation was 3rd March in the flat, Jason talking about you not being sucked into violence and the explanation you gave to the jury on Friday, "well that is because I was talking about keeping your nose clean in business and he wanted to show to me he would be clean for business, out of football and into drugs."

A. I think there is a general, certainly, a general message we are trying to give to Jason over in relation to our potential drug deal well into the New Year was that it would not be a good idea to get your hands dirty and therefore bring it on top for us, which would be a reasonable line that serious drug dealers would give to anybody who would come to work with them.

Q. Maybe you would know but on this case, Mr MacIntyre, you were saying, were you not, on Friday that Jason's warning to you and his lack of interest in violence was because he was interested in business and that you said was the explanation for his words on the March 3rd meeting.

A. I think it is, you know, like I said —

Q. No. Is that what you said before you add the commentary, so that I can get it right, is that what you were saying on Friday?

A. I said in the context of working with me as a fellow potential drug dealer he — I felt that part of his attempt to remove himself from the world of football violence was related to potential work with us. There is no doubt about it.

Q. The other part you had not yet thought up when you explained it on Friday?

A. No.

Q. What is the other part today, then?

A. No, my view hasn't changed at all in this.

Q. I know but you did not share it with us on Friday, so what is the other part that you share with us now today?

A. No, if I had been given the opportunity on Friday I would have been happy to share it then. Mr Marriner on several occasions even after Leicester —

Q. I am asking about March 3rd , please, the meeting in the flat?

A. — on several occasions had said that he was keen to leave this world behind and on several occasions he said to me, once he said, "I am trying to tell the lads," I thought trying to was a very interesting verb there. Another occasion is he says, "My problem is I am so passionate about it." It is quite clear at some stage and particularly into early to mid 1999, he was struggling but the problem is that Jason, the hooligan in Jason unfortunately rode rough shod over some of those attempts

Q. The reason why you did not tell us on Friday is that you did not get the chance, did you just say that?

A. Well, I felt that if the court, erm, dealt with it specific I would have been happy to detail it then, absolutely.

Q. You had the time to tell us one reason because it is from a two-part excuse, is it not? One part of the excuse you said, "if Jason said such words his evidence would be a struggle." The second part of the excuse is he wanted to demonstrate to you he would be clean for your drugs business.

A. I think it was, erm, a couple of issues involved there but —

Q. I did not ask you that, I was asking you about why we did not hear it on

Friday. Was it an invitation for you to repeat the commentary? I asked you why you did not say it on Friday.

A. I wasn't specifically asked it.

Q. Of course you were not we did not know what your excuse was, but once you had given one excuse what has stopped you telling the other, or had you not yet thought it up? Had you not yet thought it up on Friday?

A. I wasn't given an opportunity or I wasn't asked the question. I am sorry I can't tell.

Q. You have in advance of your evidence to this jury struggled to find a way to write off the words of Jason which are recorded on certain tapes. You came up with one excuse on Friday and you have doubled up today, that is the better position, is it not?

A. I think the definitive position is with Jason's own words: "there is no value in it without your mates."

Q. I want to know your position, Mr MacIntyre, I am discussing your position not his?

A. It is entirely coloured by both Jason's actions and his words.

Q. No, Mr MacIntyre, you are not really close to me. Your position in coming up with one excuse on Friday and adding one today is that you struggle to explain away words that have been recorded on tape which expose your whole case against Jason. That is the position, is it not, your position?

A. That's absolutely not the case.

Q. I am asking you again please about Bloody Sunday. Those words which turn out to be hearsay, what you were told afterwards that you never witnessed, those words about a plan to attack, do you realise that if they were said they might be the single distinguishing feature between the criminal offence of affray and a person's right to counter-demonstrate. Do you realise that, the importance of that?

A. I am not a lawyer.

Q. Let us take it together — of course not. There is a passage in your witness statement that we now discover together is hearsay, something that you are not a witness to at all but something you have been told about afterwards. You follow that much, do you not?

A. Yes, I do.

Q. Do you realise that if, for example, no-one was to take the bottle bits seriously, then Jason talking about his knowledge of plans to attack might be the single feature that distinguishes between a jury saying guilty of affray or a man's right simply to go and counter-demonstrate. You know its importance, do you not?

A. I absolutely take your word on that.

Q. Would you like to comment on how interesting it is that the single distin-guishing feature between someone being guilty of affray and just wishing to counter-demonstrate turns out to arrive in your witness statement with no hint that you were not a real witness of it. Is it not strange because you are not biased are you, Mr MacIntyre?

A. I did the statement and I am here in the court to help the Court, that is all I can say.

MR WOLKIND: I can hardly hear you, I am sorry.

JUDGE BYERS: You have given him three of your comments; you are not biased, are you?

MR WOLKIND: Yes. I could not hear him, the last thing, I was not complaining. I said I could not hear his last answer.

JUDGE BYERS: That is the one piece of evidence that distinguishes the one from the other and the third one that it was only, that there is no hint in there that it was not something he overheard and all he has said is I cannot help you.

MR WOLKIND: Yes, I could not hear him, that is all. I was not complaining about the answer. You dropped your voice so much I could not hear you. Did the policeman never tell you as he took the statement on any previous occasion that he was interested only in matters you witnessed, and that he was not there to waste his time and your hearsay? Did he never tell you that?

A. I only wrote the statement to help the Court. That's all I can say.

Q. But you ran up to the other marches, did you not?

A. We were in the group, middle to back of the group, that took across to Trafalgar Square, lingering around the back.

Q. You ended up on the front line?

A. We did end up on the front line.

Q. Did you commit the offence of affray?

A. No, I did not.

Q. But you, I suppose, feel secure in the knowledge, because you say so in your book at page 151, that you did not commit any offence by running up to the march?

A. Well our intent was not to attack, our intent was obviously to witness and that's why we are here.

Q. We are discussing why you were there, not why you are here now. You ran up but please tell the jury what Jason Marriner did when you let the pub which was different or worse from anything you did that you saw — because I know you would not want to tell us what anyone else saw?

A. Well Mr Marriner ran up to the front of the demonstration and was attempting to break through the demonstration.

Q. What did he physically do?

A. I wasn't exactly up at the front but I saw Mr Marriner race up to the front and try and attack the march.

Q. What do you mean try and attack, what did he physically do?

A. He was waving his hands and shaking and that's all.

Q. You said he was trying to break through, how do you break through by waving your hands?

A. Well he was running aggressively.

Q. And you were running what?

A. Well, in fact, I was trying to run as slowly as I could still remaining in the group because I was trying to maintain this passive member of the group without ever obviously trying to do as little as possible and trying to look after my fellow BBC journalists who were also in the group with me.

Q. You were not the very last one, were you, throughout as you ran?

A. I can't recall. There were some people behind us.

Q. Were you running passively, did you say?

A. No, I was trying to be as passive as possible as we jogged and we walked — we walked and then we (inaudible) up and in the front of the march ran at great pace.

Q. Imagine, please, that anyone on the other side perceived the people running as a threat, that you would have been part of that threat, would you not, by your mere presence, you would add to the numbers that they saw approaching them?

A. I think that's for them to comment but clearly anyone part of that group may have been considered a threat.

Q. Here is your chance, please, to tell the jury what Jason Marriner did to try and break through the lines as you claimed?

A. Well, that was my view and I wasn't at the front of the demonstration, so I couldn't exactly see what Jason was doing.

Q. Mr MacIntyre, just in case anyone might suggest that your view is a wholly biased one you keep just asserting rather than giving details, here is your chance, give us the details of what Jason Marriner physically did to try and break through? Do not just assert, give us the details.

A. I do not know what Mr Marriner did at the front of the march but I know that he ran up and his intention was to attack the march and to disrupt it; and I saw him run aggressively towards it.

Q. Well how from behind did you know he was running aggressively, rather than like you, running passively?

A. Well, if you are waving your hands and shouting obscenities then — and at some speed towards the march, when I — he had told me that he was intent upon, my view, attacking, then that added it up to me.

Q. When did he tell you that?

A. Well he said that he had — his intent was to use this bottle as ammunition.

Q. A bottle; so is there nothing other than a bottle that you have that his intention being expressed to you that he was going to attack the march, just the bottle?

A. No, the bottle — his actions — the bottle clarified it for me. Also the conversation he had with Mr Atkinson.

Q. You did not witness that, did you?

A. Which I did not witness.

Q. What you did tell us on Friday is that in the pub there was a fifteen minute conversation, wide ranging, with Jason Marriner. Would you like to tell us a single sentence from that conversation which shows his intention to attack the march, one sentence please?

A. The bottle conversation which – -

Q. Apart from the bottle, please?

A. Well for me the bottle conversation was very indicative. More than that Mr Marriner and his evasive tactics avoiding the police and, erm, indicated to me that there was some reason to avoid the police. There were other counter-demonstrations at the march legitimately which were policed and were — but I presume that if a legitimate counter-demonstration would have taken place there would have been no need to coalesce and hide in a bar before launching an attack.

Q. I was looking for a single sentence within the wide ranging 15 minute conversation you would like to share with us that show Jason's intention to attack the march, not the bottle please.

A. Well that for me was the defining moment.

Q. "I noticed Marriner was drinking a bottle of Ballygowan Irish mineral water. On seeing this I said to Marriner, 'What's this Fenian water mate?' 'I do not give a fuck, that's ammunition mate. A bottle is a bottle to me I do not give a fuck as long as it hits one of those cunts'." Mortifying moments?

A. That for me suggested Mr Marriner was intent upon attacking the march. These other comments to me after the day clarified —

Q. No, the 15 minute conversation, please. Share with us another sentence, what were you talking about, it was wide ranging?

A. I can't recall specifically the nature of the conversation.

Q. Surely you were interested and on your evidence, surely, he was excited about his plans to attack the march?

A. Specifically I can't recall, but the defining line for me was the ammunition line.

Q. So if we leave aside your witty comment and his witty reply, you have nothing to offer us from a 15 minute conversation to show his intentions to attack the march?

A. Within those 15 minutes I can't recall anything else of significance.

Q. Then we move on from the 15 minutes to your evidence that you did not see him ever with a bottle — going to take it chronologically — we move on from that, do we not? Then we move on to Mr MacIntyre running passively but Mr Marriner running aggressively, because that is a serious piece of evidence from you.

A. Well I wasn't waving my hands about and shouting obscenities.

Q. But what was he shouting, individually, Jason's voice, if you could tell from behind in the crowd, you tell us what he was shouting, please?

A. I think they were all, erm —

Q. No, Jason I said.

A. They were shouting aggressively at the march. They were calling –

Q. I am sorry to interrupt, I must keep miss-hearing you, you keep saying they, I was asking you about Jason, please. What was he shouting?

A. Erm, Fenian bastards.

Q. You recognised his voice, did you, from behind?

A. Jason has a distinctive voice. There were a number of things that I had heard Jason shout.

Q. Go on then list them?

A. I can't recall specifically but there was, erm, the whole gang were shouting and I could hear Jason at one stage shout Fenian bastards.

Q. Do not drift over to the whole gang again please. But where within any of your witness statements, your many statements, do I find your list of things that Jason shouted?

A. I am just saying that is a recollection one word Jason used.

Q. Sorry, perhaps I was not clear, where in your witness statements do I find your list of things that Jason shouted at the march?

A. Well —

Q. You want to turn over the page, will you not, to catch up with the chronology. Just tell me where I find it?

A. Well I can't recall whether it is there or not.

Q. Have a look and you can tell us and help us.

A. It doesn't change the fact that that is what I heard.

Q. No, but you are keen to help us, you have told us that many times before, so look and help, see if you can find it?

A. Well if it is not there it does not mean –

Q. I do not know, look and help, catch up with the chronology from when you left the bar. You will find that on page 16 at the bottom and 10 at the top, and I know you will limit yourself to Jason. Is there anything there about how Jason moved to the other side, whether he ran aggressively, is there anything there?

A. I mean, I am just saying what I heard.

Q. I know. But you do not mind me asking you about the statement, do you?

A. Not at all.

Q. Thank you very much. So can you tell us again, please, or tell us for the first time is there anything there about Jason running aggressively; and then I know you will want to look for your list of words that Jason shouted in your witness statement, see if you can find it?

A. Well it says, "The marchers were at the top of Whitehall and it is where persons from the group who had been in the Tom Crib shouting abuse and lunging towards some of the marchers."

Q. Because your witness statement is all about and, the case, is all about Jason Marriner and Andrew Frain. Is it not?

A. It is really to do with the occurrence of the march, absolutely.

Q. So with that as background, that the case and the investigation is about Jason Marriner and Andrew Frain, did you take the opportunity to say amongst those marchers who was shouting abuse and lunging, I saw Jason Marriner, do you say it there?

A. I do not say it therein the statement.

Q. Is it not strange, Mr MacIntyre, as you tell us now that you saw Jason running aggressively and shouting abuse, is it not strange that you do not say it to the police? Where is it? Where is it in the statement?

A. Well I had done a number of statements for the police.

Q. Take your time, look through all of them and tell us where it is?

A. — and it is a comprehensive statement over the year or so, interactions, more than a year with Mr Marriner and that's what I recall from the day one of the phrases that he used.

Q. Mr MacIntyre, but why have you just told us that you made a number of statements, what has that got to do with anything, what is your point?

A. That there are details left out, I am happy to fill in the blanks as best as I know them right now, absolutely.

MR WOLKIND: You are very happy to fill in the blanks in the case that you bring against Mr Marriner, are you not?

MR VAUDIN: I am sorry. Your Honour, really I think this is a bit much. He brings no case against anyone. He is a witness for the Crown, I remind my learned friend.

MR WOLKIND: You understood why I have said that, did you not, because you are totally biased and your interests run parallel to this prosecution. I have not forgotten the police themselves bringing the case, but your interests run parallel and you are biased, are you not?

A. No. Your Honour, can I get a glass of water?

JUDGE BYERS: Yes, of course.

MR WOLKIND: Can we see where we have reached on this point. In this witness statement where you found time to recite a conversation you never witnessed, did you find time to mention that you saw Jason Marriner running aggressively and shouting abuse? It is not there, is it?

A. Well I've mentioned it in the context of the group of which Jason was a part, but specifically not. But I am happy to clear up any matters if I can, like now, obviously.

Q. Mr MacIntyre, that is kind of you, but that is not the point. The point I am asking you is how did you come to miss out the fact that you specifically saw Jason Marriner running and you specifically recognised his voice? How did you come to leave it out of your statement?

A. I can't recall the circumstances but as I say I am happy to clear up any details now.

Q. Would you be kind enough to leave out your repeated claim that you are happy to assist us and instead concentrate on my question. You made a long statement on this occasion, did you not, it goes to 15 pages?

A. Yes, I did.

Q. You found time to recite a conversation to which you were not even a witness but came from something you were told by another person?

A. I think that statement involves a number of evidential areas and including the Chelsea to Leicester car journey.

Q. One area specifically includes your awareness that persons from the group were shouting abuse and lunging towards some of the marchers, yes? In the context of an investigation into Jason Marriner, do you think you could have found time to say, "I saw Jason was amongst them and I heard his voice saying Fenian bastards and other things"?

A. Well, I am obviously happy to say I heard that now.

Q. You are delighted to make it up now, are you not, as you are doing, not just happy, you are delighted to make up anything that will hurt Jason Marriner in front of the jury? Would you like to add anything else that is not in the statement that he did that day? Perhaps you saw him with a bottle. Did he throw a bottle at the other marchers?

A. I can't testify to that.

MR WOLKIND: Would you be happy to make it up now?

JUDGE BYERS: That is not a question.

MR WOLKIND: Extract 17 please. Your Honour, this is the one I have mentioned many times. It is early March. It lasts perhaps 15 minutes. There are transcripts, so it is the entire 3rd March and we are keen the jury see it all.

JUDGE BYERS: Yes, very well.

MR WOLKIND: Can I hand out copies of these transcripts. There are 6.

JUDGE BYERS: Have you seen these transcripts, Mr Vaudin?

MR VAUDIN: We were given one copy this morning. I am not sure what was being put to this witness a moment ago about hearing shouts and so on but, of course, my learned friend did not have a copy of the exhibits in front of him which might have assisted him particularly MIC1, MIC2 and MIC8.

MR WOLKIND: I am going to stop my learned friend.

JUDGE BYERS: No, I have to point, Mr Wolkind.

MR WOLKIND: I put here shouts for photographs. He can make a comment when it is his turn.

JUDGE BYERS: Mr Vaudin, the point is well made. If he is being asked about comments made by people vocally then photographs will not necessarily help. I shall be directing the jury in due course as to the essence of affray and the fact that it involves numbers.

MR VAUDIN: Yes. Your Honour, I was simply making a point those are the stills of the film if we see it. I do not think it is fair to the witness.

JUDGE BYERS: Yes, I understand that, but the time for re-examination comes later (video is played back) Have we actually reached the transcript on the tape yet?

MR WOLKIND: 'W' means woman in this and there is some early talk and I think we have just reached that line. Let us see together if we can sum up what was happening there at least in parts. That conversation featured your increasingly desperate attempts to get Jason Marriner to talk in favour of football violence, did it not?

A. No, it did not. There was the conversation — we had finished pretty much all our interactions with Mr Marriner at that stage and wanted to see if he could more clearly and concisely in a stable, sound and picture environment and that was the purpose of that last meeting with Mr Marriner.

Q. Yes, you have told me your purpose. I was discussing what happened in the event. So leaving aside Donal MacIntyre's wish for his TV programme and discussing what happened in the event, it featured your increasingly desperate attempts to get Marriner to talk in favour of football violence, did it not?

A. No.

Q. It did not feature any struggle by Jason Marriner as to whether he is for or against violence, did it?

A. There was no desperate attempts we were just keen to engage Jason on subjects which he had talked to us in the past.

Q. I promise I will not be shy to ask you if I want to know about desperate attempts. Did it feature any struggle by Jason Marriner as to his views on football violence?

A. There were a number of moments where Jason had said that he was going to leave this world behind.

Q. No, the struggle, not one side being against it, the struggle, you know, things in favour as well as things against, one of the two excuses you have offered to us today as I described them?

A. Well, Jason himself had told me but not specifically in this flat.

Q. No, no, this occasion, I am asking you whether it featured the struggle?

A. Well, I mean the previous answer I had given which you are referring referred to a number of occasions that Jason had said that he is so passionate about it he is trying to — it is a drug. "There is no value in it without your mates," which is a line he used in the Leicester pub. So my view is formed over a number of meetings.

Q. Does this occasion feature him as being against violence, because he is apparently interested in going into your drugs business?

A. I think it was a factor in his decision about being, erm, — trying to pull back from football hooliganism, obviously.

Q. We will reach the passage soon that you may be referring to, but let us just look at this first, please. Page 1, nothing of significance I wish to ask you about. Page 2, is the first mention by anyone of violence of football hooliganism form you. About 8 lines down he said, "The Polish were really up for it." Is that the introduction of violence coming from Mr MacIntyre?

A. Yes. That was related to a meeting we had had in a pub in Manchester with Mr Marriner and a couple of hooligans from the north region who Jason was introducing to each other and so that was a back ref.... — I was referring to that conversation.

Q. I was asking you if that was the introduction of that subject into this conversation?

A. Yes, it is. And that conversation had taken place not too in the distant past.

Q. That is right. Answer first and your commentary afterwards might be a working arrangement between us. Page 3, is this you, about a third of the way down, telling some story you have made up about trouble with a Millwall geezer and I have corrected the words there, I now read it out. "I saw some Millwall geezer the other day trying to give it a large one." You probably heard that yourself, did you not?

A. This was what Jason had told me previously in a car journey from Manchester. Sam wasn't very good about a Millwall altercation which he was involved in and I was attempting to get the story again, except this time in a stable sound environment.

Q. You achieve that, because you go on explaining it was just down in Chiswick, one of the pubs in Stroud Green, it should be. You tell the story of your bravery in the face of this Millwall hooligan, do you not, and he responds with the 16 years old story or whatever it would be by then of the march on Millwall's old ground.

A. Yes, that's correct.

Q. Then going over to your boasting on Page 4 where, "I would have had this bloke except for the fact that he" — I do not know how your boast would have ended. But that is what you say at the top. Then we come to his advice: "the thing is, Macca, I am not being funny, blah blah, do not get yourself sucked in. Do not even get yourself because you've only got to get nicked. I just let people go. Yeah, yeah, yeah. Love you mate." So in other words, you are the one who is boasting you would have got stuck in for the purpose of your story and he is saying let people go on and just effectively ignore them. Have I summed that up fairly?

A. No, that is Mr Marriner saying at that point, and I feel that's in reference to the, "I am coming, drug deal," where it would have been appropriate for him to keep his powder dry.

Q. Because in the very next sentence from you, "If you are doing business...." It is about business there, is it not, that means the drugs business?

A. Yes, it does.

Q. "If you are doing business today you have got to keep your nose clean." That is your point about doing the drugs business, not getting caught?

A. Yes.

Q. Did you realise how brilliant it was of Mr Marriner to know in advance that you would be introducing in your next comment the drugs business?

A. The nature of that entire meeting was related to the potential drugs deal.

Q. See if you are able to answer this clearly, please. By the time Mr Marriner advised you not get yourself sucked in, effectively let people do what they want but do not get involved in violence, by that time is the drugs business mentioned anywhere in this transcript?

A. It is not mentioned in this transcript up to this point but the whole reason for the meeting was to arrange and make arrangements about a prospective drugs deal. That is why we were there.

Q. Is there any hint in his words, "The thing is, Macca, I am not being funny etc...."that he is referring to the drugs business, from the words themselves, not your theory?

A. No. I mean, the only reason why we met Jason that day was to specifically discuss the arrangements related to the dugs deal. That predicated the meeting, that's why we were getting together, so the whole conversation is in that context.

Q. So what it means then is because the reason for getting together was the drugs business that would influence anything Marriner said that day, is that your theory?

A. Well I certainly think it would go some way to influencing his behaviour that day, that's my view.

Q. Because your view is totally biased against him and you are looking for an excuse to write off his views on football violence, are you not?

A. No, I mean, I've said the reason why we got together that day was to discuss a drug deal. I have already said that I felt that Jason on a number of occasions offered himself some relief and to offer then to put a break on that by saying, "There is no value in doing it without your mates." He is so passionate about it and it was a drug to him, and I think in this case this whole meeting was surrounding a potential and lucrative drug deal and this was in March or June, I am not quite too sure on the date here, and it is some time after the primary evidence material which we had gathered.

Q. Mr MacIntyre, why do you mention it is after the date of the primary evidence you have gathered when it would hardly be something that could influence Mr Marriner, why do you mention that?

A. Well, because we had — the key thing we were interested in was in witnessing people organise football violence. We had witnessed that and we wanted to create an environment where Jason would talk freely about his past events.

Q. Yes, but you are repeatedly telling us about how you want to construct your television programme. If I bring you back to the discussion on Mr Marriner being on trial here, it does not matter that you had gathered in your evidence when we consider how Marriner responded, does it, that is your business, that is your TV programme?

A. We took a view and we made a television programme on the basis of all the evidence we had gathered.

Q. Reading on in your response, "But if you are doing business you know you have got to keep your nose clean, but you know, frankly, my plan is actually at the end of the day, you know, unless, you know, you are being smart/naughty, be simply smart. Once I am over through, over June, bits of July, no problems, I couldn't care." Then you go on, you do not pause there to see whether he wants to talk about the drugs business, do you?

A. We were waiting for Mr Atkinson and another colleague who was pretending to be Mr Atkinson's brother to arrive to discuss the drugs deal and the proposition was that if Mr Atkinson's brother liked Mr Marriner then the deal would –

Q. I do not want to hear about the proposition, tell it in re-examination if you are asked a question about it. Do you remember what I asked you?

A. Could you repeat the question?

Q. I am happy to because I know you will concentrate on it. You did not pause there after you had brought up the subject of business to see if he responded but you go on to violence. "I had to go away. They put me away or locked me away for affray. I couldn't care less, you know, I couldn't, you know." You have brought it back to violence, have you not?

A. That's the question, yes.

Q. He says, "Now what's the value in that? I mean an old pal of mine have just been put away for affray, got 3 and a half years." Now just pause there, please. A number of times you have said to this jury that when he said, "What's the value in that" he talks about "What's the value without your mates."

A. Well, I am referring to a recorded statement Mr Marriner said in the Leicester pub.

Q. I see, you are not sticking to this subject?

A. No. I mean I did say earlier that the two reasons which I had given related to the drugs deal and also related to him trying to get away but not being able to escape from the hooligan within him, but one of the reasons he gave himself was that there was no value in it without your mates, which I suppose gave reason to the other people in the car.

Q. Can we spot that reason here, in this sentence? I was not sure if that was meant to be an example of that reason because we are discussing 3rd March, "What's the value in that? An old pal of mine have just been put away for affray, got 3 and a half years." Can we spot your second part of what I call the excuse there?

A. No. I mean, my views on that are formed from several meetings with Mr Marriner.

Q. Thank you. Affray, he is being charged. You say, "Well the thing is once they put it with football" — you are obsessed with football violence, are you not, for the purpose of this meeting?

A. Well, I was doing a programme about the organisation of football violence and Mr Marriner's football hooliganism, so obviously I was keen to continue to bring him round to football and football violence.

Q. The football hooligan as you described him, I politely informed you it was not football it was a pub. He carries on, "No value in that," and then he talks about the attitudes of people who are in prison saying, "Switch off, be happy and, like, they have got a few quid to come out to." Do you then take him back to specific violence again by brining up Copenhagen?

A. Yes, I do.

Q. "I loved Copenhagen" you boasted "surrounded by 40 of them, you know what I mean. Rolled over, gave my best, came off as well as anybody came out." So you are boasting how you did. He accepts defeat with his comment, "I came off second best." Do you see that?

A. Yes, I do.

Q. Then going over the page, please, as we get to the end of Copenhagen I know you will be able to answer this very directly. Does he mention anywhere going back and getting revenge on any of the people who had beaten him up?

A. He doesn't here but he did when we travelled home from Copenhagen and he said it to me explicitly.

Q. "Then at the end of the day, you know" — this is a third of the way down on Page 5 — "I am not going to pretend I am a hero but I have never been a bully, never really pushed people when they are down and all that, you know."

A. Yes, I can read that.

Q. Then there is you advancing the justification for a fight. "If you are up for a fight, you are up for a fight and so on." Marriner: "The older I have got the more I am not interested in football violence. The days are over. The 80s have gone. It is time to get on in life, you know what I mean. It is fucking — they have gone, you have had your good days." Can you hear a distinction between the 80s and the late 90s when you were actually talking to him?

A. Well, in 1998 he told me himself that he had been involved in, erm —

Q. I am sorry, I asked you if you could hear then in that sentence, what are you talking about?

A. Well, I am putting it in context.

Q. Forgive me. I am asking you in that sentence if you can hear the distinction and you are telling me about something else. Please answer whether you can hear the distinction in his reply? Mr MacIntyre, if you want me to pause after every question so that you can say something new which is bad about Mr

Marriner I will do it. But the question is this, as you read his answer: "The older I have got the more I am not interested in football violence. The days are over here. The 80s have gone. It is time to get on in life, you know what I mean, it is fucking dead gone. You have had your good days." Can you spot there a distinction for Jason Marriner between the past and the present?

A. Yes, if I could put it in context. Mr Marriner is still discussing about the 80s having been gone and is trying to get on with life, and if I had accepted that at face value, then I wouldn't be giving myself credit for hearing what he said to me himself about being involved in an incident some months before we even started this football investigation where he said, "If I had not been tooled up I would have been nicked along with my other pals who were later convicted for the offence." So that's the context in which we viewed this – –

Q. Say it again. "If I had not been tooled up." Have you got confused or did I miss-hear? I am sorry, say it again?

A. "If I had not been tooled up" i.e. if he had been tooled up or my interpretation was that he would have been arrested for that offence along with everybody else who were there. So that is the context of which I viewed Mr Marriner's statement at that time about the 80s suddenly been gone in the context of him talking to me about the 90s, in fact early 1998.

Q. I know you do not want to mislead and this time perhaps by accident but can we clear it up please. Perhaps the words in your version would have been, "If I had been tooled up I would have been nicked."

A. Yes, if he had been tooled up.

Q. Yes, all right. You had it the other way round before but on this occasion perhaps you were misleading by accident. Then your next long passage here. "It's good crack remembering though all the same, it's great." Crack does mean just sort of enjoyment, does it not?

A. Yes, it does.

Q. The pleasure in company as you go on to say, "I love hearing those stories." Did you realise that you to Mr Marriner, who knows, to anyone else, had the pleasure of your company came over as a sort of idiot groupie who enjoyed hearing stories?

A. I mean that's where — I think I came across not as an idiot groupie but as what we were. Mr Marriner would not contemplate involving himself in a drug deal with an idiot groupie only in somebody who he perceived as being my undercover guise as a drug dealer.

Q. Mr MacIntyre, each to their own idiot groupie when it comes to enjoying stories of other people's violence look, for example, to fit in with that picture. There are you boasting how you stood up to a Millwall fan, if only it had not been for some little problem you would have dealt with him. So did you not realise, perhaps, that you gave the impression of being a little hanger on and a wimp when it came to violence, even if you were excellent in your drug deals. Did you not realise that?

A. That's specifically for Mr Marriner to say.

Q. In response to that, Mr MacIntyre, you were provoking stories and boasting and claims which were not true?

A. Mr Marriner told me many times — and I wanted to — about some of the stories and I was keen to hear them in a static sound environment because as you know the sound in uncontrolled situations as like the pub and the car are very difficult.

Q. Mr MacIntyre, why does it matter? We are not discussing whether you make your television programme with better pictures or sound, why do you keep telling us that please?

A. Because the whole pretext for that particular meeting was to give us and discuss previous things which Mr Marriner had told us happily but not in quite the clear sound context it is very difficult to hear.

Q. I am sorry, who asked you about the pretext? Why are you telling me?

A. The meeting has a context and I am happy to tell the context to the jury.

MR WOLKIND: You have told it ten, fifteen times, why are you telling us about the pretext, who cares?

JUDGE BYERS: You asked him originally about the pretext for this particular conversation.

MR WOLKIND: Not about needing to get a better sound and vision.

JUDGE BYERS: No, but you did ask him about the pretext for it and he has already mentioned a better sound and vision in relation to a conversation that took place coming back from Manchester.

MR WOLKIND: Can we take it, Mr MacIntyre, you set this up because you wanted better sound and vision and that unless I ask you or challenge you on that maybe you will consider your answers and exclude us from hearing that again? Did you not realise the danger that by setting yourself up as someone who enjoys the good crack and that is great and you love hearing those stories that you would get what were you apparently interested in, particularly if they want to get in with your drug dealing?

A. We had got all that we needed to make a television programme. Mr Marriner had spoken about his past, his present, and we had witnessed him organising football violence. There was no need for us, evidentially, for our programme and for our purposes to get more stories. The only requirement for us was to try and improve the quality and pictures of Mr Marriner's words.

Q. The sound, you have not reminded us of the sound as well. Early on you adopted the guise of a drug dealer, is that right, from the start of your meetings with Mr Marriner?

A. Yes, we did.

Q. If it turns out that he would be interested in getting to know affluent drug dealers with their flash cars and wads of money, it was wads of ready money, was there not?

A. We carried cash and we were happy to show that we were amply supplied.

Q. So the flash car and wads of ready money. If he was interested or tempted to get to know such people and if such people also appeared to be idiot groupies or hangers on who wanted to hear all about violence — you know some people get a vicarious thrill, do you not, through hearing stories of violence?

A. That may be the case.

Q. Did you not spot — you the investigative journalist — the obvious danger that you were being fed lines to keep in with you, and that you were being teased and boasted to, did you not realise?

A. Mr Marriner and the first time when he specifically mentioned football violence to us and related to the Copenhagen pub, we had pretty much not a great deal of interaction with him up until then and he was quite happy to talk about it and demonstrate to us at that pub at that time that he was a hooligan.

Q. Forgive me, prior to the Copenhagen pub you were already in the guise of the flash drug dealers with the flash cars and the ready money, were you not?

A. Yes, we were.

Q. You helped him to go over to Copenhagen, did you not?

A. We bought a ticket which he paid for.

Q. Yes, you helped him. It is convenient someone does the work for you. You helped him to that extent, have you not?

A. Yes, we did.

Q. Had you not realised that by pretending to be flash drug dealers, and as I suggest was fascinated by the stories of other people's violence, there was the danger when you deal with an affable friendly chap who likes a good story you would be fed a good story?

A. That's — we were always aware that we do not turn somebody who isn't a football hooligan to a football hooligan. But we do not sit somebody down and etch a Chelsea headhunter tattoo on somebody's right arm. Mr Marriner was a football hooligan before we met him. He organised football violence while we were there and we broadcast the programme as such.

MR WOLKIND: Do you erase the tattoos if they are not a hooligan, is that your job? What date did he get the tattoo? The next questions are about a completely different subject which I would be grateful if I could finish soon after lunch.

JUDGE BYERS: Yes, very well. 2.05 then please, members of the jury, and 2.05 for you please. If you would like to leave the court you are free to go. (luncheon adjournment)

MR WOLKIND: May it please, your Honour. Can we see extract 34, please. I do not have a date for this nor a transcript. (extract 34 is played back in court) Thank you very much. Obviously I cut it off there when you have gone on to tickets and you are more than welcome to hear the rest of it if you want. But does it start, that extract, with you discussing having been with Paynie and Danny Walford, is it as well, to the Machester City/Millwall game?

A. Yes, it does.

Q. If Jason had not been there and he begins to tell you, does he not, about trouble at Birmingham —

A. Yes, he was telling me about, I think, a fight between some Birmingham supporters and Chelsea supporters. I can't recall.

Q. — one might have thought he began to describe violence involving Chelsea supporters, that this was an example of him talking about violence he was involved in?

A. No, I think he says that he wasn't there.

Q. That is why I just said to you as he began, do you see, before he had reached the point where he explained he was not there, but you, Mr MacIntyre, but for the fact that he goes on to explain he was not there that would be one of your examples, would it not, of Jason Marriner that you had present to help the jury being involved in violence.

A. Well Mr Marriner said he wasn't there.

Q. I am not sure whether it is particularly complicated so I will try again. It must be my fault. But for Jason Marriner saying he was not there you would seize on that, would you not, as proof that he was involved in violence?

A. No; if Jason Marriner said he wasn't there we did not say he was there.

MR WOLKIND: You are either incapable or you choose not to answer my question, but for....?

JUDGE BYERS: Mr Wolkind, I am sorry, it may be me being stupid but I do not see that the witness has not answered the question. You are asking him he would seize upon that as being an example of Jason Marriner being involved in violence and he says, no, he says he was not there.

MR WOLKIND: No. I have not asked that question once. The question I have repeatedly asked is: but for Jason Marriner saying he was not there you would have seized on it as material? IN other words, where there is material where you cannot be completely contradicted, you would take it in a wholly prejudiced way against Jason Marriner and use it as evidence that he is involved. Here you cannot do it because he told you he was not there.

A. No, that's not the case.

Q. You began to describe the violence you had in these terms of relish, wild, good, ruck, great, great day out, do you remember that?

A. Yes, I do.

Q. He began to describe the violence in terms which sounds like he was interested too. He began that way, did he not?

A. I could hear it again but I am quite comfortable Mr Marriner said he wasn't in Birmingham, that he wasn't involved in the fight, and I am happy to take it and agree with that.

Q. Forgive me, I have not asked you that, have I? I asked you whether he too began with terms that sounded as if he enjoyed the violence. You do not need to go on to questions I have not asked, see if you can deal with the one I have asked?

A. I do not have the transcript of the conversation.

Q. There came a time, as we all know, when he said I was not there.

A. Yes, that's true.

Q. As early as November 5th in a pub in Copenhagen, Mr Marriner made it clear that he knew right from the start that you were at it, meaning you and Paul were crooks, do you remember he said it as early as November the 5th?

A. Yes, in a pub in Copenhagen Mr Marriner said that the first time he saw us he knew we were at it which gave us some comfort, safety comfort, that he recognised the stereotype we had given him.

Q. I am just going to separate your answer from the commentary. The answer to my question is as early as November 5th Jason was telling you he had known from the first time he had seen you that you were at it; from getting the date, it is as early as that, is it not?

A. That's correct.

Q. Indeed it led you to express some satisfaction when you were in the car with Paul the very next day; and we see that on extract 14, please. Can I ask you to pause for a moment. I have been told it is 14 but I am not convinced that it is. My writing, 24. (extract 24 is played back in court) The world of investigative journalism there is no-one who can achieve what Donal MacIntyre and Paul Atkinson can do, that seems to be the proposition that you agree to because you are fucking phenomenal.

A. We have just — to put it in context — come back from Copenhagen where we have been in the company of Chelsea headhunters, and we felt we had for the first time gone out and travelled in their company and that our guise as under-cover dealers have protected us and Jason was being very comfortable with us.

Q. It is far more than being in the company of headhunters and Jason being comfortable, it is far more than that. Your colleague says you can control him and now we get everything you want from him. It is very specific, is it not, as to the relationship between you and Paul and Jason?

A. The relationship is to make sure that Jason is comfortable to be able to talk to us as he would to one of his own and we were very comfortable that Jason had felt comfortable enough to go to Copenhagen with us. And he had just told us in that car journey how he had gone about and sought revenge and beaten up a number of people in Copenhagen and we felt that that was an admission which had not been heard before.

Q. Not had beaten up, because I know you do not want to mislead. He did not tell you he had beaten up, do you remember, that was the question that the phenomenal no-one else can do it, investigative journalist, had not actually asked. So you do not know he had beaten up anyone, do you?

A. Mr Marriner told us on that specific car journey that he went about and grabbed some of the — the other English supporters and went about — and I am not quite too sure of the language he used, but my understanding was that he grabbed anybody he could find.

Q. But I thought the language was that he went looking for other people. When I asked you whether he had found someone else and even worse if he had actually touched them you explained it would have been too dangerous to have asked that extra question. So you are not telling us, are you, that he ever told you that in fact he did touch anyone else?

A. Mr Marriner said on that specific car journey on the way home from Heathrow Airport after Copenhagen, that after he had been beaten up he went back to the pub and I don't know the exact words but he went about and grabbed anybody he could find.

JUDGE BYERS: Do you want my note of it?

MR WOLKIND: Certainly.

JUDGE BYERS: what he said was that after he had said that he had got beaten up in Copenhagen he said he explained how he had gone back and having grabbed people, how they had rounded up people and beaten them up in Copenhagen.

MR WOLKIND: When we heard the words, did we not, from looking at the film, he had not said any such thing, had he, in the car? Is that what you claimed to the jury before we heard the film?

MR VAUDIN: We have not seen that film yet.

MR WOLKIND: Have we not seen the film?

MR VAUDIN: No, we have not. It is available. We can show it if you wish?

MR WOLKIND: How kind and so can you? Your Honour, I am sorry that is entirely my mistake that allows me to put a different matter to you. Is it your evidence — and Mr Vaudin is keen that we see it, so that we can see if your evidence is accurate — that he told you he had beaten people up?

A. Well, I can't remember the specific words but certainly it was clear to me that he was indicating that he had gone back, grabbed some members from the pub and gone out to beat people up. That was my recollection of his statement.

Q. See if you and I start the story from where he has grabbed people. Imagine he is not all boasting, all right? So I want you to imagine that he is telling the truth and not trying to impress some idiot who is interested in violence vicariously, please imagine that. Can you tell me if you would know the difference between looking for people to beat up and actually finding them and beating them up? Can you see the difference?

A. Yes, I can.

Q. Thank you. Which of the two meanings did he give to you?

A. Well, forgive me, but I can't recall the exact words apart from the impression and indication that he went out and sought revenge. But as I say the tape recording is definitive on that issue. I can't recall the exact - -

Q. Yes, but we did not have the tape recording at that time, you see, and I want to know whether you are perhaps choosing your words carefully, leaving it open for the jury to believe that he had confessed to you that he had actually beaten people up. So doing your best to be fair, Mr MacIntyre, you have now chosen the word sought. You agreed with me you knew the difference between looking for and finding, did he only look or did he find and then beat up, which is it?

A. My impression is he went out and grabbed. My recollection of the conversation —

Q. No, we start from the grab. Do not go through that again. Start from the grabbing. He has gone out, did he only look or did he find?

A. I think the tape will demonstrate it better than my recollection.

Q. I want to hear it from you?

A. My recollection is that he said he went out and he grabbed some guys from the pub and went out and sought any old guy he could find. I think the tape is perhaps more accurate in the sense.

Q. You have said that. You have offered that several times. Remind us, please, the reason why you did not ask him what damage is inflicted is the danger of being a phenomenal undercover reporter and investigative journalist?

A. I think we are talking about two conversations, one was in the pub coming home from Copenhagen and the other was in the flat some months later, some considerable months later.

Q. Mr MacIntyre, I am talking about one conversation. I am talking about the conversation in the car soon after which we just saw you and Mr Atkinson explaining that no-one else could do what we did and how phenomenal you are and fucking brilliant and so on. It is the same occasion, is it not?

A. Yes.

Q. So perhaps you can answer without bringing in another conversation months later. So concentrating on these events, please, this is the occasion where you did not ask him the extra dangerous question of whether he actually found and touched anyone in Copenhagen?

A. I can't recall.

Q. Well did you or did you not ask him that?

A. I can't recall. I don't know the transcript of the conversation.

Q. But you told me on Friday that you did not ask him that because it would be just too dangerous to have asked him that question?

A. That was in specific relation when you were asking me why I had not asked the question in the flat some months later. This is now in the car and Mr Mariner had said he had gone out and to my impression sought revenge, so I felt I felt I did not have to ask the question, he had said it as much to me. That's my best recollection of events.

Q. Sometimes people go out and look for something, they may or may not find it and you will never know if you are not there or you do not ask. Just remind us, please, you were not there when he went out?

A. I wasn't there we he came to the pub.

Q. Confirm, finally, as you leave this point, you did not ask him in the event whether he found?

A. No, I took his view that his statement was adequate enough for me at the time, bearing in mind the conditions.

Q. The reason why it is adequate for you — so that we can expose again to anyone — is it is just vague enough for the programme and your prejudice in giving evidence now. You leave it vague rather than getting an answer that contradicts what you want. That is your technique, is it not?

A. No, it is not.

Q. That is why I was so careful in the question I asked you before in saying about the Manchester City/Millwall and then the Birmingham violence. But for Jason saying, "I was not there," that would have been prime MacIntyre material to distort?

A. Absolutely nonsense.

Q. Why is it, please, when I have asked you about Mr Atkinson's words that he can control him you three times used the word comfortable. Can you face up please to what was said in your presence, the boast was that you could control him, not comfortable that you said three times, control? It was said, was it not?

A. That word was said. That was said in the context we had just dropped Jason off having spent three days in his company and we had finally felt we had crossed a hurdle now being comfortable in the company of the Chelsea head-hunters and dropped them off and we were able to put Jason in a position where he was comfortable with us and increasingly comfortable with me so that he would involve us, recognise us as people who he could talk freely with.

Q. The guise you adopt throughout all your evidence in this case in front of the jury is rather a soft man who may not be so bright so that when I point out that you said comfortable three times you slip in comfortable another three times in a row. It is a fake what the jury see now, is it not, Mr MacIntyre, this is the role you have adopted for your performance in court?

A. I am telling the truth as I know it.

MR WOLKIND: So when I asked you whether you could face the word control out comes comfortable three times so that it looks poor little Donal MacIntyre does not quite understand.

JUDGE BYERS: No, that is a comment.

MR WOLKIND: I am not going to make submission on that because it is a question, it was meant as a question but your Honour rules. It is a guise, is it not, it is a little pretence?

A. No, it is not.

Q. Why is it that when I asked you if you could face the word "control" your answer would only go each time as far as comfortable. Do you have a problem in saying that you and Mr Atkinson felt that they could control that man?

A. No, we were controlling an environment to protect us to allow Jason to feel free and comfortable with us. That's why we went in with an appropriate guise as undercover drug dealers so that he would feel comfortable talking with us about his football activities which is why we did not go in as football hooligans into that world but as another guise.

Q. Share your fears with us now please, Mr MacIntyre. If you were to face up to the words, control him, not nothing about environment but control him, then the jury might realise that you were manipulating him and getting out of him stories because it sounded like you wanted stories and you were a little violent groupie.

A. No, Mr Marriner was a football hooligan before we met him and we were keen to let him know that we were comfortable and creating an environment where he would feel comfortable with us and that is what our undercover guise was all about.

Q. Then Mr Atkinson continues or the two of you in a duet performance finishing off each other's words. "Now we get everything you want. No-one else can do it." That is quite a boast, is it not, to get everything you want from Jason?

A. We were keen that Jason was a headhunter and we knew that if we got to know Jason then he would introduce us to others in that world which in fact he did; and that we may have been slightly excitable having dropped Jason off, but I have no problem with the jury seeing that material, obviously.

Q. Who raised that?

A. I was just demonstrating the fact that I am not embarrassed by it, we had just dropped off Mr Marriner having spent three days in the company of him. I have been beaten up, Mr Atkinson had been beaten up, it was a tense time.

Q. The programme about the Kent Care Home was a fraud, was it not, it was a fake presented by you?

A. No, it wasn't.

Q. You cheated consistently in its production and its presentation?

A. Absolutely not.

Q. It was a disgrace made for your ego, was it not?

A. Absolutely not.

Q. You know as a result of what I describe as a fraudulent programme there was an inquiry conducted by the Kent police?

A. Yes, there was.

Q. It was conducted, was it not, by an acting inspector, a Mr Costello?

A. Yes, it was.

Q. He, of course, was able to interview people that appeared on the programme and analyse the TV programme itself and the underlying material?

A. He interviewed some of the production team. He did not interview any of the experts which appeared in that programme.

Q. I did not mention the experts, I was thinking about, for example, some patients and some workers.

A. I do not think he interviewed some patients. I understand he interviewed some workers.

Q. But you had taken a camera into a home in Kent which cared for severely mentally handicapped people?

A. It was a broad range of impairments, that's the case, yes.

Q. As a result of your programme 42 severely mentally disabled people were moved and 84 people were made redundant. As you no doubt hope you got it right, do you not?

A. As a result of our programme the Social Services conducted their own investigation and after the police themselves had found five incidents of assault on five different residents, these assaults were admitted. The council after our programme conducted their own inquiry and have subsequently closed down the home permanently. Before the programme was broadcast residents in that home were kicked in the head, bullied, humiliated, they had fire extinguishers turned on them and they were insulted and called dirty and filthy. After our programme that was no longer the case. I am very proud about programme and remain so.

Q. But your programme on the Kent care home is a fake and an embarrassment for which you defend as strongly as you can because you know you were condemned by the police who investigated it. I know you do not want to mislead but the home was closed down within 24 hours of transmission of your programme well before the police investigated — you said after the police investigated — it was closed down within 24 hours, was it not?

A. But to put it into context, nobody actually closed the home down initially, what happened was that after the programme the Local Authorities who had residents in that home and who were actually paying the bill for residents in that home withdrew the residents from that home and they were then placed else-where. What is indisputable even on the police —

Q. I need to stay with that before you go on otherwise we will get lost.

A. Sorry, I am just saying on the point of closure I think it is important to put into context, is that what is indisputable is before our programme was broad-cast people were assaulted in that home. It is in fact a care home not a home where there is any number of assaults acceptable; and I remain incredibly proud of that programme and I am currently suing the Kent constabulary for libel relating to some comments that they made on the programme.

MR WOLKIND: We know.

JUDGE BYERS: Yes, but he is not to know that you know in fairness to him.

MR WOLKIND: I bet you are. You have read the newspapers, have you not, where the fact that you are suing was published? I bet you have read those, have you not, Tuesday 21st of this month, have you not read it where the fact that you are suing was published?

A. Yes, I have.

Q. Thank you. But what you are going to do in your approach is to assert that you saved people from being assaulted or hurt in the same way as you will assert that Jason Marriner is a football hooligan. Would you mind if I made some suggestions about your evidence?

A. If I could just answer that first statement. Is that what I can assert is even in the police's own terms people were assaulted in that home. They did not complain, they did not go to the police because they could not. The police went in there and found that there were five assaults on five different residents by two workers, some of the most long standing. They also found that five or six other workers had acted completely inappropriately and recommended that in total seven or eight workers should never seek employment in the care industry again. These residents have now moved to a safer place and I am incredibly proud of that programme and remain so.

Q. Mr MacIntyre, can you hear me say that I have heard you say that now about the number of assaults?

A. Well, I think what is definitive is that assaults were admitted in that home: It is not conjecture, it is not me saying that. These assaults were admitted and there were five cautions and in order to caution people the assaults have to be admitted. So if there is any dispute about the facts there can be no dispute about the fact that assaults had taken place in that home.

Q. Can I ask you about other matters — and will you take it I have heard that and perhaps you will not mention it again unless it is germane to a particular question. So if you are ready now to answer questions. Is it right that the programme was misleading?

A. No, it was not.

Q. Is it right, more specifically, that on several occasions critical footage had been cut out or information withheld which explained why the staff acted as they did and often justified their actions?

A. No, that's not true.

Q. Is it right that sequences shot several hours apart were spliced together to give an impression that an unfeeling event had taken place where it had not?

A. That's not the case.

Q. Is it right that the allegations that dangerous forms of restraint were used by staff were not substantiated by any of the film, Mr MacIntyre, the film of which you are so proud?

A. Indeed, some of the Government's main experts and advisers in relation to the field of restraint for those with learning difficulties absolutely and totally concur with us that there were restraint practices used that can kill. More than that — excuse me, it is a very important point here — the police's own report states that the workers in that home were trained with a technique which is known as pindown which they say themselves is a technique which has been the subject of some considerable controversy because of deaths which resulted in its use.

MR WOLKIND: Just take a breath. Does anything that you have told us justify your lying, cheating and faking in that programme?

JUDGE BYERS: Mr Wolkind, no, no, pause. You will have to split that up. You will have to ask him if he lied, you will have to ask him if he cheated in that programme before you put it because he may not accept.

MR WOLKIND: I have already suggested that at the start it has been refused but now we have had the explanation so many times of the findings of the police I am asking you whether you think that justifies the programme as I suggest lying, faking and cheating?

A. Mr Wolkind, you have called me a drunk, a liar, a cheat, you have also called me soft. Now being called soft is not an insult and it wasn't an insult for those people in that care home, they had no crime. They were beaten up, they were assaulted, they were kicked in the head and I myself remain true to that programme. I am very proud of it and I am quite sure that in the fullness of time when the full issues are brought before a court, a libel court, that the truth of that programme will be borne out.

Q. Did you capture on film a resident being kicked in the head?

A. Yes, my colleague, Mr erm — my colleague had captured that and that assault was admitted and received a caution for that.

Q. Yes, I was going to ask you about that. A total number of prosecutions, please, as a result of your programme?

A. Because the residents had admitted it –

Q. No, give us the total?

A. Well, there were five admissions of criminal assault.

Q. Mr MacIntyre, is there a problem with the question, total number of prosecutions, please?

A. There were no prosecutions.

MR WOLKIND: You see, can we have an answer before the commentary.

JUDGE BYERS: Mr Wolkind, sometimes people do not understand what a caution means and what a caution avoids.

MR WOLKIND: Your Honour is entirely right and that helps the jury. But it was unnecessary for you, was it not, Mr MacIntyre, because you were very clear before to explain that a caution means an admission of guilt. So you had no trouble understating my question even if it could have been a bit more helpful for others.

JUDGE BYERS: Yes, but it goes a little bit further than that, because if somebody admits their guilt and is prepared to accept a caution in those circumstances a criminal prosecution does not follow. It may be that in circumstances where the police would have prosecuted such a prosecution is avoided.

MR WOLKIND: Yes, of course we do not know whether they would have prosecuted or not one would never know that.

JUDGE BYERS: Yes, we do not, but you have made the point and so has Mr MacIntyre, so let us move on.

MR WOLKIND: I think together we have agreed no prosecutions and you have told us many times about the cautions. Let me also ask you, the police findings were unable to justify MacIntyre's opening commentary: "There was a culture of neglect when some of society's most vulnerable are assaulted by those looking after them, where restraint methods are used that can kill." Is that a criticism you accept that you sold something to the public and it could not be justified by the police on investigation?

A. I am not aware of what experts the police used to come to their decisions. I am aware of the experts we used and these experts are government advisers, they were head of Mencap and these were some of the most expert professionals in this arena. I stand by those words.

Q. You mentioned experts before so I ask you were the experts alongside you throughout your undercover guise at the home?

A. The experts before broadcast had been given underlying footage and saw some of the restraint techniques, they saw people being kicked in the head, they saw workers admitting turning fire extinguishers on to residents and indeed threatening to turn on fire extinguishers. They saw residents — workers calling residents disgusting and filthy. These people are not in control of their faculties, they are in care, this is a care establishment and beyond a shadow of a doubt no decent care establishment can stand people being threatened with fire extinguishers and assaulted.

Q. I invited you perhaps to answer a question before the commentary and so I will ask you again in case you forgot it. Were those experts alongside you during your time at the care home. You went on to comment about something else but were they alongside you?

A. They were not.

Q. Thank you. Did those experts get all of your film so that like the police they would be able to tell if you were cheating and cutting and editing, did they get all of your film?

A. The Social Services who investigated the programme related to the Brompton Care Home and who indeed unlike the police actually spoke to the psychologist who worked in the home who told us and told the Social Services that the restraint practices at that home were in the very bottom of bad practice. More than that the Social Services talked to workers there, they talked to us and they had their own experts and they have closed and confirmed that the Brompton Home is not a fit place to look after vulnerable people.

Q. That is in answer to what question?

A. That is in answer to the fact culture of neglect.

Q. No, no, that is in answer to what question I asked you?

A. The question asked.

Q. Which was what?

A. Which was the context relating to the comments related to neglect and the police criticism.

MR WOLKIND: Mr MacIntyre, what was the last question I asked you that led to that commentary?

MR VAUDIN: Your Honour, really my learned friend is arguing with the witness. He is also not asking questions he is making comments expecting the witness to answer. Now he is expecting the witness to remember the last comment he made, with respect, if we could have some restraint.

MR WOLKIND: I am very wounded. I asked a direct question. Did the experts get all the film? I have no doubt Mr Vaudin is taking notes, such a poor interruption. The question was: did the experts get all the film? I suppose they did or they did not, really?

A. The Social Services experts received all the footage.

JUDGE BYERS: He has actually already answered that question when you asked him the first time, were the experts alongside you? His answer was the experts were given all the underlying footage.

MR WOKIND: No, I did not hear all the under, I did not hear the words all the underlying footage.

A. Your Honour, it is just a slight difference the Social Services received all — their expertise — all the underlying footage.

MR WOKIND: Yes, I am sorry, I was asking about the experts. Is that the same as the experts?

A. Yes, it is.

Q. I wonder if you agree with this, that with such a large amount of material, because you shot some 41 hours, one per cent of which being for the actual broadcast, it was imperative the footage that was selected was truly representative. Concentrating on that question, you would probably agree that is a fair point, is it not?

A. The television programme is a half an hour to 45 or an hour long. It is quite clear we could not broadcast the 90 hours of mini discs and the 42 hours of footage, so it was reduced. And the fact I was very keen and I think I wrote in a memo before broadcast that we did not want all the difficult material broadcast before the people because some of them we held some harrowing material back.

Q. Just popping back to the question. I wondered if you agreed with the idea that it was imperative that the selective footage was truly representative? You have not answered that at all or touched on it.

A. The material that we broadcast was representative of the assaults and the mistreatment which took place in that home. I am of the opinion that the assaults in any care home does not — is completely inappropriate and wrong, any number.

Q. You have said that many, many times.

A. But it is important.

Q. It is important we have not forgotten it, you have said it ten times. We have not forgotten your view.

A. But in terms of, I think it is just the one point of being representative, I think, you know, there can be no sense that one assault one day can be equated with a fine food the next day and any assault in a care home in my view is completely and utterly unacceptable.

Q. Now dealing with the finding, please, of the police. Viewing the programme makers performance that they discovered notable misrepresentations, do you accept notable misrepresentations in your film?

A. Absolutely not.

Q. One of the people you filmed was a lady, a senior carer, telling you what your duties would be. Do you remember that?

A. Yes, it was.

Q. Your commentary over that, so that the viewing public would hear it was this: "Denise tells me that my duties will include giving life saving injections and that she intends to teach me how to administer the drug even though she is not a nurse." The full unedited material however makes it clear that that lady does not tell you that your duties will include administering insulin and that she does not propose to teach you how to inject it. You faked it for the viewers, did you not?

A. That's absolutely not the case. On my first interview in the home I was told by the head of the home that my duties would include injecting insulin. On that day that particular worker told me that she would teach me how to inject insulin. I studiously avoided, obviously, and would in no circumstances have injected anybody with insulin at all.

Q. But nobody is asking you that. Not at all the issue that we are discussing, is it, discussing whether you faked accounts you give, including your evidence now. You see, no-one is asking you about whether you actually give insulin, so concentrating, please. Am I right at least on the first part of my suggestion to you that your commentary said, "Denise tells me that my duties will include giving life saving injections and that she intends to teach me how to administer the drug even though she is not a nurse." Is that part of your commentary?

A. Yes, it is.

Q. Am I also right as the police found that the full unedited sequence makes it clear that that lady does not tell you that your duties will include administering of insulin and that she does not propose to teach MacIntyre how to inject what I described as your fake?

A. That's not the case. What I was told on my first interview by the head of the home, the person who ran the home, was that my duties would include the injecting of insulin. I think the police may have sent the second part of the conversation but not the first part, so she quite clearly then said she was going to teach me how to inject insulin and it was quite clear that even the head of the home thought it appropriate that that would be part of my duties.

Q. That was filmed, was it?

A. Yes, it was.

Q. That has been missed by the police, subsequently?

A. Well, I cannot speak for the police.

MR WOLKIND: Well they are either missed or they are lying, I guess.

MR VAUDIN: Your Honour, they are not giving evidence.

JUDGE BYERS: He cannot answer for the police and we will leave it at that.

MR WOLKIND: No, I accept that. I will take it as far as he passed the material. Your Honour is right. One of the allegations made in the programme, am I right, concerned abuse of the patients by the staff and a particular worker was secretly filmed taking a mouth organ from a resident after insisting he could only have the mouth organ for ten minutes, do you remember that sequence?

A. Yes, I do.

Q. Then we see or the viewing public saw the carer clench his fist in front of the face of the patient and saying these words: "Tomorrow you can have that as well." Do you remember that?

A. Yes, I do. I remember it exceptionally well.

MR WOLKIND: I have not asked you the commentary yet, you will have a chance.

MR VAUDIN: But, your Honour, he is not being given the chance because he is being asked further questions.

JUDGE BYERS: No, Mr Vaudin, it is better that these questions are allowed to run.

MR VAUDIN: Yes, but they run and then they do not run again so that the witness cannot answer. I think it is not fair.

JUDGE BYERS: But the witness will be given an opportunity to answer and I shall see to that.

MR WOKLKIND: Mr MacIntyre, has there been a single occasion when I have not given you the chance to explain to me what you want? We normally get that first but if I have ever stopped you, has there ever been a time?

JUDGE BYERS: I do not think we need go through a catalogue, Mr Wolkind.

MR WOLKIND: I was trying to be helpful but I did not know what Mr Vaudin was referring to.

JUDGE BYERS: Let us just leave it at that, you ask your questions relevant to the cross-examination you wish to pursue and the witness will answer them.

MR WOLKIND: Now despite what you chose to display for the public the unedited footage tells a very different story indeed, does it not? It is a general proposition and then, of course, you will get your chance. Do you agree with that proposition?

A. No

Q. The edited segment, the bit that was broadcast is made up in fact of two separate sequences shot several hours apart. In neither of the sequences does the care worker actually take the mouth organ away Am I right on that?

A. I don't think you are correct on that, I don't think it was several hours apart. I think what is important is that some people call this the mouth organ sequence, I call it the first sequence. I defy anybody to show me the health care manual which thinks it is appropriate to wave a fist in front of a 30 year old man and saying, "I give you some of this." The care worker involved, Mr Jeremy Cadbee(?) —

Q. I was not mentioning names on purpose, did you notice that?

A. I am happy to mention the name.

JUDGE BYERS: Let him answer the question.

MR WOLKIND: No, forgive me, a name has been mentioned in public and it is my duty to draw to your Honour's attention it may not be appropriate. I have to do it now not later, I am sorry.

JUDGE BYERS: But the witness has been asked a question about a particular sequence, if it is necessary for him to state the name of the person who was involved in that sequence and it was probably mentioned during the course of the broadcast, I do not know, then there is no reason why he should not mention it during the course of an answer.

MR WOLKIND: I invite your Honour to reconsider that with the greatest respect for this reason. I have said the carer and the patient and I thought that was appropriate as we are discussing other people and I shall continue to do that. If your Honour says he can mention names then I do not argue it further.

JUDGE BYERS: I do not allow him to mention names but if he happens to mention a name then it is not right that the flow of his answer should be interrupted, that is the problem.

A. I think what is important to know is that specific worker was specifically criticised for that specific incident by the police in their own report. He was also criticised on three other occasions and the police advice to him has been not to seek employment in the care industry ever again. I stand by their views on that matter.

MR WOLKIND: Please understand I do not accept that it is their views at all. In this second sequence, which is spliced into the first, the patient does not even have the mouth organ. And tell me if this is right, the sound of it playing has simply been added to make viewers think that he is playing it, the sound is then shut off to make viewers think that the carer has taken the mouth organ again. In other words for you, I suggest, on what we have seen from the football case such as with the telephone box, just standard trickery to deceive?

A.   That incident is about a care worker waving a fist in front of a man with a mind of a two year old. Aggression to care worker — by care workers, whatever way, is completely and utterly unacceptable. I take the police's view that that behaviour was unacceptable.

Q.   Let us see if you have the police's view right or whether you are trying to mislead even now as you talk. "The clenched fist is not the threatening gesture that was portrayed to viewers. The investigating officer, the detective inspector it is secretly filmed in discussion with MacIntyre. The care assistant did utterly unacceptable things about the residents which suggests that he was quite unfit to be caring for them."

A.   Mr Cadbee –

Q.   I have not even finished yet.

A.   You are quoting there not from the police report, you are actually quoting from the Sunday Telegraph, I think there is a difference. I think there is a difference if you are quoting from the Telegraph or the police report. I am quoting from the police report.

Q.   Just pausing. Continue in this way, "Although we viewed everything he was filmed doing very carefully, we couldn't actually find him doing anything wrong. He seems in fact to have been a good carer." Here we come to the crunch. Tell me if this is right, Mr MacIntyre, do not worry about sources, just tell me if this is right. When you look at the unedited footage you can see that his gesture of putting his fist in front of the patient was not threatening, it was a game that the patient enjoyed playing. In the unedited film you can see the patient smiling. It is trickery and fake, is it not, for the sake of a good programme?

A.   It is absolutely not the case that the patient, the resident (because he is not a patient, he is a resident) was smiling after that incident, it is absolutely not the case. And more than that in their own report whatever is quoted in the Telegraph and I understand that is a quote from the Telegraph, in the police's own report they criticise as inappropriate that specific incident and I defy anyone having viewed all the underlying footage in a right mind to describe that particular worker as a good care worker.

JUDGE BYERS: Mr Wolkind, you have put a piece of a report and I have allowed it to be put without intervention. I think it is only right that we should know what the source material is that you are putting.

MR WOLKIND: Actually it is not, with respect, in law which is why I keep saying, suggestion, I am asking him to react to suggestions.

JUDGE BYERS: I understand that.

MR WOLKIND: I am not going to unless your Honour rules in the absence of the jury because the law –

JUDGE BYERS: But it has become an issue, has it not?

MR WOLKIND: I have heard comments and I have disagreed with comments that certain things are said by the police when I have said they are not. But I hope I have stuck within the parameters of what I am allowed to do in the situation.

JUDGE BYERS: We will leave it at that.

MR WOLKIND: Yes. There was, was there not, a good reason for the rule that that particular resident was only allowed his mouth organ for certain minutes, he got so excited that playing it could bring on epileptic fits for him. You knew that, did you not?

A. That may very well be the case but there is no rule which allows a worker to wave fists in front of residents saying , "I'll give you some of that." I saw another — some days earlier — in front of the same resident another care worker do exactly the same thing. Now obviously that care worker is no longer at Brompton and that is a good thing.

Q. See if you can understand why I am asking you these questions. It is not to test whether there was misconduct at the care home — just hold that very tight whilst I tell you what it is for — it is to test whether you are a person who can be trusted. So let me explain it another way. If you see an assault in a care home on Monday, Tuesday, Wednesday and Thursday you are entitled to be outraged at that misconduct. Do you have that so far? It does not allow you to lie about what has happened on Friday. Do you understand why I am asking you the questions?

A. I do not accept we lied.

Q. But you do understand that I am not asking what your views are on violence because you are probably against it. I am asking whether you are lying now as you lied in the presentation of the football programme and the presentation of the care home programme?

A. That's absolutely not the case.

Q. What you claimed in the care home programme was that certain restraint methods used by the staff can kill. Do you remember claiming that?

A. Yes, I do.

Q. By the presentation of this programme a particular resident was made to look like a victim of an unprovoked assault and in relation to him an expert in restraint, so called, was interviewed on the film.

A. That is — which particular incident are you referring to?

Q. A very tall gentleman, six foot four suffered from a form of psychosis, threatened the nurses before, fractured a woman care worker's jaw and had thrown a 40 inch television across a room, does that remind you of who the resident was, trying to make a bid for freedom by running to the fire escape when he was restrained. None of that was told to the viewers, but does that identify the person?

A. I think that was an incident where there was mayhem in the home when I was looking after another resident who was being called disgusting by other care workers.

Q. You demonstrated to the experts for the purpose of the film the restraints that were being used?

A. I think — yes, I did.

Q. I want to ask you about another particular incident and you may remember this because it involves a female resident. The film was shown of two care workers putting a female resident in a wrist lock for no apparent reason. There is no reason given, it is part of a footage for the film.

A. No, it was to demonstrate a wrist lock that was being used in the care home inflicting pain; and in that particular incident the resident was put in a wrist lock long after a minor incident occurred, it therefore inflicted pain after an event rather than restraint.

Q. What about this as the truth please. "The resident was about to attack the man filming the sequence and in the unedited sequence, in other words, what we do not get to see normally, in the unedited sequence you see the resident move to hit the man.

A. The carer involved there who was my colleague Ben Anderson.

Q. That is the sequence.

A. And what happened was one of the residents was, erm, slightly moved towards Mr Anderson. There was no danger. The care worker involved — and this is her the way she behaves said: "Don't you attack that man," escalating a minor event into a major happening and she put the resident into a painful care lock, a lock, and walked her down the stairs. Now restraint procedures are required in care homes but they must always be used appropriately.

Q. I am not asking you about proper procedural occurrence about the TV programme, do you see?

A. That's absolutely the context of that moment.

Q. Mr MacIntyre, you say that is the context so I will ask you again. Does misconduct, as you see it, justify lying or faking? I ask it because you keep saying that is the context.

A. We did not lie or fake.

Q. But at least we are concentrating on the issue. Did the film show the carer taking the resident's arm saying, "Don't attack anyone." Was that broadcast?

A. No, that wasn't broadcast. The nature and the reason why we're demonstrating that particular picture we're making a point about the wrist locks which people use in that home and that was why that picture was used.

Q. But that is the same technique as you have in justifying footage in the football programme. You talk about what your purpose was, but what about the fact that it misleads?

A. It wasn't misleading. We were demonstrating a point and in any event her behaviour was entirely completely inappropriate and it was completely wrong to walk somebody down there in pain long after an incident. This is somebody with a mental age of less than two. So when they do something or lunge forward they forget the incident and it was the care worker herself who defined the incident as an attack which it wasn't and she defined it and that's what bad care workers do, they escalate minor events into major happenings and then they put them into locks. That particular worker I believe has actually been cautioned.

Q. You say the worker defined it, you know you have read the police report as well. It is a fair description, is it not, that the resident was about to attack Ben Anderson, the carer says, "Don't attack anyone," none of this is shown on the screen, All the screen shows is the resident saying, "I will" and one of the carers saying, "You won't" as she puts the resident in a wrist lock. A shade misleading that one did not know that there was an earlier attack and an earlier statement from the carer, "don't attack anyone," a shade misleading by your standards?

A. Not at all. It is the possible failure of training and expertise in that home which allows care workers to act inappropriately and to register minor events as attacks. Now a good care worker would never have walked down that resident in continuing pain after a minor incident. It was that worker who defined the incident, a care worker who defined the incident as an assault, and this, the resident, with a mental age of two or so said, "I will," but this is a care establishment which just should not involve restraint but not pain.

Q. Mr MacIntyre, you were keen to claim what the police report said on other occasions. Now I have heard you repeat again it is the care worker. You are not suggesting, are you, that the police have not also described it as a resident moving to attack, you are not claiming that, are you?

A. I am claiming that the —

MR WOLKIND: No, no, concentrate on my point, please. Are you claiming that the police have not said it?

MR VAUDIN: Your Honour, my learned friend is using the word mislead, with respect, he is misleading in asking the question in that manner. The police can only repeat what they are told. The police were not there and misleading this jury to believe that a report by the police was made as a result of the police witnessing anything. They were not, with respect.

MR WOLKIND: Forgive me, that is entirely wrong that report is based on the unedited material.

JUDGE BYERS: Ask the question again.

MR WOLKIND: I do it, Mr MacIntyre, only because it is a point you made before. You have emphasised on this point that it is the care worker describing it as an attack. I have been putting to you the suggestion that it was an attack, it is one of these occasions when you are going to say please do not describe it as an attack.

A. No, I think that the point being that on some occasions the police at one stage believed that there were assaults in the home. They accept that people were threatened and they accept that five people were assaulted and cautioned. On other occasions they seemingly — they also accepted – -

Q. No, no, this occasion, what are you talking about? We are not talking about the five assaults, we are talking about this occasion.

A. I am demonstrating the contradictions in the police's own report.

Q. Mr MacIntyre, can you tell us what the thing was on this occasion?

A. In relation to what, this? I haven't got the police's report in front of me.

Q. Right. So it is not one of those occasions where you are going to claim that the police do not say it is an attack?

A. No, the police take the version of events, erm, the wrong version of events.

Q. Yes, seeing all the unedited material and not just talking to witnesses. They see the material, do they not?

A. What can I say — and they speak for themselves — is that the Social Services experts in this regard brought in their own experts and they closed down the home permanently. They found it unfit for care. The police can have their own view, but even on their own terms there were five assaults. Any assaults in a care home is wrong. More than that a year before we went into the home the Social Services did their own report which said that the one home in that area which had given them the most problems and most concern was the Brompton Care Home.

Q. Maybe that was the springboard for you faking the TV programme. Maybe that inspired you but you faked it, did you not, as you faked the football programme? The end of the football season was 10th May, 1999, do you remember the last match?

A. Yes, I do.

Q. Who was that?

A. That was Chelsea/Spurs.

Q. At Spurs, was it not? What you describe in your book as the traditional end of season clash?

A. Yes.

Q. I do not know if that is actually right whether fixture lists always stay the same, I have no idea, but that is how you described it. Then you go on to say, it is page 206 of your book: "The better described as the supporters' organised end of season scrap." Have you got, "Revenge to be extracted," and it is really their last chance in a football context at least because it is the end of the season. So you point out revenge to be extracted, do you see that?

A. Yes, that's revenge relating to the —

Q. I have just asked you a point. I have not asked you to tell a story about it for the moment. Does it say revenge to be extracted?

A. Yes, it does.

MR WOLKIND: Mr Vaudin, please, if you have an objection. There are reasons why I ask in those terms. Do you want to object?

MR VAUDIN: If I were to object, your Honour, each time my learned friend does something he should not do, I would be on my feet every two minutes. I am not doing that.

MR WOLKIND: I am dying for you to say what the objection is here.

JUSGE BYERS: Mr Wolkind, it may be helpful to move the matter on swiftly to ask about the extract and then ask him what he meant by it.

MR WOLKIND: I am not going to ask him what he means by it on this occasion, Mr Vaudin can if he wants. But you say revenge to be extracted and you make a further comment, "The match is completely superfluous." That is about six lines down on 207.

A. Yes, it is superfluous to the intention of some of the football hooligans who were intent on having a fight there.

Q. Prior to that match Jason gave you some advice, did he not?

A. Erm, I can't recall. He could have done, yes.

Q. Yes, I have noted it, but I expect it is on the same page. I will see if I can take you to it. The next paragraph, second line into it, "Even he told me to keep your head down." So he did not tell you to get one of those Spurs fuckers for me or anything like that. On the contrary Jason's advice, keep your head down. I am sorry if I do not have it. It is the second complete paragraph 207, second line. "Even he told me to keep your head down," do you see that?

A. Which paragraph, sorry?

Q. The second complete paragraph on that page.

A. Oh the second complete, sorry.

Q. It is the second line within that, "Even he told me to keep your head down." This last opportunity for violence, the traditional end of season scrap, Jason's advice to you is to stay out of trouble, is it not?

A. The advice was to keep your head down because it could have been a very dangerous fight.

Q. Let us confess to the jury what his part was, please, in the Spurs/Chelsea last opportunity for violence end of season clash, his part.

A. Mr Marriner played no part whatsoever on that day.

Q. Why is that?

A. That's for Mr Marriner to say.

Q. No, tell us. He did not go to the match, did he?

A. No, he did not, no. That's what I meant earlier.

Q. But that match is also significant because by chance on that last day you suspected and worried that other people had guessed you were not a genuine Chelsea supporter?

A. They say I was concerned that without the patronage of Jason Marriner and Andy Frain that we would stick out like sore thumbs.

Q. You have been to a match without him before, have you not?

A. Yes we had, but we had not –

Q. Name that match, what was that; how long ago would that have been?

A. We went to Derby without….

Q. He was there, I know you may not have meant to mislead on that occasion, he was there but did not go with you, did you not know that, the Chelsea/Derby match?

A. This is December 12th 1998?

Q. Away or home are you discussing, which one are you discussing away or home?

A. December — I am not too sure what date.

Q. You only went to one Chelsea/Derby match, did you not, you went without him, did you not?

A. Yes, December 12th, I think it was.

Q. Now that we move on four, five months and you are on your own and look at page 210 please, we are going to deal with the moment when you decided that enough was enough for your role as a Chelsea supporter and to do it justice that last paragraph on 210 do you want to read it or shall I read it?

A. I'll be happy for you to read it.

Q. Thank you. "The game is up. I walk away. Took me nearly a year to get there, just a few seconds to leave it behind. I'm no longer a headhunter. It is over. I've crossed to the other side of the road and meet up with Paul. He looks at me. We shake hands, firm handshake and then we hug. We are safe." Did you write that yourself?

A. I did, yes.

Q. "A misplaced word could have you killed." That is no exaggeration, that is another part of the book we looked at today, is it not?

A. That's absolutely the case.

Q. So let me end, please, with some questions that rather follow on from that. There came a time when Jason Marriner discovered as well or heard from others that you were not a genuine Chelsea supporter but an undercover reporter?

A. That's true.

Q. Will you share with us, please, remembering the degree of danger we discussed this morning, the misplaced word could have you killed, could you share with us please the chilling words in the telephone message left on your machine by Jason Marriner. I have it as 60, that is in a witness statement dated 5th May, continuation sheet 15, it is numbered at the bottom 60. Can you have it in front of you please?

A. Sure, I am happy to say that from —

Q. Could you have that in front of you, the commentary can come afterwards. I have asked you to tell us his words. So I have asked you the words and it begins, "He simply said" and then we go into quotation marks. So what were his words then?

A. He said, "Macca, it's Friday afternoon everybody knows about the programme." That was it.

Q. You have missed out the hesitations, so I will just read it again so we have its full chilling effect. "Macca, it's Friday afternoon, it's, er, everybody knows about the programme." He rang off, is that right?

A. That was a message left on the phone.

Q. "He rang off, as you could tell, and neither Paul nor myself had any further contact with him." Those chilling words from the man who organises football violence: "Macca, it's Friday afternoon, it's, er, everybody knows about the programme." Did it make it on to the TV programme?

A. No, it did not.

Q. Did it make it into your book?

A. I don't know whether it is in the — no, it did not, because the book was finished more or less. No, it did not.

Q. What do you mean, the book was finished? What are you talking about?

A. Well, I mean the — because the football investigation was over.

Q. No, no, you said the book was finished?

A. Yes.

Q. Do you mean the book was finished before that call?

A. No, it wasn't, the final book wasn't finished but my, er, the substantive book which is a book which finished our investigation was over, in fact it was over pretty early on.

Q. You have just slipped, did you not, you wanted to give the impression, Mr MacIntyre, that it is a matter of timing that the final contact with Jason did not make it into your book, but it is not a matter of timing, it is because it is a fine illustration that the picture you drew of Jason Marriner is false and that is why it cannot make it into the film, cannot make it into the book and makes it into the evidence, now I have asked it to you and proves that you have mislead us all, does it not?

★★★

We hereby certify that the above is an accurate and complete record of the proceedings or part thereof.

Signed: SMITH BERNAL REPORTING LIMITED
File:300101/JB

_____

So now you decide.

ACKNOWLEDGMENTS

To my good friends:
Paul "H" Hopping
Nicky Olpin
Steve Paget
Paul Treherne
Alan Glazier
Sid Rabbetts
Ray Kennet
Ricky Alboni
Micky Greenaway
Barry Johnstone
Simon Gillard
Mark Ash
Leslie Costa
Linda Costa
Kath Scott
who all died too young -xxx-

Special thanks to my legal team: Michael Wolkind Q.C., Adam Budworth junior counsel and to my solicitors James Saunders, Martin Fisher, Huw Jones, Tom O'Gorman and Helen Leadbeater. In my opinion we won 4-0.

And to Rob Potter for helping me with my book.

Aaron Keppel, Aaron Smith, Abley Diop, Adam Fisher, Adam Kidson, Aitken, Al Kelly, Alan Ash, Alan Cooley, Alan Foskitt, Alan Hopping, Alan McCaffrey, Alan Paramasivan, Alzi Paramasivan, Alan Pearce, Alan Reid, Ale Scotti, Alfie Summers, Alfie Summers Jr., Andrew Burke, Andrew Darby, Andrew Harper, Andrew Heywood, Andy Barnet, Andy Cruickshank, Andy Bedwood, Andy Frain, Andy Garner, Andy Gardner, Andy Harris, Andy Hills, Andy Linton, Andy Turner, Anthony Hillsted, Anthony Jones, Army, Aruhn Maharajh, Ashley Hayles, Barry Coffey, Barry Costa, Barry Esden, Barry Nutall, Basher, Battersea Bill, Beau Courtney, Ben Usher, Billy Brown, Billy Chamberlain, Billy Collicot, Billy Fisk, Billy Holiday, Billy Hussain, Billy M, Billy Payne, Billy Steadman, Billy Whiteley, Blucky, Blue, Boatsy, Bob Anderson, Bob Chamberlain, Bob Furber, Bob Holiday, Bobby Keane, Bobby Tompkins, Bobby Watson, Bonny, Bonny Dave, Bonzo, Boz, Brendan McGirr, Brian Fullocks, Brian, Furlong, Brian Gowers, Brian Gray, Brian Hall, Brian Houshby, Brian Tuff, Brian Wright, Brownie, Brummie Dave, Budgie, Bully, Buster Bloodvessel, Bruce Peak, Bubs Skully, Busby, Butch Alboni, Calvin Ewing, Cammy, Campo, Carlos, Carl Beresford, Carl Hammond, Carl Stenhouse, Carlo Darlington, Cass Pennant, Charlie Bronson, Charlie Summers, Chris Collins, Chris from Kilburn, Chris Griffiths, Chris Harwood, Chris Kempton, Chris Kidd, Chris Radwell, Chris the Greek, Chris Henderson, Chris O'Neill, Chris Whalley, Chonker, Chunker, Cliff Summers, Clive James, Cockney Tony, Cola, Colin Bell, Colin Gault, Colin Prior, Colin Barrett, Colin Reno, Colin Salmon, Craig Bonsall, Craig Crook, Craig Daley, Cutler, Daisy, Dale Thomasson, Damian McSorely, Daniel Beam, Daniel Twin, Danny Agnew, Danny Godfrey, Danny James, Danny Taylor, Danny Young, Darren Alboni, Darren Barnwell, Darren Brewer, Darren Crew, Darren Kerr, Darren Harman, Darren Ormiston, Darren Rowe, Dave Brown, Dave Casselars, Dave CFC UK, Dave Courtney, Dave Cox, Dave Cruickshank, Dave Dunne, Dave East, Dave Martins, Dave MacPherson, Dave Nye, Dave Paget, Dave Picknall, Dave Powell, Dave Sim, Dave Wallis, Dave Whitewick, Davey Carrick, Davey Duke, Davey Gilmore, Davey Mason, Dean Brewer, Dean Cox, Dean Hillier, Dean Lingham, Dean Russell, Dean Scott, Dean White, Del Goody, Dennis Shail, Dennis Flemming, Dennis

Houlihan, Dennis Sheridan, Dessie O'Flynn, Dickie Parrot, Digger, Dinksy, Dipps, Disco, Dixie Hobson, Don the Gas, Donk, Duck, Eddie Barnes, Eddie Collis, Eddie Crispin, Eddie from Ulster, Eddie Tang, Eddie Wilds Everton, Eion McSorely, Fitz, Flynnie, Ford Davey, Fred Wilson, Frankie Fullbrook, Gappy, Gary Alleway, Gary Baker, Gary Bradley, Gary Brunning, Gary Cambridge, Gary Cooper, Gary Ewing, Gary Gibbons, Gary Glazier, Gary Gurson, Gary Humphreys, Gary Jenkins, Gary Long, Gary Maguire, Gary Mills, Gary Sumpter, Gary Tompkins, Gary Winslade, Giles, Gilly Shaw, Ginger Bob, Glen Hall, Graham Stack, Graham White, Grant Griffin, Graham Moore, Graham Mews, Graham Payne, Graham Russell, Greg Myers, Guy Hammond, Hanif, Harry Hogg, Harry Holland, Harry Robertson, Harry White, Harry (whine bar), Hayden Bowers, Henry Doe, Hickey, Hoody, Howard Marks, Ian Drummond, Ian Duncan, Ian Freeman, Ian Holloway, Ian Kiernan, Ian McLean, Ian Sim, Ian Thompson, Ian Tovey, Imad, Ivan Collier, Jack Bravado, Jack Russell, James Bavin, James Cooley, James Ince, James Keye, James Kielty, Jamie King, Jamie Osborne, Jamie Robertson, Jamie Walford, James Wilde, Jason Collins, Jason Fenton, Jason Howells, Jason Hyland, Jason Scott, Jason Solomon, Jason Watson, Jason Weeks, Jay Davis, Jay Kelly, Jay Usher, Jay Willis, Jed Chamberlain, Jeff Battersby, Jeff Chelton, Jeff Scafarde, Jeff Sharp, Jeremy Richardson, Jerry Edmonds, Jimmy Keane, Jimmy Smith, Jimmy Stockin, Jim Stradlin, Jimmy Summers, Jimmy White, Jimmy Wright, Joe Butts, Joe Dowling, Joe Smith, Joe Slater, Joey Pyle, Joey Pyle Jr., John Anslow, John Calender, John Duke, John D'Urso, John Heather, John Holland, John Hollifield, John Jo O'Neill, John Kelly, John Laverick, John Leftley, John Mapletoff, John McNeil, John Mortimer, Johno, John Pidgely, John Wigmore, John Wilson, Johnny Helps, Johnny Sawyer, Johnny Sawyer Jr., John Wakeling, John Wallis, Johnny Blisset, Johnny Frankham, Johnny Matthews, Johnny Smith, Julian Classey, Justin Hughes, Justin Merrit, Keith Herman, Kelly, Ken Gilmour, Kenny Goodwin, Kevin Baker, Kevin Bushnell, Kevin Challenger, Kevin Cressey, Kevin Faithful, Kevin Gadsby, Kevin Glarvey, Kevin Houlihan, Kev Lanigan, Kev Maskell, Kev Sweeney, Kev Wesley, Kilburn John, Kingsley, Kristian Warby, Luckan Sinclair, Lance Hargreen, Lee Booter, Lee Colvin, Lee Devins, Lee Hillier, Lee Kidd,

Lee Kerr, Lee Jackson, Lee Orme, Lee Payne, Lee Scott, Lee Spence, Lee Whitelock, Lenny Hagland, Lenny Pidgely, Les Brum, Les Strong, Les Winslade, Liam Galvin, Lipsey, Little Tommy, Lol Aherne, Maggy, Mal Vango, Malcolm Allen, Malcolm Carle, Manny, Marc Abrey, Marcus Fuller, Mark Abley, Mark Alleway, Mark Andrews, Mark Bamford, Mark Beam, Mark Bennett, Mark Campbell, Mark Carter, Mark Dane, Mark Dimbleby, Mark Drummond, Mark Fish, Mark Gregor, Mark Hickmott, Mark Hunt, Mark C., Mark Lord, Mark Marsla, Mark Monks, Mark Osbourne, Mark Parsons, Mark Peak, Mark Quigley, Mark Silbury, Mark Ward, Mark Wilson, Mark Wotton, Mark Wright, Martin Bats, Martin Denslow, Martin Steadman, Martin Ward, Martin Willis, Matty Clear, Matty Dormer, Matty Green, Matty Gould, Matty Morris, Matty Osbury, Matty Peak, Matty Robson, Matty Shadbolt, Matty Wigmore, Max Free, Max Scotti, Meady, Martin Denslow, Martin King, Martin Travis, Martin Ward, Max Free, Mensi, Michael Penny, Mick Berry, Mick Collins, Mick Gadsby, Mick Maguire, Mick McSweeney, Mick the Badge, Mickey Cavanagh, Mickey Forrest, Mickey Gray, Mickey Hemmings, Mike Bish, Miles Cruickshank, Miles Saward, Millwall John, Mugsy, Murdo, Muzza, Nathan Twin, Nathan Wharf, Neil Carvey, Neil Fearnley, Neil Fisher, Neil Lucas, Neil Holland, Neil Phillips, Neil Watkins, Neil Wright, Nicky Hills, Nick Godfrey, Nick Owen, Nicky Penny, Nick Travis, Nigel Hobson, Nigel Smith, Nigel Venus, Noel Barrington, Norman Parker, Noski, Ollie Crompton, Ollie Moeni, Paddington, Paddy Forrest, Palmer, Para Paul, Pascal, Pat Doland, Paul Atkinson (Rampton), Paul Blackmore, Paul Brooker, Paul Carney, Paul Coles, Paul Costa, Paul Cushion, Paul Dane, Paul Dowsit, Paul Gowans, Paul Hardy, Paul Keenan, Paul Levingstone, Paul Manvelle, Paul Maguire, Paul O'Donovan, Paul Reid, Paul Riley, Paul Scarborough, Paul Sharp, Paul Walsby, Paul Winter, Perky, Pete Summers, Peter Brown, Peter Lynch, Peter MacBeth, Peter Russell, Peter Volks, Peter White, Phil Hall, Phil Papaelias, Phil Riley, Philip Shields, Pieman, PJ, Porky, Pops, Rab, Ralphy, Ray Atkinson, Raymond Hill, Ray Harris, Raymond, Hill, Reza Moeni, Rhys Hefford, Richard Evans, Richard Linton, Richard Saxford, Richard Stringer, Ricky Ewing, Ricky Graves, Ricky McNamara, Ricky Steadman, Rob Allen, Robert Hoffman, Rob Honeyball,

Rob Kiernan, Rob Ratcliffe, Rob Sumpter, Rob Sylvester, Robert Songhurst, Rocka, Rocky Alboni, Rodney Croney, Roger Crunchy, Rog Fabharwal, Roland Terry, Rolesy, Rolls, Roly, Romford Lee, Ronnie Borg, Ronnie Herbert, Rory Quigley, Roy Page, Roy Shaw, Russell McFadden, Russell Weeks, Sam Hickmott, Scatty, Scott Green, Shaun Baker, Shaun Bowman. Shaun Fullocks, Shaun Kidson, Shannon, Snide Sid, Silent Jason, Simon Bennett, Simon Brown, Simon Lawley, Simon Williams, Skeeny, Skippy, Skitsy, Sonny Ayinde, Spats, Spencer Allen, Spencer Willmott, Spider, Stacky, Steffan Bauldoff, Stephen Burke, Steve Alboni, Steve Blackmore, Steve Bradley, Steve Choules, Steve Clarke, Steve Clayson, Steve Collis, Steve Dunne, Steve Flatman, Steve Fogarty, Steve Gilmartin, Steve Healey, Steve Humphries, Steve Hyland, Steve Keane, Steve King, Steve MacPherson, Steve Nuttall, Steve Nye, Steve Parker, Steve Payne, Steve Proctor, Steve Reno, Steve Skully, Steve Taylor, Steve Thomas, Stuart Glass, Stuart Holloway, Stuart Monks, Stuart Shooter, Suitcase Eddie, Swiggy, Syksey, Tel Gallacher Terry Butts, Terry Curtis, Terry Heather, Terry "Tess" Mann, Terry Newman, Terry Parks, Terry Turbo, Tim Rice, Timmy Lyons, Tom Furber, Tommy Capliss, Tommy Doyle, Tommy Keane, Tommy Tobin, Tommy Williams, Tonto, Tony Atkinson, Tony Covelle, Tony Freeman, Tony Harris, Tony Ludby, Tony King, Tony Murphy, Tony Newman, Tony Noland, Trav, Trigger, Troddy, Tuse, UK, Untold, Vaughn Jackson, Vince Drake, Vince Stapleton, Vince Stapleton Jr., Vince O'Flaherty, Vinny Hillier, Vinny Lynch, Wally Stockin, Walshy, Warren Glass, Warren Jenkins, Will Browning, Will Mason, Willy Reid, Winston, Yeti, Yoksi, Ziggy, Zorro.

I've tried my hardest to remember you all but if I have forgotten anyone who should be included please accept my sincerest apologies.